"Ted Kim has a bold vision for renev
rope. In a manner that is both highly
vocative, he sets forth his vision with :
practical wisdom. Reading him has fo.
that I have been taking for granted. In t
me some new reasons to be hopeful abo   ‥‥‥omplish
in Europe—and beyond that in the globa. ∪ııurch."

—**RICHARD MOUW**
President Emeritus, Fuller Theological Seminary

"I wish to congratulate Ted on presenting such an ambitious and wide-ranging discussion of so many issues facing Christian faith in western Europe today. His style is punchy, to the point, and easy to read. The text moves along at a fair clip. Many of his points are insightful and challenging. As often the work of an 'outsider' to the region can bring fresh insight which the 'locals' may not perceive. There is much to learn from many points Ted makes. We do not have to agree on everything to learn from each other. There is much food for thought for those who care to reflect. I recommend Ted's book to you."

—**MALCOLM CLEGG**
Lecturer, Evangelical Higher Theological Seminary, Poland

"As a long-time missionary and educator to Europe, I was excited to read Ted Kim's book, *Save Europe*. Kim shares my heart and passion for post-Christian Europe. The majority of books that I have read regarding mission in Europe have offered diagnosis of the spiritual crisis. However, Ted Kim not only gives a diagnosis of the spiritual ailment in Europe, which has implications throughout the West, but he also offers a missional prescription to reintroduce Christianity. As a Korean pastor and scholar, Ted Kim is not attempting to introduce an American version of Christianity into Europe. Rather, he seeks to deconstruct Christianity in Europe to the fundamental elements—i.e., the word of God, the Holy Spirit, the fellowship of Christians, and charity. Kim re-visions church that is uniquely European, yet authentic, missional, and deeply spiritual for a secular society that long ago rejected the construct of Christendom... *Save Europe* is refreshing and encouraging. I agree with Kim that the best for Europe is saved for last."

—**BLAYNE C. WALTRIP**
Assistant Professor of Global Mission and
Church Development, Pentecostal Theological Seminary

"Ted Kim discusses the situation with Christianity in Europe with projection to the entire world. He asserts that the truth of the gospel must be recovered by churches in Europe to bring people back to faith and church. He touches on many issues of church life and Christian living. You may not be in agreement with everything Ted Kim states, but his conclusions and ideas are thought-provoking and calling to action."

—**VASILY DMITRIEVSKY**
Professor in World Missions and Intercultural Studies,
Dallas Theological Seminary

"In *Save Europe*, Ted Kim pointedly outlines the emptiness of Europe's post-Christian identity and grapples with how the gospel can restore a sense of grounding to Europe's present and future. Similar to Paul in the book of Acts, Kim has heard the Macedonian call from the European West and wants to motivate a generation of people to save Europe through prayers, academics, the arts, and public theologies. While one may not agree with all of Kim's assumptions, suggestions, and conclusions, the reader will glean multiple gems. The book's prophetic focus on the gospel for a post-Christian context makes this text relevant and compelling."

—**KIRSTEN S. OH**
Professor of Practical Theology, Azusa Pacific University

"This is surely is a necessary volume. We Americans rarely think of Europe as a needy mission field. They are not 'colored' enough for that. A terrible and costly mistake. God needs us there, and I am pleased that Ted Kim has responded to his leading."

—**WILLIAM E. PANNELL**
Professor Emeritus of Preaching, Fuller Theological Seminary

"Should Europe be evangelized again? Should the gospel be preached again in Europe when there are innumerable places on earth where the good news has not been preached even once? Yes, says Rev. Ted Kim. That's the thrust of his new book, *Save Europe*. This book is hugely relevant at a time when there is a certain cold apathy creeping into the church at large with regard to winning new souls and new grounds for Christ. While acknowledging the accomplishment of the European church as monumental, he also emphasizes the need to reinstate the gifts and calling of the Europeans. This book is a must-read for evangelical Christians."

—**ROBIN SAM**
Editor, *The Christian Messenger*

"Europe has become the most difficult mission in the world today. Secularism poses a new kind of challenge for Christian missionaries. As a servant of God, Ted Kim is rightly concerned about this and, in this book, offers the type of help that can only come from a non-European. His passion is exactly what is needed to re-evangelize Europeans. This book will not only cause readers to see Europe as the mission field that it is, it will also convict them to pray. This is a book for everyone concerned about God's mission in the world, which should actually be every Christian in the world."

—**HARVEY C. KWIYANI**
Lecturer in African Christianity and Theology,
Liverpool Hope University

"As Ted Kim says, he is not writing so much academically as prophetically to stir up Christians for the Great Commission. The author has a passion to see the gospel touch the old continent again in a new way. . . . The biblically based argument is encouraging: God has not given up on Europe. He wants to give it a new opportunity. . . . Yet, the gospel of peace still needs to penetrate the hearts of the Europeans! Ted Kim's book calls us to do the job!"

—**MARKO HALTTUNEN**
Director of Conference Centre, Iso Kirja Bible College, Finland

Save Europe

Save Europe

Reintroducing Christianity
to Post-Christian Europe

Ted Kim

RESOURCE *Publications* • Eugene, Oregon

SAVE EUROPE
Reintroducing Christianity to Post-Christian Europe

Copyright © 2021 Ted Kim. All rights reserved. Except for brief quotations in critical publications or reviews, no part of this book may be reproduced in any manner without prior written permission from the publisher. Write: Permissions, Wipf and Stock Publishers, 199 W. 8th Ave., Suite 3, Eugene, OR 97401.

Resource Publications
An Imprint of Wipf and Stock Publishers
199 W. 8th Ave., Suite 3
Eugene, OR 97401

www.wipfandstock.com

PAPERBACK ISBN: 978-1-7252-7933-9
HARDCOVER ISBN: 978-1-7252-7925-4
EBOOK ISBN: 978-1-7252-7928-5

All Scripture quotations, unless otherwise indicated, are taken from the Holy Bible, New International Version®, NIV®. Copyright ©1973, 1978, 1984, 2011 by Biblica, Inc.® Used by permission of Zondervan. All rights reserved worldwide. www.zondervan.com The "NIV" and "New International Version" are trademarks registered in the United States Patent and Trademark Office by Biblica, Inc.®

To my beloved wife and precious son

Contents

Introduction | ix

1. Europe Is a Major Mission Field | 1
2. Europe's Spiritual Condition Has Been Left Unattended Too Long | 7
3. History Is Not Over | 15
4. The Gospel Can Go around the World One More Time | 21
5. What Happened to the Western World? | 34
6. The Unique Situation of Europe | 55
7. Options for European Christians | 72
8. Recovering of the Gospel | 83
9. Major Issues of Christianity in the Twenty-first Century | 111
10. Restoration of Christianity in Post-Christian Europe | 139
11. A New Paradigm of World Mission | 169
12. Lessons for America | 172
Closing Words: Secularists Have Answered the Question for Us | 178

About the Author | 183
Bibliography | 185
Index | 191

Introduction

EUROPE IS GOING THROUGH an identity crisis of unprecedented nature. Europeans are fearful of losing their Europeanness amid this crisis. The European Union was established decades ago in the hopes of creating a collective identity for Europe. After decades of experiment, Brexit attempted to build a new identity by exiting from this Union. During the COVID-19 pandemic, the European Union could not help the member nations to prevent or combat the virus. Instead, each country had to fight on its own. With or without the European Union, Europe is not sure of its place in the world. What does the future hold for Europe?

The decline of the Christian faith in Europe is not just the loss of European identity, but the loss of the European psyche. The decline of Christianity is no longer just an intellectual discussion but an existential concern. The intellectual giants who pioneered the modern and secular Europe are all dead, and their descendants must decide how to live in an increasingly empty world. When Notre Dame burned down, many Parisians must have felt as if they had become orphans. Human beings are not so strong that they can live with the disappearance of familiar persons, institutions, and symbols. Deconstructionists may have felt the satisfaction of shedding the vestige of the old world, but they have not replaced the old world with anything.

God is the source of life. The further a person moves from God, the further he removes himself from life. When the prodigal son went to a faraway country to live, a famine struck. It was not a coincidence that a famine came to the man who went away from the father. For a short while, his rich inheritance could support him. But once his inheritance ran out, there was nothing that could offer any sustenance.

The Western intellectuals shined the brightest when they advocated the independence of humanity. They were most eloquent and distinguished when they challenged the centuries-old Christian values and beliefs. But that was their limit. They could not go any further and replace God, Christ, or the Christian values with anything. The hard-won liberty of man in itself cannot tell us why we should love one another or why we should live and not die. Secular philosophy cannot tell us what awaits us after we go through our current pain. The natural and inevitable destination of Western secularism seems to be the capitalist and consumerist culture. Instead of going to church to pray, postmodern homemakers go to shopping malls to talk to friends over a bagel and a cup of latte. For men, football and baseball stadiums have replaced churches as sacred meeting places.

The film *Good Bye, Lenin!* satirizes the liberty imposed on former East Germany after the Wall came down.[1] Superior West German consumer goods instantly replace inferior East German products on the supermarket shelves. East Germans watch helplessly as their old world disappears. The collapse of communism is immediately followed by consumerism. Compared to the grandiose promises of communism, western democracy offers nothing except cold and impersonal commercialism.

Modern secular culture has not offered any substitute for the family values that it ridiculed as being bourgeois. When the sex revolution started in the 1960s, men and women thought that finally they could be liberated from the traditional family obligations. By staying single, men hoped that they could satisfy their fantasies in absolute freedom. But it was all rhetoric with little substance. Even Hugh Hefner, the quintessential playboy, not only got married but also bequeathed his empire to his daughter. The symbol of sexual freedom could not live his life outside the boundary of the family. As Don Corleone says in Godfather, a man who doesn't spend time with his family is not a real man. Those who abandoned their families searching for better alternatives had to crawl back, hoping that their families would take them back.

Music fans are surprised when they hear their idols mentioning God and religion on the stage. Eric Clapton often brings out a gospel choir on stage to sing choruses for his "Holy Mother." Ozzie Osborne, the prince of darkness of rock, greets his audience by saying, "God bless you," leaving his fans puzzled about his religious orientation. The rebellious can only go so far from the presence of God. After a long wandering, they must come back at a certain point. Those who looked to the celebrities

---

1. Becker, *Good Bye Lenin!*.

to guide their experimental lifestyle will be disappointed. It was the fans' critical error to expect their idols to guide them in their journey away from the traditional Christian values.

People hoped that modern art and music would establish a viable alternative to the conventional art and music style. Abandoning the traditional style, modern artists and musicians tried to develop new and different expressions, except that many people found them ugly and unappealing. It is incomprehensible why some art lovers are willing to pay high prices for abstract works of art that, to ordinary people, look strange, dark, and depressing. Likewise, so-called modern music has no beginning and no end. The audience cannot tell what keys modern music is on. They cannot hum it or whistle it by memory. It does not sound either beautiful or sensible. Though artists try to justify anything in the name of art, when art rejected the Christian interpretation of life, it is forced to go elsewhere where there is no standard for beauty, goodness, or meaning.

The series of events from the Enlightenment forward have gradually eroded Christian faith in the minds of Europeans. Christianity has been continually on the retreat for centuries. No other continent has experienced this kind of constant spiritual decline. The rest of the world thought that perhaps the highest standard of culture and sophistication of Europe took its toll. Though churches are small numerically, Europe still has the highest theological scholarship and Christ-based ethical standard, people thought. Decades have passed, and there is still no sign of change. Europe is like a barren woman. It is unable to give spiritual births. She does not seem to be praying with tears like Hannah, either.

What is happening in Europe is no longer just Europe's problem; it is a problem of the Christendom. The name of Jesus is at stake. If Europeans cannot bring back Christianity on their own, they need the cooperation of concerned Christian brothers and sisters from other parts of the body of Christ.

The coronavirus pandemic of 2020 demonstrated how vulnerable European states are. Europe is no longer the mighty civilization that it once was. The signs of the waning began to appear earlier. The world was incredulous when Great Britain began to sell its national name brands like Rolls Royce and Bentley. Waiting for the European powers to return to their former glory is like waiting for Godot.

When the 007 James Bond franchise started in the early 1960s, the idea of a British secret agent saving the world seemed believable.

However, after several decades, a British secret agent's role in the postmodern world has grown smaller and less credible. In *Skyfall*, one of the most recent 007 episodes, the archvillain scornfully challenges the loyalty of the captured James Bond: "England! The Empire! MI6 (chuckle)! You are living in a ruin as well. You just don't know it yet."[2] No other film portrays the current state of Britain this honestly and painfully. It takes a European screenwriter to speak candidly about his own culture. A branch severed from the tree cannot survive. The immense identity crisis of the continent ultimately stems from its loss of faith. Spiritual problem lies at the bottom of all other issues.

Unlike other issues of identity, Europeans cannot restore Christianity by political will or social consensus. Restoring faith is not like repairing an old work of art. Emphasizing the legacy cannot bring faith back. For instance, the French government outlawed the wearing of burqas by Muslim women in public. Such laws cannot help to bring back the disappearing Christian faith in the hearts of people. Provoking a sense of rivalry with Islam does not create a love for Christianity. Having lost the zeal for Christianity, Europeans can only watch the rise of Islam in their midst with helplessness. Do Europeans have the will to resurrect Christianity in Europe?

Nostalgia cannot resurrect Christianity. Protecting the Christian heritage is not the same thing as recovering faith. One cannot find God in the past. God is always in the present; otherwise, he is meaningless. He did not say, "I was what I was," but "I am what I am." One cannot gain faith by going back to the traditions. Faith does not work that way. Faith requires a personal relationship with God, who exists in the now. The decline of Christianity in Europe is partly due to churches' failure to help people establish a meaningful relationship with the living God.

Europe is a continent of contradictions because the memories of the past contradict the present reality. There are glorious relics from the era when Christianity ruled the lives of the European people. These come in conflict with the conspicuous lack of faith in the hearts of people. This conflict produces irony, which is visible everywhere. Harvard, the synonym of academic prestige in America, began as a theological seminary in 1636 to educate clergy in the American colonies like Oxford and Cambridge in Britain. As Harvard became the bastion of secular learning, it gradually lost its Christian affiliation. How the university originally

---

2. Mendes, *Skyfall*.

started could not guarantee what it would become. Now Harvard has little to do with Christianity that created it. The branch declared independence from the root.

Is this the inevitable destiny of Christianity in the world? Is the west taking the lead of the rest of the world? Having given birth to high values, culture, and ethics, will Christianity disappear from the center stage, leaving only its memories behind? Christians in the rest of the world will loudly shout no. The custodians of Christianity have failed to preserve the integrity and power of the faith. What the western churches have been unable to do, the rest of the Christendom must try to restore. The Anglican bishops from the Global South, for example, are the bulwarks against the precipitation into radically progressive decisions by the Anglican Church.

Even though Europe's churches have become objects of grave concern for the Christians in other parts of the world, Christians in nonwestern countries are hesitant to meddle with the spiritual affairs of the west. In the past, missionaries from the west brought the gospel to the Global South and Asia. Financial help also came from the western churches and charities. Theology students from the Third World came to study under the eminent theologians in Europe. Europeans are not only at the forefront of culture but are also white. Being white is still the badge of intrinsic superiority in the world.

As a result, the rest of the world silently watches what is unfolding in Europe, wondering what will happen next. The crisis seemed to deepen. Europeans do not seem to know how to own up to their situations. Christians in other parts of the world cannot sit idly by while Europe is committing spiritual suicide. What occurs in Europe affects not only the Europeans but also the integrity of Christianity itself.

Prophet Elijah demonstrated the reality of God on Mount Carmel. He did not attempt theological discussions with people. Instead, Elijah showed them the existential urgency of believing in Yahweh by having the fire of God fall upon the altar. When they saw it, people repented of their apostasy and came back to the Lord. People are not much different now. Instead of emphasizing religious traditions, we must convince them of the reason to believe. Instead of reminding them of how people once believed in the past, we should show them why they must believe now. Faith requires an existential context. One desperately needs faith when thrown into the belly of a fish, or the lions' den, or blazing furnace. There are areas in people's existential conditions that only God can fill.

How can we introduce the presence and power of God to people? We do it the same way that the first Christians did it—by the Holy Spirit. The Holy Spirit searches all things, even the deep things of God. What God has prepared for those who love him, he has shown it to us by his Spirit. When people brought a paralytic man lying on a stretcher, Jesus announced, "Take heart, son; your sins are forgiven" (Matt 9:2). How did Jesus know the man's hidden spiritual need? Other people only saw the man's external need, his physical condition, but Jesus saw the inner problem of sin before he turned his attention to the physical condition. Jesus saw the inner problem by the Holy Spirit. One can never know the real needs of the inner man by looking at the external condition. Only the Holy Spirit reveals them.

The basic human condition has not changed. People still need affection, meaning, and self-worth. As Kennedy said, we breathe the same air, cherish our children's future, and are all mortal. There is ample room in each of us that God can fill. If anyone thinks that the room is already filled, he is mistaken. When the rightful owner comes, the false owner must vacate. When the Israelites entered Canaan, the earlier inhabitants had to leave. As the lyrics of *Save the Last Dance for Me* state, "But don't forget who's taking you home, and in whose arms you're gonna be." The last dance is saved for the Master.

Many Christians thought that the Great Commission applied only to the Third World mission fields. The sobering fact is that Europe is emerging as an enormous mission field of the twenty-first century. The most serious spiritual contest in the twenty-first century will take place on this continent. Europe needs not just missionaries, but earnest prayer warriors, Christian intellectuals, artists, writers, and opinion leaders. We have seen enough of anonymous Christians. The European community is like the Macedonian man who appeared in Paul's vision, asking him to come over to help. No one person or church can carry out this enormous task; it takes a whole generation of faithful people. Though the work seems overwhelming, we will know how to do it once we agree on the goal.

This book examines the spiritual situation of western Europe from the missionary and pastoral perspectives. Already many people have written books and articles about the state of Christianity in Europe. Most of these writings offer diagnosis instead of a cure. Academics tend to dwell on diagnosing the condition but not finding a cure. The remedy proposed in this book is reintroducing Jesus Christ to Europe. Taking

Europe back to the past is not a viable option. Neither is trying to restore the Christian roots. Instead, we need to reintroduce Christ to Europe. Reintroducing Christianity means reintroducing Christ. We can never go beyond him. If Jesus is not good enough for Europe, Europe is beyond redemption. We are confident of better things. We must believe that the grace of Jesus is enough for everyone and every circumstance.

This book differs from many books and articles written on the topic in that it proposes a prescription and not just a diagnosis. It takes the exhortation of a few to encourage the rest. Joshua and Caleb, though they were few in number, inspired the entire nation of Israel to believe in their spiritual destiny. This book hopes to give encouragement and vision to any European Christians who need them. Negative thoughts are contagious, but so is faith. For decades, negative thoughts have prevailed in Europe; now, let us spread faith in Europe to bring back Christianity.

This book speaks to pastors, church leaders, seminary professors and students, seekers, and anyone else who wants to understand the place of Christianity in the west. The same proposition applies to the United States, Canada, Australia, and New Zealand. It includes many references to films and current affairs to make it easy to understand what could otherwise be an arid subject. Any portions of the book can offer sermon ideas or discussion topics. It has more than ten-years-worth of material from prayer, study, and preaching. It is not academic research but a prophetic message to the Christian brothers and sisters in Europe who are concerned about their Christian identity.

Why is a Korean-Canadian pastor so concerned about the spiritual condition of Europe? I am like a volunteer for the Spanish Civil War or the Kurdish war of independence. What is happening in other parts of the world concerns all of us. It is important to Jesus. Therefore, it is important to us. The world is our parish, as John Wesley said. Did the Macedonian man appear in my dream, asking me to come over and help? The situations are different now. Someone who sees his neighbor's house on fire does not require a vision from God to go and put out the fire. At the time of Paul, there was no real European person who could ask Paul for spiritual help. Thus, an imaginary Macedonian had to appear on behalf of the Europeans in Paul's vision. In our time, by contrast, there are plenty of Europeans who are aware of the continent's spiritual need. H. Dan Beeby, a former British missionary to China, said that they who evangelized other nations could not understand their own culture. He cried, "Come and help us."³ It takes more than an understanding of culture, but a belief in God's unchanging faithfulness to bolster the tilting wall of the church in Europe. Jesus has not revoked the Great Commission. Jesus's command to us to go into all the world and preach the gospel is still binding on us.

Secular scholars have found the solution for us. The cure exists where we have suspected all along. Comparing the European conditions to the United States, secular scholars have discovered two reasons for the decline of Christianity in Europe: Europe's lack of competition and lack of religious plurality.⁴ Though the clergy have been reluctant to acknowledge them, secularists have confirmed their suspicions. The cure demands that the churches in Europe stop depending on the protection and privilege by the states. It also requires that multiple denominations and churches compete for people's hearts and minds, instead of passively expecting people to come to church. The world is active at preaching its values. Why should the churches be passive in its mission? This is an obvious conclusion. Churches operate by the same principle all around the world.

Secularists have found out that the supply of religion, not the demand for it, increases the religious activity of society. This discovery agrees with the principle of the New Testament. Jesus commanded the disciples to go into the entire world and preach the gospel. He did not tell them first to investigate the spiritual demand of people. Apostle Paul did not research people's spiritual needs first and then decided to preach the gospel to them. Paul preached the word of God regardless of the apparent lack of the spiritual needs of gentiles. The supply of the word of God inspired the demand for God in people's hearts. God did not send his Son into the world because the world asked for him. God sent the Son to the world on his initiative, and this act created the most remarkable spiritual revolution the world had ever known.

---

3. Beeby, "White Man's Burden," 7.
4. Finke "Supply-side explanation," 27.

— 1 —

Europe Is a Major Mission Field

THE AMERICAN STAND-UP COMEDIAN David Chappelle said, "Chivalry is dead." Then he added, "Women killed it."[1] Though intended to be funny, this joke is a very keen insight into people's responsibility for their loss. Chivalry refers to men's gentlemanly conduct toward women, but women in their independent spirit rejected it, making chivalry superfluous. Who stands to lose from this result? Chappelle's statement resembles what Nietzsche said about God: "God is dead." Then Nietzsche added, "We have killed him."[2] No man can kill God or bring him back to life at will. Nonetheless, if a man chose to eliminate God in his world, he has only himself to blame for his loss. By killing God, the modern man committed spiritual suicide. This suicide has taken place over a long period, and its effect is becoming more and more visible. The absence of God in the world did not produce the independence of man, but the alienation of man. It is like a divorce. A divorcee may have thought that he could be free after the divorce, but he finds himself alone and not free. Unlike a divorcee, the modern man cannot look for a substitute for God.

Nietzsche's ominous statement seemed to predict the decline of Christianity as an inevitable result of humanity's progress. The profound changes in the values and thoughts of European society since the Enlightenment have led to the decline of Christian faith in Europe. On the other hand, there are also some not-so-profound reasons. The flesh opposes the spirit. There is nothing profound about the deeds of the flesh. The

1. Davechappelletv, "Chivalry Is Dead," 00:14–00:24.
2. Nietzsche, *Gay Science*, 181.

natural mind does not appreciate spiritual things. That is what happened in Europe. It is not as mysterious as we think. The appeal of the secular lifestyle has pushed away the sacred demands of the church.

God is not someone whom man can kill or bring back to life at will. What Nietzsche thought the modern man had killed was not God, but the dominance of Christianity in modern culture. Nonetheless, the real power of Christianity does not rest on its cultural dominance but on the word of God and the Holy Spirit. Christianity was never meant to be the dominant culture of the world. Instead, it must go against the dominant culture. The success of Christianity became its own poison. Christianity should lose its preeminence in the world to save its true self. Christianity needs to be small to be great again.

Anyone will leave a church if services are dull and unappealing to his heart. On the other hand, people will come back if something touches their hearts. Basically, three conditions must be met for churches to grow. First, the congregation must not fall asleep during sermons. Second, they must come back the following week. And third, they must bring their friends. When these three conditions are satisfied, churches will grow. When such an obvious principle is lost, churches have only themselves to blame. Preserving Christianity is not very complicated.

We are not talking about the marketplace of religion or spiritual consumerism, as some pastors fear. Instead, we are talking about introducing Jesus Christ to the post-Christian world once again. The gospel took one trip around the world. When the gospel reached the end of the world, we thought the task was over. But the job is not over. We must do the work one more time. Like Peter, who fell into the water after attempting to walk on water, we must recover the faith we once had. Who is to say that one attempt at world evangelization suffices? We must go back to the basics like praying, preaching, and practicing faith. If anyone is contemptuous of these tasks, he is contemptuous of the Great Commission.

Whenever people discuss the topic of the loss of European identity, the subject of the Muslim immigrants comes up. People seem to believe that the influx of Muslim immigrants is responsible for the loss of European identity. But the truth of the matter is that Europe began to lose its Christian identity long before the Muslim immigration. Europeans cannot blame the Muslims for their loss of identity. Instead, it was the loss of faith that led to the loss of cultural identity, and this loss of identity produced timid immigration policies. The political leaders of Europe cannot talk about defending the "European values" without knowing what they are. The loss of faith is like taking the cornerstone out of the building called Europe; there is no foundation to support the structure, and the collapse is predictable.

It does not ordinarily occur to people that a problem can have severe and deadly consequences until it is too late. They expect their comfortable lifestyles will continue indefinitely. The COVID-19 pandemic of 2020 was not taken seriously at the beginning. Nobody imagined that an epidemic from one part of the world could spread to the rest of the world, crippling the whole world, locking people in their homes, and bringing about grave economic ruin. Spiritual problems can do a more severe damage to the souls of people.

Throughout the history of Judeo-Christianity, deadly wars have raged for the souls of humanity. The Israelites in the wilderness were always vulnerable to the temptations of idolatry. Elijah had to prove before the people of Israel that Yahweh, and not Baal, was the true God. Apostle Paul cautioned the Galatians against false gospels. Apostle John warned that the antichrist was already in the world. Wars for the souls of men are not theoretical, but real and fierce. Defeat has deadly consequences. The emptying of the church pews in the western world demonstrates not just a cultural phenomenon but spiritual loss. Protecting the faith is always a grave task throughout the history of Christianity. One of the many titles of the British Monarch is the Defender of the Faith. But no queen or king can defend the faith in modern society. Each soul must be won through deliberate and effective ministry—one person at a time. Otherwise, Christianity in Europe will be regarded by people as an antiquated institution like the monarchy.

Discussing the condition of Christianity in western Europe gives us a sense of crisis, dread, and resignation. We feel that perhaps Christianity is on its way toward extinction. Europeans have tried Christianity for two thousand years and have reached their final verdict, it seems. Such fear is unfounded and uninformed. Christianity is not headed toward extinction when viewed from a global perspective. Europeans are not authorized to issue the final verdict. It would be presumptuous for them to think so. The judgment is not about Christianity itself, but about Europe's performance as the custodian of Christianity for two thousand years. It is like the master coming back to see what his servants have done with the talents he gave them.

Not all the servants have suffered a deficit because Christianity has experienced rapid growth in other parts of the world—in Africa, Asia, and Latin America. Christianity still has a very powerful presence in the United States. Hence it is not just in the "poor" Global South where Christianity is thriving. Eastern Europe has already experienced a society without churches. The experiment with communism in Eastern Europe was not just an experiment with communism but also an experiment with the church's absence in society. After several decades, communism gave up, and the church returned. Christianity has demonstrated higher survivability than ideology.

The shifting of the gravity of Christianity from Europe to the Global South has been going on for several decades, but Europeans are paying attention to it only at this time because the Christian immigrants from the Global South display different attitudes toward Christianity. Europeans pay attention to the church growth in other parts of the world not because they are impressed by it, but because they find it odd. Europeans cannot imagine that God must be behind any of the extraordinary Christian revivals in the Global South. They merely ascribe them to sociological or psychological factors. Christians from the Global South who thought that the robust church growth in their countries might impress the Europeans are disappointed to see the expressionless faces of European observers. It is almost irrelevant to the Europeans because such dramatic church growth is so different from their everyday experience. Their lack of interest accentuates the depth of their spiritual condition. They cannot easily feel what Christians in other parts of the world feel. They cannot believe that God can do the same thing among them.

The flourishing of Christianity in the Global South is a little cause for optimism for the future of Christianity. The west has been a model for democracy, education, science and technology, economics, and culture for the rest of the world. If it has taken Europe two thousand years to lose its Christian convictions, can the rest of the world not follow suit in a hundred years? What Europe does today, everyone else might do tomorrow.[3]

Nonetheless, a sense of dread is sometimes spiritually useful because it makes people take their faith more honestly and seriously, driving them to depend on God instead of themselves. It helps them to think about what it means to be Christians. It makes Christians humble. No longer can they hide behind the number and size of churches. They should have been humble sooner. The loud voice of the American evangelicals in the

---

3. Davie, "Europe," 76.

political arena points to the misplaced confidence in their number and influence. Europe does not want to learn from America in this regard.

Instead of focusing on how to bring people back to church, Christians must focus on bringing Jesus Christ back to church. What they lack is not the know-how and techniques of church growth. Elijah had to endure three-and-a-half years of poverty and humility at a widow's house even though he was a prophet with magnificent gifts and power. During the time of smallness, Elijah had to learn obedience and humility. In the same way, Moses had to go through a harsh discipline in the isolation of the desert. The man who wanted to save his people in Egypt had to persevere forty years of obscurity in Midian shepherding his father-in-law's flock.

The lean years are the time for the remnant to seek God's face truly. It is the time for Christians to come back to humility. Humility does not reside in success. It is no difficult thing for God to bring about a revival in Europe. Church pews are not empty because God is dead. But Europeans need to bring Jesus back to their midst. Their affiliation to Christianity can no longer be just cultural or traditional. A man is not a Christian because he was born into a Christian culture, but because he really believes. Personal faith has to be renewed and confirmed. To become reacquainted with Jesus may feel awkward after all this time. It is like a marriage renewal where long-wed couples reconfirm their commitment to each other. Older Christians need to confirm their allegiance, not to their parish churches, but Jesus Christ. Young people need opportunities to hear the gospel again. Those who already believe but are not actively attending church must find their spiritual home. Such is the Lord's will.

The freedom of religion necessarily presupposes a secular society. Secularism and Christianity are not opposed to each other. When a state determines its official religion, people are deprived of choice, and hence freedom. Only when people are free to choose their religion their faith is meaningful and authentic. Secularism, therefore, is not antithetical to Christianity. Instead, it is in the secular context that authentic Christianity can thrive. Secularism is the water from which Christians catch people.

Christianity cannot be reinvented, but churches can. Churches have to be reinvented to accommodate the unchurched. Churches cannot expect people to change without changing themselves. The Gothic towers, stained glass windows, high ceilings, and clergy vestments have outlived their usefulness. It is painful to see old church buildings being sold off, but God does not dwell in buildings made by men. Churches have to be lean and clean to be able to move to where people are. Allegiance to denominations has little meaning to the postmodern generation. Ministers must deconstruct Christianity to the very fundamental elements because only those elements will survive in the post-Christian era. Those essential elements are the word of God, the Holy Spirit, the fellowship of Christians, and charity. Ministers should be willing to shed all other aspects as excess baggage. The sequel to this book will talk about the New Church of the twenty-first century—the church that is stripped down to its essential requirements to minister to the postmodern man.

If history should repeat itself, we will be able to present Christianity to Europe one more time. Apostle Paul said, "It is no trouble for me to write the same things to you again" (Phil 3:1, NIV). It should not bother us to preach the gospel once again. The Bible is full of incidents when people had to do certain things for the second time to make them work. King David had to bring the Ark of Covenant to Jerusalem twice. It did not work until the second time. Jonah had to be sent to Nineveh for the second time to fulfill his mission. Peter had to go through the catching-of-the-fish routine once again to finally accept his calling. In the parable of two sons, the older son said yes to his father's instruction but did not obey him. In comparison, the younger son first said no but repented and obeyed him. The first reaction is not always to be trusted. The first result is not always credible. The only time that the second chance is not available is when salt loses its saltiness.

— 2 —

Europe's Spiritual Condition Has Been Left Unattended Too Long

When the COVID-19 epidemic started in China, the rest of the world regarded it as somebody else's problem until the epidemic reached everywhere. Soon the whole world began to panic. No country was left unaffected by this deadly outbreak. The decline of Christianity in Europe was somebody else's problem for more than half a century. The decline continued steadily to the point where it cannot be ignored. It is no longer somebody else's concern. If one part of the body suffers, every part suffers with it (1 Cor 12:26). Like a virus, the spiritual ailment of Europe may spread to other parts of the world. Who can guarantee that what has happened to Europe is not the precursor of what will happen elsewhere?

People have attributed the current spiritual situation of Europe to secularization. Blaming secularization is a cyclical way of explaining the problem. Secularization means that the place of religion has diminished, while the influence of the world has increased. The term does not distinguish between cause and effect. Secularization can mean both the cause and effect of the decline of Christianity. The decline of the faith led to the increase of secularity and, inversely, the increase of secularity led to the decline of the faith.

Let us assume, for the sake of discussion, that the decline of the faith in Europe is due to secularization. What we have to realize is that secularization is not unique to Europe. Secular temptations existed at every age in every place. The same temptations exist in other religions, too. All religions must combat the same earthly temptations. Attributing the

European spiritual decline to secularization is not convincing because the United States experienced the same kind of secularization without the same consequence. Numerous revivals took place in America to offset the effects of secularization. Christianity is alive and well in America. Latin America experienced an explosive growth of the pentecostal movement during the past several decades. Christianity was embraced fervently in many Asian countries where secularization, westernization, and evangelization occurred together, proving that religious decline does not necessarily accompany westernization. And the growth of Christianity has been phenomenal in the continent of Africa, which has become the new "heartland for world Christianity."[1]

Secularization is not unique to Europe. The rest of the world has undergone the same westernization and modernization process without losing its religious convictions. Spiritual revivals occurring in the rest of the world have spared the continent of Europe. Western Europe is the only part of the world where the old secularization thesis seems to hold.[2] We must find the reasons for Europe's situation elsewhere. What is the reason for it? Are Europeans, by nature, less religious? Has the modernization process hit Europe more strongly than the rest? Were the historical events of the twentieth century too traumatic for Europeans to maintain their faith in God? Is the reason spiritual, cultural, or intellectual?

When D. L. Moody went to speak at Oxford more than one hundred years ago, students snickered about Moody's accent while Moody preached. After Moody gave an altar call, no one responded. If Moody had preached the same sermon in America, many in the audience would have stood up and come to the altar. Knowing that Europe's spiritual soil was not the same as that of America, Moody repeatedly encouraged people to come forward. Finally, one student came forward, covering his face with his jacket out of embarrassment. Encouraged, other students came along, also covering their faces with coats.[3] Europeans express their religiosity differently than America.

Europeans accepted Barack Obama with tremendous enthusiasm in Berlin after his electoral victory. The Nobel Prize Committee awarded him the Peace Prize, not for what he had done, but for what people expected him to do as president. It is understandable why Obama was

---

1. Wandusim, "Christianity in Africa," 92.
2. Davie, "Europe," 65.
3. Pollock, *Moody without Sankey*.

popular in Europe. He is not a typical American. Barack has qualities that defy the conventional Americanism which Europeans disdain. Much of the so-called "European identity" is to be found in its objection to Americanism.[4] It is difficult to imagine George W. Bush or Donald Trump receiving the same kind of welcome in Europe.

Reinhard Bonnke was a phenomenally successful evangelist in Africa but not in his home country Germany. To his compatriots, Bonnke seemed too simplistic and dramatic. His sermons appealed to the African and American audience, but not Germans. Fellow German pastors could not warm up to Bonnke's style. Ernest Angley, a famous healing evangelist of America, was arrested in Scandinavia for practicing medicine without a license because he prayed for the sick. Few Americans or Asians would equate praying for the sick with practicing medicine. Though Americans often ridiculed Angley for his exaggerated style, no one would think of arresting him for practicing medicine without a license. Europeans do things differently than the rest of the world.

Imitating other people's methods in religious matters is not likely to work in Europe. Europeans are not used to disclosing private affairs before others. The Old World is more reticent than the New World. Europeans attach more importance to modesty than Americans. The way that Americans do things seems a little too noisy, expressive, and emotional, even though the American way of practicing faith has been embraced in other parts of the world, like Singapore and Africa, without much objection. While no one would deny the personal character of faith, the "privatization of faith" is not valued so highly in other parts of the world. Europeans find it difficult to share the common religious sentiments with others.

Another reason that it is difficult for the impulse of revival to penetrate Europe is that Europeans are too familiar with Christianity for their own good. Europe's experience with Christianity has been longer than any other part of the world, except Ethiopia and Asia Minor. To a person who has already been there, a newcomer's enthusiasm may seem superfluous and excessive. It may seem strange to Europeans to see foreign missionaries and preachers come into their countries to reintroduce Christianity.

Such a reaction is understandable. Nonetheless, even a seasoned doctor needs another doctor to care for him. Christianity does not belong to any one nation or civilization. It is neither Asian nor Occidental. The Chinese government objecting to Christianity on the ground that it

---

4. Kumar, "Question of European Identity," 91.

is a western religion should remember that fact. Likewise, those in the west who think that they own Christianity because it was part of their culture for a long time should realize that fact. Christianity has its own identity. It may rest with a culture for a period of time, but that does not give it ownership over Christianity. The Holy Spirit is like wind, said Jesus. You hear its sound, but you cannot tell where it comes from and where it goes. So is everyone who is born of the Spirit, said Jesus (John 3:8). The fact that the Holy Spirit rests upon a group of people does not mean that he will stay there forever. Likewise, the fact that the Holy Spirit is absent from a group of people does not mean that he is gone forever. Sometimes, the wind of a new revival comes from the outside. Because the universal church is the body of Christ, members of the body should care for one another. It involves not only giving care but also receiving it.

Europeans are suspicious of religious hype. Like in other trades, preachers resort to hype to sell Christianity. Granted that it is difficult to excite people spiritually without hype, the public cannot often distinguish between the real Holy Spirit and hype. After people realize that what they thought was from the Holy Spirit was, in fact, hype, they grow suspicious of anyone who peddles spirituality. Such suspicion often leads to cynicism. Cynicism is a terrible stumbling block to accepting any presentation of faith. Once a culture is accustomed to cynicism for a long time, it is difficult to recover the lost innocence. The loss is costly. It is for this reason that Jesus said, "Unless you change and become like little children, you will never enter the kingdom of heaven" (Matt 18:3). It takes God's grace to turn around the cynical mind.

Those who try to preach the gospel in Europe should be careful not to approach people as complete novices. Instead, they should find ways to present it so that even those who consider themselves well acquainted with Christianity can discover new perspectives. When Apostle Paul met some believers in Ephesus, he asked them, "Have you received the Holy Spirit since you believed?" It turned out that these Ephesian believers had not even heard of the Holy Spirit and did not correctly understand the gospel. Hence, Paul presented the gospel to them anew and baptized them. And then the Holy Spirit came on those disciples when Paul laid his hands on them. Even in Christian circles, there are many instances of incomplete conversions, near-misses, insufficient understanding of the gospel, as well as ignorance and indifference. Although we should not treat people as novices, there is always room for instruction, illumination, and progress for everyone.

No person should be presumed to be a genuine convert on the basis of church affiliation or religious background. Brad Pitt's question to the new tank driver in the film *Fury* is to the point: "Art you saved?"[5] Almost everyone will flinch at such a question. The tank driver in the film is no exception. He replies, "I was baptized," to which the gunner retorts, "That's not the same thing." Baptism is not necessarily the same thing as salvation. No person can state with authority that he has been saved because the authority to save rests with God alone. Nonetheless, Jesus declared to the paralytic man that his sins were forgiven. If a person can know that his sins are forgiven, he can also know that he is saved. Perhaps the most valuable contribution of evangelicalism was emphasizing the born-again experience and the assurance of salvation. Even for those people who have been attending church for their whole lives, obtaining the assurance of salvation by a conscious acceptance of Jesus Christ as Savior and Lord brings about a definite spiritual renewal and conviction.

Nothing will intrude on the privacy of a person as much as inquiring about his salvation. The reason many Europeans may squirm at such a personal question is understandable. However, it is this kind of straightforward approach that will take people out of spiritual passivity and bring them to an active faith. When Jack Dawson asks Rose if she loves her millionaire fiancé in the film *Titanic*, Rose is offended. She replies, "You're being very rude. You shouldn't be asking me this."[6] Rose is right; Jack's question is very rude. Still, she finds the question offensive because she cannot answer it confidently. Sometimes, we have to dispense with polite mannerisms to get to the spiritual truth.

Motivation and momentum are necessary to turn around the great ship called Europe. A big boat takes much time and force to turn around. Steve Bannon, the founder of Breitbart News and the former Republican campaign strategist, set up a political consulting firm in Europe to help the causes of the European parties in preparation for the 2019 EU Parliament election. It was much before he was indicted for shady dealings. Some people asked what an American political philosopher was doing in Europe. He involved himself in Europe's political movement because he felt that there was not enough motivation coming from the Europeans themselves. If someone lacks the motivation to change an unacceptable

---

5. Ayer, *Fury*.
6. Cameron, *Titanic*.

situation, someone else who shares the same belief can offer the necessary motivation. Regardless of the merits of Bannon's political involvement, it is significant that a non-European felt it necessary to take part in the European affairs in the 21st century.

Sometimes one does not have enough know-how and persistence to do what one must do. Experience suggests that Europe needed outside help from time to time in the 20th century. Outside help in the past was limited to military and political spheres. Times are changing. Europe now needs spiritual assistance, not because Europeans do not have faith, but because they lack the will and power to stir faith in people's hearts. In the body of Christ, we are all members of one body. No one is more valuable than others. We should have equal concern for each other (1 Cor 12:25). God gives special honor to the parts that lack it. It is almost fashionable for Europeans to resist whatever has to do with America. It is not considered politically incorrect. In the popular Netflix drama series "Emily in Paris," a young career woman from Chicago brings her can-do American attitude to a Paris marketing firm and realizes how much her French colleagues resist and scorn her American ways. An interesting question would be, if Emily were not an American but from a non-western country, would she still face resistance and scorn from her French officemates? When Christian brotherhood and encouragement come from non-western countries, will it still be fashionable to refuse them? The European intellectuals may not know how to respond to this new situation. Times have changed.

For something to be achieved on the national scale, momentum is necessary. It is one thing to have a motivation, but another to gain momentum. Momentum is built when enough people move in concert for a common cause. In the United States, the name Billy Graham became a household name for the born-again message of Christianity. When Billy Graham held an evangelistic crusade in any particular city, churches in that city pooled their efforts together to help the crusade. Often, Billy Graham's evangelistic association could buy one hour of air time on major television networks to broadcast his crusade meetings. No other minister enjoyed that kind of recognition and cooperation in America. This success was due to the single-hearted dedication, for over half a century, of the remarkable evangelist. It is just one example. Many other people and institutions have provided valuable contributions to keeping the Christian faith alive and active. Europeans must ask themselves if they have such people. This difference perhaps explains why the US has managed to keep its faith alive while the rest of the western world could not.

Compared to other spheres of endeavors, Christians are modest and even passive in the way they work. Business, finance, public entertainment, education, scientific research, and even crime and terrorism freely cross national borders. Christianity is reticent and inactive in comparison. It is a surprising phenomenon in this era of globalization and information. The most recent changes happening in the world have spared Christianity.

Churches in Europe resemble the woman in the gospel of Luke, who was bent over and could not straighten up for eighteen years. Until Jesus healed her, no one could help her during her long ailment. Many of the patients Jesus healed had been sick for a long time. The woman with the issue of blood had been sick for twelve years. The man at the pool of Bethesda had been sick for thirty-eight years. Similarly, Europe's spiritual condition has been unattended for too long. Everyone knew about it, but few people stepped up to help. Is it because Europeans are at the top of the totem pole? Is it because the conventional world mission paradigm dictates that a more affluent nation must help a poorer nation? Do Europeans consider it beneath their dignity to receive support from outsiders?

Many of the literature on this subject gives the impression that they have left Jesus out of the discussion altogether. They seem to believe that Jesus does not have a role to play in the current situation. It is as if people assume that Jesus does not care. If we leave Jesus out, we have nothing positive or optimistic to say about the future of Christianity. Someone should bring some measure of faith to the table of discussion. The discussion about Europe's spiritual condition and destiny should not be just academic or theological, but prophetic. If a person has no prophetic insight to add to the discussion, he has no place in the discussion. The conspicuous absence of faith confession in the discussion on European Christianity in itself exposes the fundamental problem. Contributors look at it from sociological, historical, philosophical, psychological, and even biological perspectives, but few speak from the standpoint of faith. They all speak the words of men, but few speak the words of God. After all, the church belongs to Jesus Christ. He called it "my church" (Matt 16:18). If we leave him out of our discussion, how does church belong to Jesus? Because the church is his, he will play a role in the church. Believing it is the beginning of the much-desired change.

God told Abraham that if there were ten righteous men at Sodom, he would not destroy Sodom for their sake. If God could find ten believing people in Europe today, he would not forsake Europe for their sake.

The migration of people from the Global South may supply such ten believing people in Europe finally. The just shall live by faith. We need ten righteous people in Europe, crying out to God to come and help them. Europe must be saved once again.

— 3 —

History Is Not Over

JESUS SAID THAT NOBODY knows the day or hour of his return, not even the angels in heaven, nor the Son, except the Father (Mark 13:32). But he gave one sign of the end: "This gospel of the kingdom will be preached in the whole world as a testimony to all nations, and then the end will come" (Matt 24:14). Based on this passage, Christians have speculated that preaching the gospel to the end of the world would bring the end. When Christopher Columbus set out to the New World, his motivation was not only exploration but also his belief that bringing the gospel to the New World would usher in the second coming of Christ. This kind of thinking has followed Christians for centuries.

In the twentieth century, it seemed probable for the first time in history that the gospel could reach the end of the world. The evangelization of the 10/40 Window greatly expanded the reach of Christianity. Missionaries were excited that Jesus could return in our lifetime.

However, while missionaries focused on the unreached people of the earth, unexpected events occurred. The existing Christian cultures began to slip away from the faith. Missionary organizations probably did not foresee this turn of events. Although the traditional mission fields accepted Christianity with enthusiasm, Europe began to depart from it. The eschatologically motivated missionary scenario was flawed. Preaching the gospel to the unreached people on earth did not complete the Great Commission. We must surmise that the history of humanity will not come to an end in any foreseeable future but continue indefinitely.

The two-thousand-year history of Christianity has demonstrated that Christianity does not move in a linear direction. There have been many detours and even retreats in its history. The loss of the Christian lands to the Islamic conquest, for instance, was one major setback. Non-Christians now occupy the birthplace of Christianity. With the seven churches of Asia Minor lying in ruins, Hagia Sophia of Istanbul, the former Greek Orthodox Christian patriarchal cathedral, was converted to a mosque. We believe in the final triumph of the church of Jesus Christ, but the road to victory is much longer than we expect.

The ends of the earth are not a geographical concept. The task of the church does not end when the gospel reaches any geographical destination. By the time we reach "the ends of the earth," other areas are again in need of new evangelization. While Africa and Asia were accepting Christianity, the western world has become a new mission field. The first became the last while the last became the first, as Jesus said. We are hesitant to say that the gospel will ever reach the ends of the earth at any particular point in time. We cannot imagine a time when no more evangelization will be necessary in the world.

We must read the prophecies of the New Testament with a grain of salt. Mixing mission with eschatology is unhelpful to understanding either the missionary task or biblical eschatology. On the one hand, the original assumption that the gospel needs to go around the world only once is in error. It is implausible that the world will get one opportunity to hear the gospel, and then Jesus will come to judge the world. This scenario is a groundless interpretation of the New Testament.

Furthermore, linking eschatology with the world mission creates false hopes about the second coming of the Lord. Jesus will return when God decides. We cannot predict this time through any sort of speculation, including the extent of world evangelization. The kingdom of God is an ideal for which we should all strive, but any human accomplishment cannot determine it. The coming of the kingdom of God is not something that can be observed so that people can say, "Here it is," or "There it is" (Luke 17:20–21). Linking the abstruse concept of eschatology with human achievement only produces confusion and error.

Nor does it make sense in any rational analysis of history. The end of history cannot depend upon a successful completion of any human endeavor, whether it is the perfection of democracy, the culmination of culture, or the fulfillment of world evangelism. Such a moment exists only conceptually, like the concept of infinity. Francis Fukuyama wrote *The End of History*, believing that the ideological evolution and western democracy have reached the endpoint.[1] He thought that no more progress was possible. That was more than twenty years ago, but no one in our time would think that western democracy has reached its final goal. Instead, western democracy in the era of Brexit and Donald Trump is going through unprecedented turmoil. There will never come a time when humanity will be able to say, "We did it." There will always be problems created by humanity, which will need all the available wisdom to solve.

Evangelical Christians are familiar with the Dispensationalists' interpretation of the end-time prophecy, involving the Rapture, the Seven-Year Tribulations, and the second coming of Jesus. Once believers get used to this school of eschatology, it is not easy to get it out of their minds. Not only did the Dispensationalists grossly misinterpret the Bible prophecies, but also falsely suspected innocent world figures and institutions of being the anti-Christ. It resembled a conspiracy theory. Those who went to church during the seventies and eighties must have seen the gospel tracts depicting the Pope, William Brandt, and the European Union (it was called the European Economic Community then) as the antichrist and the beast. The Dispensationalists' error should have been clear from their suspicious ability to turn abstruse Bible prophecies into specific scenarios. They were making up certainty where no such certainty was possible. What would the Europeans have thought about the American evangelicals' credibility if they discovered what the Americans were saying about Europe?

Evangelicals should free their minds from the Dispensationalist's false theory that the world will end in utter confusion and despair. Such a scenario means that God's creative purpose will fail, and so will Christianity. The end will come when God determines it, but the Dispensationalist theory makes Christians fatalistic and pessimistic.

Whether correct eschatological beliefs should lead to pessimism or optimism is a tough theological question. The Bible is not clear on this issue. During the Cold War, some people suggested that the nuclear strategy should not rest in the hands of fundamentalist Christians. The reasoning was that, because fundamentalist Christians believe in the apocalyptic prophecy of the Bible, they might accept the inevitability of atomic apocalypse more than those who do not believe in such prophecy. Instead of trying to avoid a nuclear war, fundamental Christians might be fatalistic about it.

---

1. Fukuyama, *End of History*.

Christians have expected the imminent return of Jesus throughout the history of Christianity. Each generation is vulnerable to the belief that the end may occur during its lifetime. The tendency to expect the apocalyptic end of the world owes itself to man's psychological condition more than theological conviction. We are afraid of the future. We cannot imagine what the future holds for humanity. One does not have to be a Christian to have a pessimistic view of the future. During the confrontation between the United States and the Soviet Union, we feared that a nuclear war might annihilate the world. After the collapse of communism, we feared that climate change, depletion of natural resources, or the rise of artificial intelligence may end the world. If not, a giant meteor will do the job. Words like "apocalypse" and "armageddon" kept appearing in movie titles. If it is not a giant meteor, robots will turn into terminators to end humanity. Billionaires are working on plans to migrate to Mars to escape the inhabitable conditions of the earth. Instead of dreaming about an optimistic future, we are afraid of it.

As long as we allow our fears to determine our eschatological beliefs, we will always make theological errors. What the Bible says about the end of history is that God will triumph despite all the trials and tribulations. The Bible is not saying that human history will end in utter failure and disaster. If that were the future of humanity, God's plan for humanity would have failed. Belief in the Lord's plan to save humanity requires overcoming our psychological anxiety. To be prophetic does not mean predicting the end, but looking into the future. A true seer should not see just the end, but a new beginning and the hope for the future.

Do we think that God's redemption of the world will be like the Americans' evacuation during the last days of the Vietnam War? As the North Vietnamese Army surrounded Saigon, US helicopters rescued Vietnamese civilians desperately waiting in the US Embassy to flee Saigon. Do we believe that Christians will be rescued from the world while the world goes down in cataclysmic destruction? Noah's flood and the destruction of Sodom were such events. The Dispensationalists' idea of the Rapture looks precisely like the US evacuation of Saigon. But there is something deeply troubling about this kind of scenario.

We do not have inside information on how the kingdom of God will come upon the earth. Nonetheless, the apocalyptic view of the end is irresponsible, fatalistic, and devoid of faith. Did God create the earth and humanity only to end it like the American evacuation of Saigon? If so, it can only mean that God will have failed.

Jesus refused to give any detailed information about how the kingdom of God would arrive. Instead, he predicted that his disciples would be his witnesses to the ends of the earth. When Jesus's disciples asked him whether the kingdom would come any time near, Jesus replied, "It is not for you to know the times or dates the Father has set by his own authority" (Acts 1:7). Jesus did not consider it essential to offer a detailed end-time scenario, other than the expansion of the gospel to the ends of the earth. It is not proper, therefore, for Christians to demand more information about the subject. Heresies go off course by trying to add more details to eschatology.

Our eschatological doctrine should rest on a deep faith in the providence and faithfulness of God toward humanity. God has not been patient with humanity since the creation of the world only to abandon us in cataclysmic tribulations at the end. The history of humanity is not ready to end yet. If God brings humanity to an end at this point in history, there are too many unanswered questions about God's purposes and providence. For all creation to give glory to God, his power and wisdom must be made manifest. On the day of judgment, all of humanity must acknowledge that God has been just. To say that God is just is to say that he is right. It means that God has been right in all that he does. The history of humanity has not yet come to a place where we can fully understand the justice of God's actions. Unless all creation can praise God for his justice and wisdom, he will not receive glory. The Book of Job ends with Job and his three friends repenting of their ignorant remarks about God's justice. The ending of Job is a mini version of eschatology. If all people cannot realize and exclaim the righteousness of God's actions toward them, God will not receive glory. God will not be pleased.

Hence, history is bound to be longer than we can imagine. We neither own time nor decide it. We do not understand the meaning of time. Before God created the heavens and earth, time did not exist. The very first verse of Genesis, "In the beginning, God created the heavens and the earth," suggests that God created not only space but also time. Before creation, time did not exist as we understand it. Thus, God created time for a purpose. What could that be? Revelation 2:21 holds the key to the biblical definition of time. Most English translations of the passage say, "I have given her time to repent of her immorality," but King James Version translated it like this: "I gave her space to repent." Here is a hint of the definition of time: the space to repent. Time is the space or opportunity to repent for the fallen humanity. Thus, the end in the theological sense means the termination of the chance to repent. This interpretation makes sense.

As long as there are people on earth who need to repent, God will allow time to continue. We cannot ask when history will end. To ask that question is like asking when there will be no more people to repent. The last day cannot be likened to Noah's flood or the destruction of Sodom and Gomorrah because those two events did not mark the end of history *per se*. History continued after the flood and the judgment of Sodom and Gomorrah. The last day, in contrast, means there will be no more time after it. God will usher in the last day after humanity has had enough time to repent. Only God knows when that will be.

Jesus's statement that the end will come after the gospel is preached to the ends of the earth does not mean that he will wait until the gospel reaches the ends of the earth to usher in the end. Instead, it means that God will not end history until all humanity has had the opportunity to hear the gospel.

— 4 —

The Gospel Can Go around the World One More Time

To be able to see our missionary imperative more clearly, we must separate it from eschatology. The belief that the end is near has terribly restricted Christians' ability to imagine and construct long-term missionary strategies. Especially after the spiritual decline of Europe, the Dispensationalist missionary scenario has been found to be lacking. The "unreached" people within the 10/40 Window cannot be the only remaining mission field in the world. The fact that Europe has received Christianity once and slid away from it does not mean that Europe has lost all opportunities to return to it. That way of thinking is fatalistic and does a disservice to the grace of God. God does not give each culture just one chance to repent and then abandons it.

Some people think that they travel the road of life only once, and whatever they passed by on the way is not worth returning to. In the film *De-Lovely*, which portrays the life of the composer Cole Porter, there is a very disturbing dialogue between Cole Porter and his friend Gabe. Cole Porter is at the point of death and does not want to be late to his own funeral. He says, "Under the circumstances, I suppose I should say my prayers." His friend Gabe retorts cynically, "Why start now?"[1] The worst thing that anyone can say to anyone about the possibility of faith is, "Why start now?"

Any time is right for belief, as long as one has time to believe. The thief crucified next to Jesus asked Jesus to remember him when Jesus

---

1. Winkler, *De-Lovely*.

came into his kingdom. The thief on the other side of Jesus probably thought to himself, "Why start now?" The cynical thief probably thought that, if believing were so crucial to life, he would have had an opportunity to believe already. The fact that he has never had such an opportunity means that it was not crucial to him. This kind of thinking is perhaps the most arrogant thinking that a person can have. How can he be sure that he has never had an opportunity to have faith during his life? He did not count it important to pay attention to it when he had the chance. Considering how much he has dismissed the opportunity for belief all his life, he should take this last chance seriously even though it comes at the last moment of his life. The thief who rejected Jesus could not come physically closer to Jesus than when he was crucified next to Jesus. But the physical proximity did not guarantee repentance. Those who reject Jesus are not necessarily distant from him. God is not so far from anyone that he cannot believe him. In the Parable of the Vineyard, some workers went into the vineyard to work at six in the morning. Some went at noon. And some did not have anyone to hire them until five in the evening— one hour before sundown. If these men thought to themselves, "Why start now?" they would have spent the entire day without a job and pay. It is better late than never. Those who went into the vineyard one hour before sundown received the same wages as those who began at dawn.

The definition of time is the opportunity given to humanity to seek God and find him. God determined the times and places for every nation so that men would seek and find him (Acts 17:26-27). Any opportunity is a welcome opportunity. For some, the opportunity comes early; for others, it comes late. What is important is that it comes.

God does not limit the opportunity for faith to just once. The Bible is full of instances where people did not obey God the first time they had the chance. If God had given up on them, they would have been lost forever. But God was gracious enough to give them another opportunity.

Korean Christians used to describe the history of Christianity as the movement of the Holy Spirit. The Holy Spirit started in Jerusalem and moved to the Roman Empire. He then moved to the rest of Europe, including Great Britain, and went on to North America. After that, the Holy Spirit went to Asia and Africa. Those who subscribed to this theory taught that the journey of the Holy Spirit was a one-way trip. Like the Dispensationalists, they believed that the end would come soon after the Holy Spirit was finished with Asia and Africa.

The gifts and calling of God are irrevocable (Rom 11:29). Jesus came looking for Peter after his resurrection because Peter's calling as Jesus's servant was irrevocable despite Peter's failures. The reason Jesus called Saul of Tarsus to serve him even though Saul was a persecutor of the church was that Saul had the calling to be his servant. The circumstances of one's life are not always cooperative with God's purposes for him. The fact that God has planned something for a person does not guarantee that all his circumstances will be conducive to fulfilling that plan. If we looked for the evidence of God's plan in our conditions, we might never discover his plan.

The history of Christianity does not follow a straight line. Likewise, the movement of the Holy Spirit is not direct. Sometimes, what was done once has to be done again. Anything having to do with humanity takes more than one try. The blind man whom Jesus healed did not receive his sight after Jesus's first attempt. Jesus had to lay hands on him again. Peter could not fulfill his calling as an apostle after just one effort; Jesus had to call him for the second time for Peter to obey him fully.

The New Testament does not state that the gospel will go around the world only once and the end will come. We do not know when the end will come. Until then, we have to preach the gospel as many times as necessary and as often as we get a chance. To do so is being faithful to God's will to save the world. To do so is the only expression of faith and obedience for the disciples of Jesus.

Generations Come and Go

Each generation is given only a finite length of time and cannot determine the spiritual destiny of its descendants. Those living in Europe now are not the same people who slid away from Christianity in the prior generations. The previous generations have died. Each person is responsible for his faith. The decline of the British churches, for example, is ascribed not to the adult defection but to the failure to keep children in the faith.[2] The believing parents cannot presume that their children are believers by default.

By the same token, unbelieving parents cannot presume that their children will be apathetic to faith like them. Sometimes, children express an interest in religion contrary to the teaching or expectation of

---

2. Bruce and Glendinning, "When Was Secularization?"

their parents.³ In the 2000 film *Chocolat*, a non-conforming chocolatier stays away from the only church in town. Still, her little daughter is unhappy about not going to church—to the dismay of her mother.⁴ Each generation lives with different religious motives and circumstances. The circumstances that led to the loss of interest in Christianity in times past are not necessarily binding at the present time. Many Christians wrestled with doubt when the theory of evolution was first introduced, for instance. But fewer people consider evolution to be a major hindrance to faith now. Those who departed from the faith on account of evolution acted too rashly. Maybe they were looking for an excuse for not believing. New discoveries are made that alter our previous ways of understanding nature. Humanity will never reach the final stage of knowledge.

Each generation of people is entitled to a fair opportunity to hear the gospel message and judge for themselves if it makes sense to them. The fact that their parents' generation lost interest in religion does not dictate their children's decision. The decision to believe or not to believe is not a collective decision but an individual one. In *Love Story*, the son of a millionaire rebels against his family name and faith. However, in the sequel *Oliver's Story*, written by the same Eric Segal, the protagonist not only returns to his father's business but also to his church.⁵ An act of rebellion in one's youth does not necessarily last throughout his life. We judge hastily by looking at only one frame of time. Michael Corleone chooses a life of violence and crime in *Godfather* 1 and 2, but in *Godfather* 3, he confesses his sins and vows not to sin anymore. Just how long can a man live away from God and expect to be peaceful? How long can a branch be separated from the vine and hope to survive? Man may go away from God, but God does not go away from him. The grace of God is irresistible, meaning that God will never give up on his people.

We are implicitly suspicious of any trend in religious matters. People can follow trends in fashion and public entertainment. Such whims are for brief public consumption. But in matters of faith, mass trends are not trustworthy. Fads are provisional and disingenuous. Jesus cannot compete with the Beatles for mass popularity, as John Lennon famously claimed. Christianity is not popular among people in the same way as iPhones or Tesla cars. Jesus distrusted his popularity among people.

3. O'Neill, "I'm a Committed Atheist."
4. Hallström, *Chocolat*.
5. Segal, *Oliver's Story*.

When the disciples exclaimed, "Everyone is looking for you!" Jesus chose to leave the area and go someplace else (Mark 1:35–39). His popularity did not determine either his mission or itinerary. If anyone thinks that Christianity is not suited for Europe because it has lost its popular appeal, he misunderstands Christianity. Popularity is untrustworthy. God's truth has never been popular with people. Nonetheless, people have believed in him for centuries upon centuries. The grass withers and the flowers fall, but the word of God stands forever.

Each Generation Must Believe for Itself

Man lives but for a short time, but his actions have longer consequences. When children grow up to take responsibility for the things they have inherited from their parents, their parents are no longer around to explain to them why they did what they did. The current generation of Europeans, for example, must live with the European Union that was the product of their parents. The current generation cannot ask the earlier generation why it did what it did because many of the key players are already dead. The responsible political parties are no longer in power. The present generation, therefore, must find new meanings and purposes for the situations that they have inherited. The future generation of Britain will ask the same questions about Brexit. The posterity will have to live with the current generation's choices.

Likewise, Europe's youths must decide what to do with the empty churches and waning Christianity that they have inherited from their parents. The prior generation's dismissal of Christianity is not binding on the current generation. Each generation must believe for itself. Faith cannot be presumed, but neither can unbelief.

No one accepts anything for granted in this postmodern era. Some people reject the gender they were born with. How much more will they resist the religion they were born with? Everything must be challenged and reinvestigated to be authentic. Faith is no exception. The decline of Christianity in the west may have been necessary for this authentication process. Even so, is it not about time that this process came to an end? Europeans have spent enough time deconstructing Christianity; they need to build it back now. The work of rebuilding it does not take place automatically. Somebody has to present the gospel to people anew.

Faith comes by hearing the word of Christ (Rom 10:17). Nothing can substitute the word of Christ. Each generation has to listen to the gospel anew. Those who are brought up in Christian homes have more opportunities to hear the gospel, but their faith cannot be presumed from their upbringing. Any pastor who tries to raise his children in the faith understands this challenge. Christianity has been Europe's religion by default for a long time. As Søren Kierkegaard lamented, one was a Christian because he was a Dane. This kind of arrangement may have worked in the past, but not anymore. The famous debate between faith and works ignores how faith happens in the first place. Before people can debate which is more important between faith and works, they must have faith first. Otherwise all such discussions are useless.

All the converts mentioned in the book of Acts were already religious people before their conversion. But their piety did not bring about personal conversion on its own. Cornelius, for example, was a devout man whose prayers and alms had risen to God as a memorial offering. But it did not automatically make him a Christian. He was instructed by an angel to send for apostle Peter and hear the presentation of the gospel from Peter. While he was listening to the gospel, the Holy Spirit came on him, and Cornelius became a true convert. The Ethiopian eunuch was also a devout man on his way back from a pilgrimage to Jerusalem. Yet he did not know Jesus. Philip had to instruct the Ethiopian man about Jesus. Only then was he baptized and became a true convert. There are many other instances. The disciples at Ephesus whom apostle Paul met knew of the gospel only partially. They knew about John the Baptist but not about Jesus. After Paul taught them the gospel accurately, they were baptized and converted. In many cases, conversions were accompanied by the signs of the Holy Spirit. Cornelius received the Holy Spirit, and so did the Ephesian disciples.

European pastors are fearful of people's callousness, thinking that presenting the Gospel will fall on deaf ears. Some European pastors fear that Europeans need not hear the gospel message again because they already know it. This is a defeatist mentality ignoring that there are two kinds of knowledge. The first kind is theoretical knowledge. For example, we all know that Christopher Columbus discovered America. This kind of knowledge registers in our brain but produces no emotive response. The second kind of knowledge is personal knowledge. When a child knows that his mother loves him selflessly, this knowing evokes a personal response. This knowing produces a sense of comfort and security.

It feels good. When theologians think that Europeans already know the Gospel but are indifferent to it, they are talking about theoretical knowledge. Those who are indifferent to the gospel have never truly tasted it. We must taste and see that the Lord is good (Ps 34:8). Unless people have felt it, they do not truly know it. There is a significant difference.

One of the robbers who were crucified next to Jesus already knew who Jesus was, but his response to Jesus was anything but faith: "Are you not the Christ? Save yourself and us!" (Luke 23:39). He had enough information to know who Jesus is. He called him Christ. But his words were not words of faith; instead, they were disparaging and accusatory. Thus, the argument that Europeans need not hear the gospel again because they already know it is mistaken. As long as the European clergy subscribe to this theory, they will not be able to do their job boldly. Presenting the gospel message to people anew is no different from any pastoral ministry. People who come to church every Sunday are already knowledgeable of the gospel and many other things. They do not come to church to learn something that they did not know before. They come to church to confirm what they already know and believe. The fact that they already know something does not preclude hearing about it again. Instead, they want to hear it again because they already believe it. Good news deserves to be told again and again. That is why it is good news. If believing people need to hear the gospel again and again, how much more will unbelieving people need to hear it again? This is a common fact of the pastoral ministry which people tend to overlook.

Saving the World Takes More Than One Attempt

The fact that the first round of Christianity eventually led to a secular Europe does not mean that it has ultimately failed. It just means that what used to work in the past is not working so well at this time. For those who lived in the past, Christianity did well. But those days are gone, and we must deal with our new reality. We must find ways to make the Christian ministry work well now. The Normandy invasion did not consist of just one wave of landing troops. There were second, third, and many successive waves of landing crafts and soldiers. To break down the mighty Atlantic Wall, the Allies had to hit it multiple times.

Why do people believe that God gave humanity just one chance to believe? Once is not enough. Even if one generation of people believed in

Christianity, there is no guarantee that the following generations will follow suit. The work must continue. The task ends only when Jesus returns, and we do not know when that will be. As it is engraved on John Wesley's tombstone, God buries his servants in the earth but continues his work. The success of ministry cannot be determined by its short-term effect but by its lasting impact. Jesus demanded fruit that will last (John 15:16). Given the limited duration of human lives, lasting fruit requires continuous and faithful ministry from one generation to the next. Sometimes one generation is less devout than others, as when the Prophet Samuel's sons did not measure up to Samuel. It was ironic because Samuel himself had replaced the ineffective household of Eli. Though Israel's faith prospered during Samuel's life, God terminated his sons' ministry after Samuel's death and, instead, instituted a monarchy in Israel. The spiritual condition of society is not permanent. That is why ministry must be continuous and persistent. It is like filling the gas tank of your car with gas on a frequent basis. It is like watering plants. Once is not enough. You have to continue as long as you are growing plants in your garden. Plants have a longer lifespan than people. Generations come and go. Therefore, teaching the faith to people must continue from one generation to the next. If churches fail at this task, a Christian society runs the risk of becoming a secular society within one generation. It is a sobering fact.

Calling one's nation Christian is meaningless in that regard. There is no such thing as a Christian nation. Until the kingdom of God comes entirely on earth, no community of men arrives at the ideal state. Even if it does, it will not remain ideal permanently because anyone can fall into apostasy. It is liken looking for an ideal church. There is no such thing as an ideal church. Even there were such a church, it will not remain so once we join it. The ideal state is something we should all strive for but never quite reach. Other religions are no different. The Constitution of the Islamic Republic of Iran declares that Iran is a Muslim nation. But it is more rhetorical than substantive. About a third of Iran's population does not believe in Islam. Enforcing it by law at the penalty of death only produces hypocrisy.

There was a time when the western world was called a Christian civilization, but that does not mean that everyone was a genuine believer during that time. Historians are skeptical that Europe was fully evangelized at any time in its history. Historical research shows that Europeans in medieval times did not attend church in any high number.[6] Mass piety was found mainly among the nobility, not the peasant class.[7] The peasant class worshiped the folklore with some Christian content.[8] Christianity was mainly an urban phenomenon during medieval times.[9]

We do not find this fact surprising because we find the same pattern in Israel's experience in the Old Testament. There was never a moment when Israel's spiritual condition was idealistic. As the name "Israel" suggests, the Israelites always wrestled with God. Moses could not control his people, even with all the miracles he performed. Throughout the history of Judah and Israel, wicked kings followed good things, and apostasy followed revivals. The shelf life of religious revival was short. Calling a nation Christian only confuses the never-ending nature of the pastoral ministry and discipline. The briefest diagnosis of Europe's spiritual condition is that the churches were not effective at the continual responsibility of maintaining faith in society from one generation to the next. The churches were not ready to deal with the rapid cultural changes sweeping the western world. Although European churches are smaller than their American counterparts or African counterparts, that does not mean that American or African Christians are better Christians. We cannot pass such judgments. Even in societies with high church attendances, there are all kinds of moral and spiritual problems among believers. Contemporary believers do not make better people than the Old Testament Israelites. We must deal with the fallen nature of man at every age in any society with no exception. Churches and ministers must always remember the gravity of their responsibilities. They need to keep their lamps filled with oil at all times because they know not when Jesus will return.

The empty cathedrals and church buildings in Europe are not monuments to the irrelevance of Christianity. Instead, they are proof that Christianity thrived in Europe at one time. Previous generations did their job during their time. David served God's purpose in his generation and then fell asleep (Acts 13:36). The previous generation of God's servants is dead and gone. It is up to the following generation to take it over. Continuing the ministry does not necessarily require the use of the same infrastructure, including buildings and organizations. Jesus taught

---

6. Stark, *Triumph of Faith*, 51.
7. Stark, "Supply-side Reinterpretation," 241.
8. Stark, "Supply-side Reinterpretation," 242.
9. Stark, "Supply-side Reinterpretation," 242.

in open fields and private houses instead of central locations. Apostle Paul chose venues other than existing synagogues to teach the gospel. We should not lament over the old church buildings that are being sold. What is being sold is real estate, not Christianity. Continuing the ministry in our time does not necessarily presuppose the repetition of the earlier methods. New churches can meet in different facilities such as theaters, seminar rooms, and private living rooms. Being tied to the old buildings creates the wrong impression that Christianity is disappearing from society when, in reality, the changing demographic and sociological conditions are calling for innovations in church ministry. While driving through downtown Bournemouth one summer afternoon, I noticed an old church building that had been transformed to an office building. The building had a bell tower with a real bell still hanging there. Wanting to purchase the church bell and ship it to Seoul, I called the office number. The man answering my call replied that the old church building had been "deconsecrated" and, thus, selling the church bell was a possibility. They had a word for a church building that was no longer used as a church. Deconsecration was one of the saddest word that I had heard, but that was the fact of life in the western world. I ended up not buying the church bell because I had to hire a crane and a crew to remove the bell, transport it, and store it, which would cost more than what I could sell the bell for. I remember that the man on the other side of the phone did not sound too happy using the word "deconsecrated." I believe that he speaks for the rest of the European society. Nobody is happy to see an old church building in the city center either boarded up or turned into something else. I have never seen a very successful transformation of an old church building. People are not happy about leaving the faith. They probably want to come back to it if they can, only if somebody could help them to come back. A desire alone cannot bring them back. Well prepared ministers and communities of faith must help them. This is the task of the believing people in Europe today.

Jesus Does Not Hesitate to Repeat His Work

During Jesus's earthly ministry, he sometimes had to repeat the same work. When a blind man came to him at Bethsaida, Jesus spat on the man's eyes and laid his hands on him, asking, "Do you see anything?" The blind man replied, "I see people; they look like trees walking around." The man was only partially healed. At this, Jesus put his hands on the man one more time. Then his eyes were completely opened, and he was able to see clearly (Mark 8:22–26). It is significant that Jesus had to do the same task twice. We must note that he did not hesitate to put his hands on the blind man for a second time. If Jesus was willing to repeat his effort to heal someone completely, why should we hesitate to repeat our job to preach the gospel? The greatest folly of the western church in the 21st century is its hesitation to repeat the work that it has been entrusted with. It discloses unbelief, fatigue, and discouragement. Christians do not believe that it will work. But we need to learn from Jesus at this point. As Jesus put his hand on the blind man for the second time to cure him completely, we must be ready to go around the world for the second time with the gospel.

The phrase "once again" can be translated into French as *de nouveau* and à nouveau. Both words mean "once again," but there are slight differences in nuance. *De nouveau* means the simple repetition of the same act, whereas à nouveau means doing the same action with specific improvement. The French translations of Mark 8:22–26 use the phrase *de nouveau* instead of à nouveau. La Bible Louis Segond says, "*Jésus lui mit de nouveau les mains sur les yeux.*" La Bible Catholique says, "*Il lui imposa de nouveau les mains sur les yeux.*" It is not a coincidence that the French Bibles picked *de nouveau* to describe Jesus's repetition of the same work. There was nothing wrong with Jesus's first attempt to heal the blind man. His power was not insufficient. He did not have to improve his method or turn up his power the second time around. Opening a blind man's eyes is a difficult task. We should not think it strange that Jesus had to do it twice to complete it. The second time around, Jesus simply repeated what he had done the first time.

Likewise, we should not think it strange that saving the world takes more than one attempt. Some parts of the world are receiving the gospel for the first time, but others, like Europe, need to receive it once again. Opening blind eyes is a difficult task. Saving men's souls is just as difficult. We should not think that the world will be saved after only one try, requiring no more work after it. Like house chores and parenting, ministry must be continuous. Jesus was able to heal everyone he laid his hands on. His success rate was 100%. But for ordinary people, even those with a special gift of healing, perhaps their success rate is 10%. Even if one in ten people they pray for is healed, that is still outstanding. What about the chances of success for saving souls? How many people accept the gospel message out of all those we reach out to? Even if one out of ten people accept the gospel, that is still magnificent. One out of a hundred is still excellent. We should not compare our efficiency with some imaginary superstar minister. No such superstar exists. Everyone must try hard to save this hardened generation. There is no special place for tired and discouraged ministers in the kingdom of God because everyone is tired and discouraged. It comes with the job. Elijah was tired and so was Moses. Even Jesus had moments of fatigue. That is why he fell asleep on the boat. Nobody said that this job would be easy. It is not easy even to God. That is why God had to send his Son to die on the cross. God had to pay a big price to save humanity. We must believe God and do our job with perseverance and grit. Then God will reward us.

Having to do it for the second time does not mean that Christianity needs some kind of change or improvement. Nothing is lacking in the grace of the Lord Jesus. Jesus's death on the cross paid for the sins of the world once and for all. We cannot add anything to Christ or take anything away from him (Rev 22:18–19). Preaching the gospel one more time means being faithful to the purpose of the Great Commission. There is no shortcut to completing God's purposes on earth.

The Disobedient Get Another Chance

Although God calls people to believe him and serve him, people do not always obey him the first time. As a result, God calls them again. He does not have to, but he does. People's persistent disobedience to God's will does not nullify God's calling. God's gifts and calling are irrevocable (Rom 11:29).

Peter experienced the grace of Jesus after failing him on the night of Jesus's arrest. Jesus had called Peter to follow him by the Lake Gennesaret at the beginning of his public ministry. Peter spent three and a half years with Jesus. He was the chief among the disciples. But when Jesus was arrested and taken to the priest's palace, Peter became afraid and denied him three times. We cannot blame Peter for what he did. Most people would have done the same thing in the same situation. Nonetheless, Peter was devastated by his failure. After he heard about Jesus's resurrection, Peter did not dare to see Jesus's face. Thus Jesus had to visit Peter personally, asking him, "Simon, son of John, do you love me?" He asked this

The Gospel Can Go around the World One More Time

question three times to match Peter's three denials. Even those who have been called once by Jesus must be called again if their failure throws them down the gorge of self-condemnation and doubt from which they cannot come out on their own.

The same thing happened to John Mark who, at one point, abandoned Paul and Barnabas during their missionary journey. John Mark was probably discouraged, homesick, and skeptical of his vocation as a missionary. But when Barnabas took him back on, against Paul's objection, John Mark obeyed. Later, Paul called John Mark useful to his ministry.

If everybody received just one chance to serve God, very few people would be serving him right now. Jesus taught about the joy of finding the lost sheep, the lost coin, and the lost son. Jesus's interest is not just in getting new sheep, new coins, and new sons. Many times, even God's people get lost. Jesus does not give up on them but looks for them until he finds them (Luke 15:4). In English, the passive tense "lost" is used, and so we cannot tell who lost the coin, sheep, and son. The implication is that God the Father himself lost the coin, sheep, and son. How he lost them is not explained in the Bible. Nonetheless, God is determined to find what he has lost. Jesus said that the shepherd looks for the lost sheep until it is found. God does not stop until he finds the lost sheep. If our missionary task focuses only on getting new sheep and ignores the lost sheep, we miss God's determination. Evangelists and missionaries should not focus exclusively on bringing new people into the kingdom of God while neglecting the lost sheep. Finding the lost sheep is part of the world mission, too. Often pastors criticize evangelists and church planters for sheep-stealing. We must realize that old sheep and new sheep often move together. If missionaries can provide new strengths to old Christians, it is a valuable job in itself. Reintroducing Christianity to post-Christian Europe involves finding the lost sheep as well as bringing in new sheep.

The accomplishment of the European church for the past two thousand years is monumental. Christianity would not have produced the same kind of results if it had been in the hands of any other civilization. But after two thousand years, Europeans have grown tired. No one can blame Europeans for this turn of events. My intention in writing this book is not to blame anyone. I could not have done a better job if I had been in their shoes. We are all in this together. We need to encourage one another and help one another to be faithful to our calling. To do that, we must believe in our gifts and calling. Our errors and weaknesses do not take our gifts and calling away. We must believe this.

— 5 —

What Happened to the Western World?

KNOWING THE CAUSES OF an illness does not necessarily cure the disease itself but will prevent its recurrence afterward. After healing the man with a thirty-eight-year-old disease, Jesus warned him not to sin anymore so that the same sickness would not come back.

What caused the decline of Christianity in the western world in the latter half of the twentieth century? People point to the year 1963 as the turning point in the spiritual condition of the west.[1] The church attendance rate began to drop sharply from 1963. The changes in the Catholic Church trace their origin to Vatican II, which took place from 1962 to 1965. The purpose of Vatican II was to bring the Catholic Church up to date, but doing so had a dampening effect on church attendance and a drop in the number of priests and nuns. It may not be fair to blame Vatican II for the steep decline in church attendance. Instead, it was the social and cultural changes that necessitated Vatican II, which are responsible for the decline. The prevailing sentiment during that time was, "Everything is changing, so why not religion, too?"[2]

The Explosion of Freedom

The decline of Christianity in the west was due to the explosion of freedom. Though the west had been free before, freedom began to express itself culturally, morally, and psychologically in the early sixties. Much of

---

1. Brown, *Death of Christian Britain*, 1.
2. McLeod, *Religion and the People of Western Europe*, 141.

this freedom was good—freedom from racial inequality, political oppression, and the old ways of doing things. Young people began to declare their liberty through cultural expressions. New cultural expressions rocked the young generation. With this explosion of liberty, people desired to throw off the constraints of traditional morality. It meant throwing off the constraints of Christianity because western morality was based on Christianity. It is at this point where Christian ethics devoid of Christian faith can push people away from Christianity. It may sound like a contradiction in terms, but it is an important point that affects all Christian societies. Although Christianity offers ethical rules, the purpose of Christianity is not to impose ethical rules, but to forgive those who could not keep the ethical rules. Jesus did not come to demand righteousness, but to save sinners. This fact is the central message of the gospel. But when the gospel element is taken out of the message of Christianity, people begin to regard Christianity as a heavy burden. People do not see God as the Father, but as a bother. It is almost inevitable that the explosion of freedom in Christian societies would cause a mass exodus of people from churches. Such exodus is a testimony to the false understanding of the gospel. We must ask when Christianity justly represented the gospel throughout its history.

Freedom is a good thing. Many of the changes in the 1960s were necessary changes in the realm of civil rights, racial and gender equality, and peace. But freedom also expressed itself in the area of personal morality. According to the Kinsey Reports, the public attitude towards sexuality in America had been very conservative up to that time. The explosion of freedom in the sixties brought about the sexual revolution.

Which one is the chicken, and which one is the egg? Was Christianity the moral force that had kept a tight lid on sexuality, so that the decline of Christianity flung the top wide open? Or did the lust for freedom make people reject Christianity? Human beings will never let their real reasons be known when it comes to sexuality.[3] Contrary to the conventional view that the west first experienced spiritual decline, followed by the family's decline a new theory suggests that the undermining of the family undermined Christianity.[4] The explosion of sexual freedom and the decline of Christianity coincided. That is what we need to know. Behind almost every human event, there is a sexual reason. To discover the reasons for

---

3. McLeod, *Religious Crisis of the 1960s*, 163.
4. Eberstadt, *How the West Really Lost God*, 6.

any significant event in society, we have to look at the role of sexuality. To say that is not to condemn man, but to acknowledge that basic human instincts are presumed in human conduct. According to the poet Philip Larkin, sexual liberty began in 1963 between the end of the Lady Chatterley ban and the Beatles' first album.[5]

The western society might have used Christianity to restrain its sexual desires. Though this is a curious psychological phenomenon, people often welcome something to rule over their natural desires. People are afraid of their latent desires. They welcome a strict belief system to control their dangerous libido—and it does not have to be Christianity. Sigmund Freud was correct in his diagnosis of religion repressing sexuality. What he did not recognize was that many people voluntarily welcome religion to repress their sexuality because removing the restraint would be like opening Pandora's Box. It would bring chaos to their lives. Hence people welcome a coherent system that could bring order and predictability to their lives.

The Cultural Revolution in Communist China condemned sexual immorality as a class enemy.[6] For the Chinese people during the Cultural Revolution, it was not Christianity but a communist revolution that repressed their instinct. Although communism robbed people of freedom, many people were willing to give up their freedom in return for order and predictability in their personal lives and society. If society could repress all people's desires equally, people might be willing to tolerate such repression. Monasteries and convents are societies of mutually agreed chastity. But it does not have to be a religious society for members to mutually restrict sexual liberty In *The Man Who Would Be King*, two former British soldiers in India vow to each other to remain celibate as they venture into an exotic foreign land in search of riches and fame.[7] What is notable is that they promised to each other to abide by this rule. A mutually agreed sexual repression is useful for social stability.

While Christianity ruled over people's morality, it kept a tight lid on their libido. Still, once they let go of their desires, they rejected Christianity. To them, it was one or the other. It was either repression by Christianity, or rejection of Christianity to do what they wanted to do. Christ was not the savior who loved them as they are, but the mother superior

---

5. Parsons, *Growth of Religious Diversity*, 233.
6. Honig, "Socialist Sex," 150.
7. Huston, *Man Who Would Be King*.

who controlled their feelings and desires. Once they chose their desires, they did not need Christ. This mentality is obviously based on a wrong understanding of the gospel. People did not understand the true gospel. Instead, they believed in the legalistic application of Christianity. Legalism was intimidated by the new expressions of freedom and tried to keep people away from them by instilling guilt. Legalism set itself as the enemy of human instinct and pleasure. People had to choose between guilt and desire, which is no choice at all. Desire will win all the time.

Legalism, or the legalistic distortion of the gospel, only offered two colors for legitimate expressions of piety—black and white—while the secular culture offered the full array of colors. There is no competition. Legalism set itself in a place to lose. Any belief system that tries to maintain itself by fighting human instinct will fail. That was not the reason Jesus came to the world. Christianity is not opposed to human desires. The first fruit of the Spirit is joy. But an erroneous interpretation of Christianity had taught a lifestyle of abstention devoid of joy. Is it any surprise that people went away from the church in droves?

Nonetheless, the explosive appeal of freedom was not long-lasting. Since then, those who have experienced sexual revolution have come to know its limitations and liabilities. The hike in the divorce rate and the AIDS epidemic followed the sexual revolution. During the last fifty years, Christians have matured somewhat in their understanding of human sexuality. Pious mothers today do not threaten their sons that they will go to hell if they watch pornography.[8] Some readers may laugh at this remark, but devout mothers indeed believed in such a strict moral code. When *A Streetcar Named Desire* first came out as a film in 1951, people probably found its story scandalous. But when we watch it again in the twenty-first century, the story is predictable and dull. People have become more sophisticated in matters of sexuality in the past 60 years. That does not mean that people have become more virtuous. It just means that human instinct does not shock us as it used to. We do not have to pretend and hide. Human instinct is not the reason for denying Christianity. People in the west should have known this fact sooner. If they had, they would not have so readily rejected Christianity to pursue their newly found sexual freedom. A more correct understanding of the gospel would have told them that God is not against them, but for them, and that God does not condemn them, but that he understands them as

---

8. Stone, *Born on the Fourth of July*.

they are. On this basis, they could build a viable personal relationship with God. Reintroducing Christianity to post-Christian societies should be based on a more candid understanding of human nature. It does not mean that the gospel condones licentiousness. It simply means that Jesus knows what we are.

The Bursting of the Bubble

The rich external expressions of Christianity in Europe grew beyond the actual substance of faith. These external expressions were the bubble that people confused with real Christianity. When more attractive cultural attractions came along, the old Christian feelings simply went away. This event defines the process of secularism. Religion simply disappeared from people's daily concerns and languages. The Christian culture was like a house of cards. What is spiritual and internal could not be preserved permanently and securely through the cultural maelstrom. What had taken several centuries to build disappeared in one generation. It was a bubble. There was not as much faith on the inside as it seemed on the outside. It might have been better if Christianity had not been the state religion of European countries. At least it would not have turned into a bubble.

The bursting of the bubble makes people sober. Now they have to decide what belongs to Christianity and what does not. For example, is Christmas a Christian holiday or just a civic holiday? Will people continue to call their names "Christian names" even though they no longer baptize their infants? Will marriage ceremonies continue to be called holy matrimonies? Will the British Sovereign still be called the Protector of the Faith? Like a divorce proceeding, post-Christian societies have to sort through what belongs to whom. It is not necessarily a painful task. It is a necessary task to define the proper domain of faith. Once the proper area of the faith has been clearly defined, the rest has the liberty to be secular without inciting guilty feelings.

In a secular society, people have the freedom of religion. This freedom includes the freedom to believe as well as the freedom not to believe. Both freedoms have to be respected and protected. The bursting of the bubble is necessary to transition from a religious society to a secular society. It is not as bad as it sounds because the religious society was religious by presumption. It did not necessarily mean that all people had genuine faith. The external appearance was bigger than the substance. It was to be expected. Even in Old Testament Israel, which was supposedly a theocratic society, not all people believed. How can we know that? The First Commandment forbade having other gods before Yahweh. Unless there were people in Israel who had different gods, this Commandment would not have been necessary. The Second Commandment forbade making idols and worshiping them. Unless some Israelites worshiped idols, this commandment would not have been necessary. The other commandments forbidding murder, theft, adultery, false testimony, and coveting would not have been necessary unless the chosen people of Israel were doing these acts. Being a chosen people did not guarantee either spiritual purity or moral integrity. If it was like that then, it is like that now.

When I moved to Toronto at the age of fifteen, my father took me to a Taekwondo academy so that I could continue my martial art training. The trainer at the academy asked me what belt I was. I replied I was a black belt. He seemed startled and incredulous. To test if I was indeed a black belt material, he told me to spar with his black belt trainee. This black belt trainee was taller and more robust than I. He soundly beat me in the sparring. The trainer told me to wear a white belt for the time being. It was utterly humiliating. I regretted telling him that I was a black belt. I should have told him that I was a brown belt instead.

No society on earth is a black belt spiritually.

A society cannot be more religious than it actually is. Modern secularism has made it necessary for western culture to determine what it is and what it is not. Religion by presumption is not sustainable. Every culture is lacking something spiritually. Even if the entire community seems to have embraced a religion, that does not mean that every member of the community truly believes Calling a country a Christian country is not a wise idea. It creates a false impression. No society on earth has ever been an entirely believing society. Even if it looks that way, there are always sins and unbelief secretly brewing in somewhere. One of the twelve disciples of Jesus was Judas Iscariot. The Puritans in the American colonies had witch trials. We look at people on the outside; only God looks at the heart. And the heart is deceitful above all things and beyond cure. If the Christian culture could be lost over *Lady Chatterley's Lover* and the Beatles' first album, it did not have much substance to it. It was not real. We had better count the loss and begin anew.

When churches were growing large in Korea, many pastors around the world paid attention to this phenomenon and tried to copy it. The church growth movement led to the instituting of church growth programs in evangelical seminaries across the world. Many pastors came to Korea to learn the secret of this church growth phenomenon. At that time, fifty of the one hundred largest churches in the world were in Korea. The largest Presbyterian church in the world was in Korea. So were the largest Methodist and Assemblies of God churches. On top of them all, the largest church in the world was in Seoul, Korea. It was the prime of the megachurch phenomenon. The Korean churches were the envy of the world. Be that as it may, not all church growth was the work of the Holy Spirit. It was the product of the unique sociological and psychological circumstances of the time. After about two decades, no one comes to Korea to learn the secrets of church growth anymore. The circumstances that led to remarkable church growth could not be duplicated elsewhere.

Those western pastors who came to Korea looking for the church growth secrets were looking for the wrong things. They thought that the secret lay in small groups and prayer mountains. What they should have examined, instead, was how Korea, in the process of westernization, was able to allow evangelization at the same time. They should have found the keys to understanding the role of faith in a secular society. But instead, they looked for quick know-how's. The Korean hosts likewise did not know what they had to show their guests. They were infatuated with the external phenomena.

People were fascinated with a bubble. The disciples of the church growth theory were observing the bubbles. When religious bubbles burst, party is over, and people have to clean up the mess. Usually, there is much mess to clean up. When the *Hour of Power* broadcast of the Crystal Cathedral was at its height, even the American Forces Network broadcast it on Sunday mornings around the world. No one suspected it to be a bubble. But there was a bubble. When it burst, the Crystal Cathedral went bankrupt, and its building was put on auction. Two institutions bid for the building, and it went to the Catholic Diocese of Orange County, which changed its name to Christ Cathedral. No one imagined that the Crystal Cathedral could be sold at auction. The steady flow of offering could not continue forever, and the church could not afford its expensive broadcasting expenses indefinitely. A church has a finite life expectancy like a person.

No church should build a massive facility and expect to fill it with people forever. A dynamic preacher may attract a crowd for a while, but nobody knows what will happen after the star preacher is gone. How do they expect to fill the enormous building? Willow Creek Community

Church searched for the successor to Bill Hybels for more than two years. Bill Hybels's charisma and leadership contributed to the growth of Willow Creek. Though he is gone, the congregation seems to think that they can carry on the legacy of the church by finding a worthy successor of equal caliber. The church growth resulted from the combination of an exceptionally talented pastor and the sociological need that he could fill. But such a combination only lasts for a season. A new pastor must find his own vision and gifts.

God is not obligated to preserve the prosperity of one particular church after its season is over. Many congregations do not realize this fact. The Jerusalem church at once had a gathering of five thousand people, but most of them scattered after James's martyrdom. The Jerusalem church never recovered its earlier size afterward. But it was not a loss for the kingdom of God because the scattered believers established new churches all over the known world. Jesus's will for the apostles was to preach the gospel in the whole world, not necessarily to bring back the heydays of the Jerusalem church. God's apparent lack of loyalty to one local church may disappoint some people. God is loyal to his work, and local churches are but tools for accomplishing it. As he raises one king and lowers another, so he raises one church and lowers another—according to his big plan.

As a result, churches should have the mobility and adaptability of a nomad. A nomad does not stay in permanent buildings. Instead, he moves from one place to another in search of grass for the sheep and cattle. His abode is not a permanent fixture but a tent. A tent can be put up and taken down quickly. Whenever churches build huge buildings expecting to always fill it with worshipers, they are ignoring the demographic and sociological changes. Church attendance began to decline in England in the latter half of the nineteenth century because of demographic changes. The many churches in rural areas began to empty out after populations moved from country to inner cities.[9] Focusing on buildings, the Victorians had not foreseen sociological changes.

Jesus did not have a central place for holding services and meetings. Sometimes he taught at synagogues, but other times he preached by the lake or in people's houses. He did not feel the need to tie his ministry permanently to one location. Apostle Paul used the same method. Whenever he visited a new city, he went to the synagogue in that city first, but often

---

9. Gill, *Myth of the Empty Church*.

he changed his venues. At Ephesus, he used the library of Tyrannus to teach for two years, during which time all the Jews and Greeks living in Asia heard the word of the Lord (Acts 19:10).

Jesus and Apostle Paul exemplified a very adaptable and mobile method of ministry. In contrast, churches began to lose competitiveness when they started to settle down in buildings built by men. People equated buildings with churches. They would say, "This church is two hundred years old." That is an inaccurate statement. They are referring to an architectural edifice, not the church. A building is a church only if people worship in it. Often there are only buildings and no congregations. They are mere structures. When people move away, ministries should follow them. Christians should not be too concerned with old church buildings sold to bookstores, cafes, or indoor skateboard rinks. What is being sold is a piece of real estate, not the church of Jesus Christ. Those who buy old church buildings do not seem very good at turning them into other uses after all. Purchasers will always be uneasy about using old church facilities for some other purposes.

Not only should churches be free from their attachment to buildings, they should be independent of the state patronage. For a long time, true religious freedom did not exist in Europe because each state determined its religion and protected it. Cuius regio, eius religio was the Latin expression that the ruler's religion dictated the country's religion. The rulers' protection was not always beneficial to the churches because churches grew lazy and began to lose competitiveness Modernization was the bursting moment of the bubble created by the protection of the state. The state churches of Europe are the ones that have found it most difficult to adapt to new changes, leading to the decline of spiritual vitality.[10] The reason that the condition of European churches differs from the rest of the world, particularly the United States, is the unique arrangement between church and state.[11] The United States established the separation of the church and state in its Constitution, which was the essence of a secular society, which in turn led to the growth of the church's competitiveness. Other nations in the world where Protestant faith is alive and well are all secular in the sense that churches do not enjoy any favored status by the state. Churches are most effective when they are lean and clean.

---

10. Davie, "Europe," 78.
11. Davie, "Europe," 78.

Christianity by Default

We often hear that the people in the west are already knowledgeable of the claims of Christianity but are not interested in them. In that sense, they argue, the non-practicing people in the west are different from the unreached people in other parts of the world. The surface knowledge of the gospel but lack of interest in it demonstrates the spiritual callousness of the Europeans.

Such spiritual callousness may indeed exist. But we cannot equate knowing the doctrines of Christianity with knowing the gospel. In this age of information, almost everyone knows something about Christianity. A cursory look at Wikipedia will provide enough information. Even Muslim clerics are aware of Christian beliefs. They have to study them to refute Christianity. Should we say that these Muslim clerics are callous toward Christianity as well?

When evangelical Christianity was introduced to Latin Americans, the majority of whom were Catholics, they already knew much about Christianity. Nevertheless, they eagerly embraced evangelical Christianity. What brought about the genuine conversion was not merely knowledge of Christianity, but preaching and believing. John Wesley had been a clergyman and a theologian before his conversion experience at Aldersgate. Despite his knowledge of Christianity, he had lacked genuine conversion. The message that Wesley heard at Aldersgate was not new in terms of content; it was unique in terms of power. The Holy Spirit used the word Wesley heard to touch his heart, stirring genuine faith. Without this spiritual dimension, mere knowledge of Christianity does not produce real faith. Missionaries in Europe should not be intimidated by the fact that people already know about Christianity. If they let the Holy Spirit touch people's hearts, there will be a new response. Paul stated that his preaching was not in persuasive words of wisdom, but with a demonstration of the Spirit's power (1 Cor 2:4).

Spiritual revival requires a climate that is conducive to the sentiments of faith in society. A spiritual atmosphere favorable to revival must arise through concerted prayer. Evangelist Carlos Annacondia of Argentina was known to lock himself in his hotel room for days praying when he was invited to hold a crusade in a city. For days on end, he would wage a spiritual war through prayer. After he feels that he has finished the warfare, he would come out of his hotel room to lead evangelistic meetings with many wonderful results. Evangelist Billy Graham had a team of intercessors who would go ahead of him and pray for his evangelistic campaigns. Where the spiritual climate is icy, faithful Christians must pray together for God to bring a revival to their city. Only then are people willing to open their hearts to the gospel.

Christianity by presumption did not work in the past, and it does not work now. Christian heritage maintained by default is not the true faith. In the New Testament times, Christianity did not exist as a tradition. Everyone became a Christian for the first time. The book of Acts is filled with instances of individual conversions. There were deliberate presentations of the gospel and explicit acceptance of the gospel. After Europe became a "Christian" continent by decree, however, the dominance of Christianity was maintained by the rule of the kings and the church, whether people actually believed or not. The Protestant Reformation was not only a protest of the abuse of power by the church but also the restoration of the nature of faith. Martin Luther eliminated five of the seven sacraments of the church as being ineffective means of conveying Christ's saving grace. Removing these sacraments meant that God's salvific power was not available in rituals without genuine personal faith. Luther did not remove the Lord's Supper and baptism because they were explicitly commanded by Jesus. Nonetheless, even these sacraments do not convey the saving power of Jesus in the absence of true faith. The born-again movement did not ask people whether they were baptized, but whether they accepted Jesus as their Savior. How much liturgy each church should adopt is up to the church, but liturgy cannot take the place of the ministry of the word, especially in post-Christian societies where people maintain the appearance of faith without actual faith. Apostle Paul said that his job was to preach the gospel, not to baptize people (1 Cor 1:17). At least to Paul, preaching the gospel took precedence over baptism. In traditional Christian cultures, there are many so-called "sprinkle" Christians. These refer to those who were sprinkled with water at infant baptism, sprinkled with rice at wedding, and sprinkled with dust at funeral. If those three events are the only times when people go to church. Christian rites in the absence of faith do not make people Christians.

Although Christianity has left behind cultural heritage and traditions, those things in themselves do not constitute Christianity. It would have been better if Christianity had not left any visible legacy. The Reformed sanctuaries used to be bare rooms with no visual artifacts, not even a cross. Polyphony was banned in church music because the beauty of harmony could take people's attention away from the word of God.

There was a reason for that. The Reformed movement believed that the only tool that the Holy Spirit used to convey grace to people was the preaching of the word of God. The Holy Spirit does not need anything else. If Europeans are attached to the culture, music, architecture, and memories of Christianity, but not to the actual person of Christ, all those accouterments are hindrances to believing in Christ.

A Stranger's Voice from the Pulpit

When people are surveyed what the first thing that comes to mind when they think about church is, they answer "boring." God would not bore people; why should pastors bore them? No one can bore his congregation into heaven. It is of secondary importance what kind of theology a preacher subscribes to. Some liberal-minded preachers are captivating to the audience despite their liberal theology. Some evangelical preachers put people to sleep.

The life of a worship service is the sermon. And the life of a sermon is the preacher. The preacher either makes or breaks his preaching. He must believe in what he preaches. What the congregation looks for in a preacher is not a demonstration of theological knowledge, or social commentary, or even entertainment. What the congregation expects from the preacher is the reminder of the reason to believe. After attending each service, congregants must leave the church feeling happy about their faith and encouraged to keep believing. If, however, the congregation cannot find from sermons the reason to believe, they will not be happy to come to church.

Simply put, people come to church hoping to catch a glimpse of God. It is the responsibility of each minister to help them to experience him—in any legitimate way. If people do not feel God at church, they have no reason to come. If they feel God at church, nothing can stop them from coming.

It is a simple principle but challenging to practice. The decline of the European church can only mean that the clergy were less than successful at helping their flock to experience God during worship services. It may be hard for some people to swallow, but this is the biggest reason for the decline in church attendance. If people feel that God is in the church, they cannot stop coming to church. All the other discussions on Christianity are secondary to this crucial fact.

The loss of faith by the sheep stems from the loss of faith by the clergy. How can men and women of God lose faith? They will lose faith if their theology does not help them to develop a personal relationship with God. Martin Luther said that wooden chunks supposedly taken from Jesus's cross were numerous enough to fill St. Peter's Basilica. Likewise, there are enough theological publications that teach anything except how to develop a personal relationship with the living God to fill the Dead Sea. The liberal theology occupied itself with the controversial modern issues and not with presenting God's love for sinners.

My college chaplain subscribed to a white man's guilt theology. His major homiletic themes were peace, liberal social agenda, and Christian ethics. Not being black, he could not speak from his own experience of pain and prejudice. Not being poor, he could not speak out of a personal experience of deprivation. Not having been a worldly man, he could not speak about the anguish of a sinner. He offered little encouragement or comfort. Instead, he usually spoke about the moral duties of Christians. He seemed to presuppose that students were held to a higher moral standard because of their Ivy League education. What he did not realize was that young people, regardless of college affiliation, had many anxieties and issues just like everyone else. What they hoped to hear from their chaplain was not what they ought to do as Christians, but how much God loved them and wanted to help them. Liberal preachers expect little from God and demand much from people.

There are kinds of sermons that lead to church growth and those that lead to church decline. Knowledge puffs up while love builds up (1 Cor 8:1). Throughout the history of Christianity, the clergy were always the best-educated people in society, and they may try to preach from the position of erudition and scholarship. But the content of the gospel is the fact that God loves us. If the congregation cannot feel the love of God expressed in the messages from the pulpit, they will not be edified. He should express the love of God because God is love. If the audience does not feel loved by God after each sermon, the preacher has not preached the truth of the gospel.

When I say to the flock, "You must love one another," I have just proclaimed the law. If I say, "Love makes the world go around," I have taught philosophy. Then what is the gospel? When I say, "God loves you," I have presented the gospel. Is it too obvious? No, people can never hear that message often enough. It is hard enough to believe that somebody loves them; how much harder will it be to believe that God loves them? It is not a trite doctrine.

Very few people come to church to listen to either the law or philosophy. They come to hear the gospel. They may not consciously know what they are looking for, but when the gospel is preached to them, they instinctively recognize that is what they need. Anything other than that will eventually turn people away from the church. Pastors should not underestimate their sheep's ability to discern spiritually. The sheep follow Jesus because they know his voice, but they will never follow a stranger; in fact, they will run away from him because they do not recognize a stranger's voice (John 10:4–5). The sheep instinctively recognize the voice of Jesus. They will naturally run away from a stranger's voice. The church in the west may have chased the sheep away by speaking in a stranger's voice.

The church must be considered separately from Christianity at this point. There is nothing wrong with Christianity, but much wrong with the church. If the church does its job poorly, Christianity suffers. The church is on the frontline between Jesus and the flocks. If the church leadership suffers a crisis of faith, the flocks will suffer the damage. The public's disenchantment with church services must have led to the decline in church attendance and the decline of Christianity.

Seminarians often joke, "Don't give me exegesis; just give me Jesus." This joke satirizes the delicate balance between scholarship and spirituality. Many preachers have embraced scholarship at the expense of spiritual power. They have no one else to blame when the sheep fall asleep. People come to church looking for Jesus. We all must keep this in mind.

The Triumph of Individualism over Collectivism

Even though the church attendance in Europe has plummeted from the 1960s, some clergy argue that the plummeting church attendance does not mean that Europeans are necessarily losing faith. They explain that more people are selecting true faith over "religion." Anglican leaders like to make this argument for some reason. Or some argue that Christians are "practicing" neighborly love instead of going to church. None of these explanations is convincing.

Why is it so difficult for people to accept the biblical mandate of attending church regularly as a natural expression of their faith? Even if people maintain their faith, how can they prove their commitment to Jesus Christ without attending church? True believers must worship God. Without attending church, how are they going to worship God? If people consider it unimportant to belong to a local church even though they count themselves as Christians, where did they learn that from?

During the coronavirus pandemic, a German reporter residing in Taiwan compared the differences in how people responded to the epidemic in Taiwan and Germany. While the Taiwanese people all wore masks in public and obeyed the government's request for social distancing, he observed that Germans did not wear masks and occasionally disobeyed the government mandate. The reporter considered the Germans' reaction as evidence of "European arrogance."[12] Aside from the condescension that European people may feel toward people of other cultures, Europeans consider individual liberty more important than collective orientation. Europeans thought it was beneath them to cover their faces to protect themselves from the virus.

Could the same character trait be responsible for the low church attendance rate in Europe? Faith is, first and foremost, a very personal matter to them—so private that they even stay away from the church. The only problem is that Christianity, as envisioned by Jesus, was not such a private matter. When Jesus criticized doing the works of righteousness in public, he was criticizing the motive to be seen and praised by people. It did not mean that Jesus intended sincere devotion to be an entirely private affair. Jesus emphasized the community of faith. He lived in a close community of faith with the disciples. He emphasized the effect of two or more people gathering in his name and praying together.

Those who stray from the group always miss out spiritually. On the day of Jesus's resurrection, Thomas did not witness the risen Christ because he was not with the disciples. Thomas suffered a spiritual loss by not being with the group. Jesus had to appear once again to convince Thomas of his resurrection. If any of the disciples were absent from the upper room on the day of Pentecost, he would have missed the outpouring of the Holy Spirit. The Holy Spirit does not give gifts to someone because he is unique; instead, the Holy Spirit gives gifts to someone because he happens to be at the right place at the right time. The relatives and friends of Cornelius partook of the power of the Holy Spirit because they were there when the Holy Spirit came on them. Asian Christians' faithfulness

---

12. Thome, "Was Deutschland von Taiwan lernen kann."

to church attendance may arise from their Confucian tradition of favoring collectivism over individualism. If so, such a culture is good because it helps people to become better Christians.

This emphasis on religious privacy is not biblical. Anonymous Christians cannot be faithful witnesses of Jesus Christ. Jesus said that if anyone is ashamed of Jesus before men, Jesus will be ashamed of him before God. If anyone confesses Jesus before men, Jesus will confess him before God. How active can anonymous Christians be in serving the purposes of Jesus on earth? LGBT+ people come out of the closet to further their causes. How much more should Christians come out of the closet? Faith should manifest itself through service, evangelism, worship, and gifts of the Holy Spirit. There must be a public demonstration of faith. If not, people are favoring their personal preferences over serving Jesus.

When people value privacy and individuality above community and public demonstration of faith, there is no place for dedication and obedience. Anonymous Christians submit to no visible religious authority. By valuing individualism over collectivism, Europeans have departed from the very principle of Jesus's teaching—that we should love one another as ourselves.

The Trouble of the Catholic Church

Discussing the Catholic Church is outside the perimeter of this book. Protestants do not want to make careless remarks about their Catholic brothers and sisters. Nonetheless, anyone who desires to understand the reasons for the decline of Christianity in Europe cannot avoid the topic of the Catholic Church because it is an integral part of European Christianity. Resuscitating Christianity in Europe is not just for the Protestants, but also for the Catholics. The Catholics and Protestants must see eye to eye in this task. To do that, they need to engage in candid dialogues, putting aside their theological disagreements. There are more things that they agree on than disagree.

It is a sad state of affairs that, if those who left the Catholic Church in America could form their separate denomination, it would be the third-largest denomination after the Catholics and Baptists.[13] We cannot imagine what the situation in Europe is like. The only difference is that, while the ex-Catholics in America joined Protestant churches, the lapsed Catholics

---

13. Reese, "Hidden Exodus," para. 4.

in Europe did not seem to do that. Such a massive loss in membership calls for intense introspection by the clergy. But no such introspection seems to be taking place. The American bishops, for example, have never devoted any time at their national meetings to discuss this problem.[14] A similar exodus has happened in South America, too. A massive number of Catholics have left Catholicism to join pentecostal churches.

Different people have different reasons for leaving the Catholic Church. To some people, the Catholic Church is not progressive enough; to some, it is not conservative enough. For those who left the Catholic Church to join Protestant churches, the biggest reason for leaving was that their spiritual needs were not being met in the Catholic Church.[15] This reason dominates over any other, such as the church's stance on abortion or homosexuality. Those who leave the Catholic Church to join Protestant churches do not necessarily disagree with the Catholic doctrines.[16]

It is safe to assume that the same situation exists in Europe. The only difference is that those who leave the Catholic Church do not necessarily join the Protestant churches, probably because there are no Protestant churches to join. Instead of joining any churches, they just stay home on Sundays. Since the Catholics take up a massive percentage of the population in Europe, Catholics leaving the church due to unmet spiritual needs must have a gigantic consequence on Europe's religious landscape. In the U.S. and Latin America, Protestant churches enjoyed certain comparative advantage over Catholic churches. Hence the unhappy Catholics could migrate to Protestant churches. In Europe, by contrast, the Protestants do not have such comparative advantage. In fact, the Catholics and Protestants are in similarly sad situations. Therefore, when Christianity is resuscitated in Europe, both Catholicism and Protestantism must rise together. That is the only logical and plausible scenario. We cannot assume that the Lord has one plan for the Catholics and another for the Protestants. If Apostle John, the author of Revelation, could write to the churches of the 21st century, he would not write separate messages to the Protestants and the Catholics. We cannot second-guess the mind of Christ, but we cannot imagine that he would have different intentions toward the Catholics and Protestants. When will we understand this and try to work together for the common purpose?

14. Reese, "Hidden Exodus," para. 5.
15. Reese, "Hidden Exodus," para. 10.
16. Reese, "Hidden Exodus," para. 13.

Although the situation is grave, it is not beyond cure. The fundamental responsibility of any church, whether Catholic or Protestant, is to meet the spiritual needs of the sheep. If the decline in the church attendance rate in Europe is due to people's unmet spiritual needs, this problem calls for more effective ministries. The problem is not as profound as people may fear. Churches and ministers have not been doing their job well. They lost their sheep by not taking care of them spiritually.

Both Catholics and Protestants must conduct the vital task of resurrecting Christianity in Europe. The same job waits for us. There is no need for competition. Protestant churches should not expect to benefit from the decline of the Catholic membership, and vice versa. We must cooperate. When the world sees the waning Christianity, it does not distinguish between the Catholics and Protestants. To the world, it is Christianity that is waning. As a result, the need to reintroduce Christianity to a post-Christian society applies equally to Catholics and Protestants. Instead of asking why the Protestants had to break away from the Catholics, we must be able to see God's wisdom in allowing more than one church to exist in the world. Diversity is better for maintaining spiritual purity and integrity. Catholics can help Protestants to be better Protestants, and vice versa. The Pope represents the whole Catholic church. The Protestants must have leaders who can represent the entire Protestantism in relating with the Catholics. No one church or denomination can cure the spiritual ills of Europe alone. We must find areas where the Catholics and Protestants may work together. The Catholic charismatic movement in Europe has been one such venue where the Protestants could be blessed in the same way as the Catholics. Catholics and Protestants can work together studying the postmodern culture of Europe. Seminary classes should be open to all denominations. Church resources must be shared when possible. The enemy of the Catholics and Protestants is not each other, but the threats posed by the post-Christian culture. If they fail to work together, both Catholicism and Protestantism risk becoming irrelevant in this rapidly changing secular society.

The Antiquated Religion

When people look at the marvelous architecture of Oxford or Cambridge, they assume that such adorable, classic architecture must be the badge of the highest scholarly standard. But the students who study and live in those old buildings know firsthand how antiquated and inadequate those facilities are. They are dark and cold with problematic plumbing and heating. Aside from being the face of the institution, the old architecture is increasingly irrelevant and redundant. In this age of information technology, what students need is not medieval-style buildings, but user-friendly modern facilities—preferably made of glass and steel.

Christianity of Europe is old. Its expressions, accouterments, style, and even language are old. The overall impression Christianity gives to the people is that it is an old institution. It is no wonder that church buildings in European city centers are turning into museums. Old buildings are meaningful only as museums and not as current houses of worship for the contemporary generation more familiar with TED-like auditoriums.

The churches of Europe have enjoyed a protected and favored status for too long. In economic terms, Christianity in Europe was a monopoly. Each European country determined its religion and supported it. True freedom of religion did not exist in Europe. It is not sure if it exists now. Churches colluded with the state for dominance and favored status in society. Ireland remained Catholic. The Church of England was the official church of England. The British House of Lords reserves twenty-six seats for the Anglican bishops. Spain and Portugal were uniformly Catholic, while Scandinavia was consistently Lutheran. France remained mainly Catholic with small Protestant remnants. Germany was either Lutheran or Catholic, depending on the states. Although the weekly church attendance is very low, the German government reportedly collected $13.2 billion in revenue for churches in 2013.[17] The problem with the state-sponsored religion is that it loses competitiveness. It becomes part of the Establishment. Instead of reforming society, the church becomes the target of reformation. For Christianity to be revived in Europe, people should be able to choose the churches they want to attend. Deconstructing the age-old remains of the religious traditions is necessary to make the church lean and clean, able to compete for the hearts of people.

Christianity in America has had to adapt to the changing times to stay relevant. The same phenomenon did not take place in Europe. The public reaction to the burning of Notre Dame in Paris discloses how much emotional attachment people have toward old institutions. Few institutions have replaced the old-fashioned religious symbols in Europe. Southern California featured the Crystal Cathedral that was a symbol

---

17. Lipka, "In Some European Countries," para. 2.

of the megachurch in the TV evangelist era. Paris has the postmodern-looking Pompidou Center, but no cathedral with such a high-tech savvy style. Whenever someone challenges the relevance of the British Monarchy, the defenders of the institution reply that the Monarchy has provided stability in the changing times. If Christian leaders of Europe give the same answers about the relevance of Christianity in the European society, their thoughts are too old-fashioned to make Christianity meaningful to the current generation.

Neither God nor Jesus is antiquated. Even though Christianity is two thousand years old, we do not worship a two-thousand-year-old God. Even to think so would be ludicrous. God's love is new every morning. His words speak to us anew every day. Churches are not playing a two-thousand-year-old tape over and over. If Jesus were physically on the earth today, he would be the most contemporary person imaginable.

The European clergy have erred by thinking that their task was to keep an old way of doing things. Traditions have crowded out the Holy Spirit in the churches. No wonder the first thing that comes to people's minds when they think about church service is boredom. We cannot bore people to heaven. Any church service that bores people is wrong. Whenever I look at the British royals' ceremonies on YouTube, I get the impression that they are excessively long and tedious. At least Lady Diana's funeral featured Elton John.

Church services must be lean and clean. No one should suppose that the New Testament church services were long and complicated. Paul's second letter to the Corinthians provides an insight into the manner of church services at the Corinthian church. "When you come together, everyone has a hymn, or a word of instruction, a revelation, a tongue or an interpretation" (1 Cor 14:26). Does the passage not look like an order of worship? It was simple and to the point—except that modern clergy would not know what to do with revelation, tongues, and interpretations. When the word of God and the Holy Spirit are present during a worship service, it is sufficient and adequate. No one will be bored and everyone will be blessed. What more does a church need? The early church was probably more contemporary and modern than the twenty-first-century church.

Anyone who thinks that Christianity is an old institution does not realize that God is the most up-to-date and relevant person in the universe. Where do people get the idea that to believe in Christianity is to follow old rules? Not only is God living, but also he is the God of the living. When God referred to himself as the God of Abraham, Isaac, and

Jacob, he was saying that those patriarchs are not dead, but living (Matt 22:32). Everything that pertains to God is not dead but living. We have only ourselves to blame for turning Christianity into an antiquated religion that no longer speaks to the contemporary situations.

Jack Dawson, a poor artist who wins a ticket on Titanic at a poker game, says, "When you've got nothing, you've got nothing to lose."[18] Christianity's most valuable asset is Jesus Christ. Apart from Jesus, Christianity has nothing. Thus, Christians should exercise their faith as if they have nothing to lose. From that comes courage and power. But for too long, churches have feared losing so much. What they fear losing is prestige, favored status in society, and sway over people. These things have become a dead weight around the chuches' neck, making them ineffective, irrelevant, and unconvincing.

So-called "educated people in the west" complain that Christianity is full of outdated doctrines.[19] Such educated people are misinformed. The time-honored traditions of Christianity testify to the historical nature of Christianity. Christianity is the only religion with a revelation that has a historical basis.[20] In religions with an ahistorical basis, such as Buddhism or Shamanism, one cannot even complain about antiquated doctrines. What people consider as "outdated" is the historical foundation of Christianity, which makes its beliefs more credible and ascertainable.

Jesus Christ is the same yesterday, today, and forever (Heb 13:8). Churches must celebrate and present the Jesus of today so that people can meet him in today's language, culture, and agenda. This does not mean that today's culture and agenda determine Jesus, but that Jesus speaks to today's culture and agenda.

---

18. Cameron, *Titanic*.
19. Linford, "Christianity and Outdated Doctrine."
20. Hendrix, "Religion of Today," 700.

— 6 —

The Unique Situation of Europe

On the individual level, European people are just like any other people in the world. They do not necessarily carry with them a unique collective experience of Christianity. The changes that have taken place on the societal level in Europe are not necessarily linked to the level of individual consciousness.[1] They will respond to the gospel according to their personal needs, understanding, and bias, just like anyone else in the world. On the other hand, Europe's collective and historical situation is unique. Europeans already have a long history of Christianity unlike the new mission fields. They already know a great deal about Christianity. As a result, one cannot assume that Europeans lack the knowledge of Christianity. If there are reasons why Europeans were disappointed with Christianity in the first place, we must take them seriously.

What could these reasons be? There are myriads of reasons. One is the state and church relations. The state relied on the church while the church relied on the state, using each other. Another is the fat and privileged status of the church which looks alien from the perspective of Jesus's spirit of poverty and charity. The third is the cultural presumption of Christianity without genuine personal conversion. The fourth is the monopoly of the ministry by the church hierarchy which has buried the talents of the sheep.

The fifth, and the gravest, is the hardening of the population. Being surrounded by Christianity has hardened people's hearts toward the actual truth of Christianity. Familiarity had bred resistance, like a vaccine.

---

1. Berger, *Desecularization of the World*, 3.

Vaccination creates a false disease in people by introducing a tiny amount of virus into them. As a result, bodies develop immunity against the virus so that when the real disease comes, bodies can resist it. Likewise, being introduced to a small dosage of Christianity has developed resistance toward the actual message of Christianity. It might have been better if people had not been introduced to Christianity at all in the first place. Reintroducing Christianity to Europe is necessary because many Europeans have an incomplete understanding of Christianity.

Faith by Default

Many of the terms commonly used in describing Europe's spiritual condition are misleading and unhelpful. In the first place, "leaving the faith" is not an exact expression. One cannot leave what one has never had. If one has never had real faith, one cannot leave it. One may fall into sin, but that is a different matter and is not unique to Europe. Instead of calling the current situation, "leaving the faith," we may call it the "loss of appeal" or the "loss of relevance" of Christianity.

Calling European nations Christian nations is also meaningless and unhelpful. Citizens have freedom of religion. To call a country Christian is to negate this freedom. Religious freedom requires that a nation be secular in its view of itself. The role of the state is to protect the life, liberty, and property of its people. The liberty includes religious liberty. If the citizens can carry on religious activities in peace, the state has done its job. What we expect from the state is to do this duty well. Going beyond this duty and requiring a country to adopt a religious identity does not suit the modern definition of a state. It clouds the issue.

Some people claim that the United States is still a Christian nation. They are making a politically incorrect statement with political purposes. They are either nostalgic or demanding that the government policies and laws reflect Christian values. Christianity does not have political ambitions, unlike Islam.[2] Anyone who thinks that the purposes of Christianity can be served by political means is a demagogue who confuses his ambitions with the will of Jesus Christ. Jesus did not intend to build the kingdom of God through political means. He refused people's attempts to make him king. "My kingdom is not of this world," said he (John 18:36). We do not want to repeat the past mistake when the secular power and

---

2. Meddeb, *Islam and the Challenge of Civilization*, 48.

the sacred power were one. The Constitution of the United States stipulates the separation of the church and state. Those who claim that the United States is a Christian nation is denying the fundamental principle of the Constitution. Although abortion and gay marriage are serious issues, the fundamentalist Christians' attempt to outlaw them through political means is religious tyranny. Even if they succeed in imposing their beliefs on others, it will not draw people to Christ that way. Faith cannot be coerced on people by law.

In South Korea, about 20 percent of the Korean population is Protestant, and another 15 percent is Catholic. It would be unthinkable for them to claim that Korea is a Christian country. It would be an insult to those with other religions or no religions. Koreans understand Korea is a religiously free country, and diverse religious ideas are competing for the minds of people. There is an implicit understanding that the best religion will win. Korean Christians are genuinely pleased and even surprised to meet other Christians. They know what it feels like to be a religious minority and sincerely hope that the number of Christians will grow in society.

Recently David Cameron publicly stated that Britain is "still a Christian country."[3] It is not clear if he was making a faith confession or a political statement geared to the immigrant communities. Immigrants to the west do not have to convert to Christianity to get a permit to stay. Then what is the use of claiming that Europe is still Christian? Is it an expression of intimidation at the high influx of Muslim immigrants and refugees? Why do Europeans remind others that they are still Christians in a threatening voice?

Jesus said that the harvest is plentiful, but the workers are few. The harvest is never meager at any time anywhere. These words apply to Europe. The influx of people into Europe only enlarges the harvest field. It is an opportunity and not a liability. The fact that Muslim immigrants are coming to Europe means that it is now possible to evangelize them even though it was impossible in their home countries. The religious plurality and diversity offer an opportunity for the dormant Christians to become more aware of their roots. We become ourselves in relation to others. The first generation of Muslim immigrants may be reluctant to assimilate. We must wait for the second generation. Sooner or later, they will assimilate out of necessity. Look at the United States and Canada, which have a longer experience with immigration.

---

3. "David Cameron Says the UK Is a Christian Country."

Many Europeans call themselves "cultural Christians," meaning that they are content to enjoy the cultural heritage of Christianity without believing it. Why would anyone be content to live with the artistic expressions and culture of Christianity while ignoring its substance? It is like being fascinated with the painting of Mona Lisa while refusing to meet the real Mona Lisa. It is like enjoying the religious music of Bach and Handel while dismissing what inspired them to compose it. It is like falling in love with the messenger instead of the person who sent the message. Cultural Christianity is due to the loss of faith. They do not believe that the original Mona Lisa exists. They are fascinated with the creation without believing in the Creator. They have lost faith in the ground of their being. Jesus anticipated this when he said, "When the Son of Man comes, will he find faith on the earth?" (Luke 18:8). It is a curious phenomenon that people have lost faith but still cling to its legacy. It would have been better for those who lost faith to leave Christianity altogether. At least in that way, their return to Christianity will be eager and authentic.

The loss of faith, howbeit temporary, was not a new thing to the apostles. While walking on the sea at Jesus's beckoning, Peter became afraid and began to sink when he saw the wind and waves. Anyone can lose faith after a moment of faith. Faith is not static but is vulnerable to many trials and challenges. The fact that one used to believe is not enough. He must believe now. Faith is always in the now. We must focus on our present situation and not our past heritage. As Jesus held out his hand to rescue Peter from the sea, Jesus holds out his hand to save those who are going through the crisis of faith. He is the founder and perfecter of our faith (Heb 12:2, ESV).

Christianity Has Not Penetrated People's Hearts

In the film *The Godfather Part III*, an insightful conversation takes place about the spiritual condition of Europe. It reflects the intellectual depth of Francis Coppola, the director, and Mario Puzo, the writer. During the dialogue between Michael Corleone and Cardinal Lamberto, a fictitious cardinal of Venice, concerning the Vatican Bank scandal, the Cardinal reaches into the fountain and pulls out a stone from the water. "This stone has been lying in the water for a very long time," he says. Breaking the stone open, he shows Michael its interior, saying, "But the inside is perfectly dry. Water has not penetrated it." And then continues, "The same thing has happened with men in Europe. For centuries, they have been surrounded by Christianity. But Christ has not penetrated it. Christ does not live within them."[4] No other film describes the spiritual condition of Europeans better than this scene. Christianity, which had surrounded the Europeans for centuries, did not penetrate their hearts. Proximity, familiarity, and availability did not guarantee true faith.

Whether such a phenomenon is unique to Europe is not clear. Was it just Europeans who were difficult to penetrate with the gospel? Probably not. Towards the end of his earthly ministry, Jesus lamented over the spiritual condition of Israel because the towns where most of his miracles had taken place did not repent. "Woe to you, Chorazin! Woe to you, Bethsaida! For if the miracles that were performed in you had been performed in Tyre and Sidon, they would have repented long ago in sackcloth and ashes" (Matt 11:20–21). The judgment on those towns would be more severe because they had seen the miracles of Jesus and yet refused to repent.

It is not the stone's fault that water did not penetrate it. Being surrounded by Christianity is not the same thing as being surrounded by Christ. If people had been surrounded by Christ, and not just with Christianity, Christ would have penetrated their hearts. I had a similar experience. I was surrounded by Christianity during my childhood and adolescence, but Christ was not in my heart. My mother sent me to a Catholic kindergarten and a Presbyterian elementary school. At the elementary school, we had weekly chapels. We started each day's classes with prayers. During the Easter season, we drew pictures to depict the Bible stories about Jesus's death and resurrection. When my family immigrated to Toronto, we began to attend church. Most Koreans in Toronto went to church because the church was the only place to meet other Koreans. It was a fad for the Korean teenagers in Toronto to go to church. But throughout all this time, Christ was not in my heart. It was not until I heard a clear presentation of the gospel by Billy Graham and consciously received Jesus into my heart at the age of seventeen that I became a born-again Christian. Since then, Christ has dwelt in my heart and my life has never been the same.

Being surrounded by Christianity guarantees no real faith. Being surrounded by Christianity can make a person a cultural Christian. Because he belongs to a church and engages in Christian activities, he may think that he is a Christian. Such thinking prevents a genuine personal

---

4. Coppola, *Godfather: Part III*.

encounter with Christ. Jesus needed to tell Nicodemus, a religious leaders of Israel, that he had to be born of the Spirit to enter the kingdom of God. It is possible for a spiritual leader, a clergy, even an archbishop, not to have been born of the Spirit. Asking a religious person if he is born again will come across as an insult. One of the issues that European Christians have with the American evangelicals is the evangelicals' emphasis on the one-time born-again experience.[5] It is true that conversion does not always take place instantly. Many people are brought to faith gradually over a period. Some are converted without consciously realizing it. Nonetheless, Jesus asked Nicodemus whether he was born again. Even if this question may be offensive to those who have been custodians of Christianity for fifteen hundred years, this question is particularly important because they have been Christians for such a long time. Familiarity breeds presumption. The concept of reintroducing Christianity is necessary to settle the issue of conversion instead of presuming it.

Some Differences between Europe and America

The secularization theory spectacularly fails over the glaring difference between Europe and America.[6] When the rising secularism hit Christianity in the west simultaneously, America had the resurgence of evangelical revival to counteract secularism. Europe had no such recovery. Scholars point to 1963 as the turning point when church attendance began to drop sharply in all the western nations, including the United States, Canada, and western Europe. Eastern Europe at that time was behind the Iron Curtain. Some people trace the decline of the old-time religion to the end of the Second World War. The exact timing is not essential for this discussion. America experienced a series of successive revival movements from the nineteenth century. The turn of the twentieth century saw the birth of the pentecostal movement at Azusa Street. The 1940s saw the emergence of many evangelists like Billy Graham, Oral Roberts, Katherine Kuhlman, and other similar revival preachers. The healing movement began at the same time. When the hippie counterculture movement arose in the sixties and seventies, the Jesus People Revival took place to counteract the dominant secular culture. Many spiritual revivals sustained Christianity in America in the twentieth century. Even

5. Paas, "Mission from Anywhere to Europe," 22–23.
6. Berger et al., *Religious America, Secular Europe?*, 10.

the sects like the Seventh-Day Adventists, the Jehovah's Witnesses, and the Mormons thrived in America during that time.

The mainline Protestant denominations in America, like the United Church of Christ, the Episcopalians, the PCUSA, the Evangelical Lutheran Church, and the United Methodist Church, have been losing membership steadily. Some of these denominations are expected to disappear entirely within a couple of decades.[7] The decline of the mainline denominations in America does not differ much from the decline of the European churches during the same period. Nonetheless, the vitality of Christian faith has not suffered a significant loss because the evangelical and nondenominational churches have absorbed those who left the mainline churches. The same thing did not happen in Europe.[8]

European churches do not have strong evangelical roots from which to derive spiritual strength, sustenance, and leadership. Canadians used to tell this self-deprecating joke: "The US has Bob Hope and Johnny Cash, while Canada has no such personalities. As a result, Canada has neither hope nor cash." Christians in Europe may feel the same way about their relative lack of spiritual leadership. While Americans have had world-renowned preachers like Billy Graham and Oral Roberts, Europeans cannot easily name preachers who represent them. Helmut Thielicke was at once a prominent preacher in Germany, but his influence was limited to Germany. Reinhard Bonnke from Germany was an evangelist of international fame, but he worked mainly in Africa, not Europe. Miki Hardy, a prominent francophone preacher, works mostly in Africa.

European Christians seem to find the American version of evangelicalism or pentecostalism from the Global South alien culturally and theologically, even though North Americans have been sending many missionaries to Europe from the 1970s. I have not read a single article written by European theologians, which had something positive to say about pentecostalism from the Global South. They all seem to think that African pentecostal services are too long, pentecostal preachers are too authoritarian, and their theology too metaphysical.[9] Even the Hillsong from Australia is viewed with certain reservations.[10] What European pastors want is some theological discussion, but both Hillsong and African

---

7. Stetzer, "If It Doesn't Stem Its Decline," para. 8.
8. McLeod, *Religious Crisis of the 1960s*, 3.
9. Paas, "Mission from Anywhere to Europe," 12–13.
10. Paas, "Mission from Anywhere to Europe," 19.

pentecostals are too preoccupied with their methods to sit down with European counterparts for a frank dialogue. Hillsong believes in the superiority of its methods, and pentecostals are busy fighting spiritual wars instead of engaging in open theological discussions with the Europeans.[11] As for the Americans, we already know what Europeans think about the Americans. They are loud, unsophisticated, and affluent. It takes Europeans to evangelize Europeans, but this does not seem to be happening yet. Oliver Roy said in his book, Is Europe Christian?, that if there could be a Christian revival in Europe, he does not believe that it will come from Europeans because they are too small and lacking in spiritual knowledge. To be able to initiate the needed revival, he said, Europeans have accommodated themselves to too much secularism. He and I share the common opinion that the much needed revival must come from the outside. The same Macedonian man who appeared in Apostle Paul's vision must appear implicitly in the visions of many servants of the Lord who may be considered "outsiders" by Europeans.

The European Protestants do not seem to have clothing that fits them. When David went to the battlefield to fight Goliath, he wore his clothes and carried his weapons instead of wearing Saul's armor. Saul's armor did not fit David. Using his clothing and weaponry, David won the battle. Europeans need a native revival movement. Even if it is not a movement, they need their expression and confession for the revival of the faith. This will not happen until they overcome their fatigue and regain will power.

Fatigue and Guilt

After carrying the weight and burden of the Christian civilization for two thousand years, Europeans are tired. Christians are tired. Churches, ministers, and political leaders are tired. Europe has lost confidence in western values—in a liberal democracy, universal human rights, and support for transnational projects.[12] All of these things are connected. The loss of confidence in Christianity leads to the loss of confidence in other values that owe themselves to the Christian faith. It is collective, not personal fatigue. As individuals, European people may seem fine. But

---

11. Paas, "Mission from Anywhere to Europe," 12.
12. Applebaum, "West Has Lost Confidence."

as a collective society, there is hesitancy and timidity. The spirit may be willing, but the flesh is weak.

Although Christianity in America is vibrant, America is relatively young—only about four hundred years old. Christianity in Korea is thriving, but the history of Protestantism in Korea is only slightly over a hundred years old. Protestantism in the Global South is still relatively young. Europe, however, has borne the burden of Christianity longer than any other nations. Europe was the epicenter of Christianity for a very long time, and Europeans have seen and done things that other countries have not.

Not all their experiences were pleasant. We do not have to go far back to look for unpleasant experiences. Most recently, the clergy sex abuse scandals shook the faithful's confidence in the church. Going a little further back, Europe fought two world wars in one century. A Christian nation committed the Holocaust against the Jews. The European civilization colonized the Global South under the sign of the cross and profited from slavery. Although it was the Christian nations that eventually abolished slavery, it was also the Christian nations that started it. There are other unpleasant events in the past, including religious wars between the Catholics and Protestants and the Crusade. It seems that the Christian civilization committed most of the violence that occurred in the modern era. The Christian nations were not more righteous than non-Christian nations.

The European governments were hesitant to react strongly to the refugee problem from a deep sense of guilt. Having exploited the Global South in past centuries, Europeans feel that they must pay for their sins by having to take in millions of immigrants and refugees from the same countries that they had exploited. It is like the British who hesitated to face up to Hitler, during the early years of Hitler's rise to power, out of guilt over the excessively punitive Versailles Treaty after World War One.

A guilt complex could be at the bottom of the Europeans' collective hesitation to recover their Christian heritage in the face of the rapid disappearance of European identity. Charlie Hebdo, a French satirical weekly magazine, carried satirical cartoons of Muhammad only once and had its headquarters attacked by terrorists. On the other hand, Charlie Hebdo carries satires of Christianity all the time, but no one complains or retaliates. Is it because Christians are used to turning the other cheek? Or is it because Christians are hesitant to respond to attacks on their own identity and heritage? Black and Hispanic people have no hesitation in expressing their ethnic pride, while white people instinctively refrain from doing so. Guilt is at the bottom of their psyche.

In *The Strange Death of Europe*, Douglas Murray mentions two things, among others, that contributed to the strange deathlike helplessness of Europe. One is guilt, and the other is tiredness.[13] Guilt stems from the sins of the past, like colonialism, slavery, and the Holocaust. Tiredness comes from many layers of European history, typical of a civilization that has reached the twilight of its natural life.[14] Murray is not the only person who suspects that Europe is dying a strange death. This death is considered self-inflicted.[15]

Whether this theory is correct is debatable. We do not welcome the political right in Europe to use this theory as the pretext for their xenophobic political agenda. Europe is not the only civilization that has reached the twilight of its natural life. Europe is not the oldest civilization in the world. Other civilizations are far older: Chinese, Indian, Egyptian, and Mesopotamian. These earlier civilizations have undergone many transformations and have adjusted to new realities. There was a time, for example, that China was called the "sick man of Asia." That was at the end of the Qing Dynasty. But no one would call China that anymore. After many trials and errors, China, though not perfect, has adjusted to the modern realities and emerged as the second most powerful nation in the world. It goes to show that each society and civilization can adapt. The fatigue and the loss of Europe's confidence must be due to its loss of faith. Elijah, the prophet of fire, grew intimidated and tired after he suffered a crisis of faith at the threats of Jezebel. If the loss of faith was the reason, nothing else can resolve this fatigue except the recovery of faith.

Sometimes Christians must be driven to the point of utter fatigue and weariness to realize that their methods do not work. Christians often substitute their plan for the initiatives of God. Whenever their plan does not work, they blame themselves and God. Their relationship with God suffers as a result. Claiming to work for God, many Christians have poor relationships with God. That is an irony.

I, too, have experienced the same problem. I thought that God made me do all the hard work while he took all the credit for himself. I often blamed him for hiding behind the scene to protect his reputation

---

13. Murray, *Strange Death of Europe*.
14. Murray, *Strange Death of Europe*.
15. Tucker, "Quo Vadis?"

in controversial situations where the world blamed the clergy and Christians. I often wondered if God was still intent on carrying out the Great Commission in the world. Has he lost his motivations along the way? Has God withdrawn from the battlefield while Christians are still fighting?

I would be lying to you if I claim to have all the answers to my questions. But as my heart continues to beat even during my weary moments, God's heartbeat goes on. He is the most determined and patient person in the universe. He does not have to use me or you or anyone else. But he patiently waits for us to catch up with him. What he desires from us is not performance or skills. He is not impressed with our results, either. If we feel tired, it is because we were running our race without him. He never demanded us to do those things that made us weary. We never quite learned to play with him, to rejoice with him, like children playing with their father. After a long day's labor, we are unhappy. We are like the prodigal son's brother. If we can overcome our personal slump by waiting on him, we will be able to overcome the downturn of the continent.

Do Europeans Have the Will to Defend the Faith?

Europeans are by and large aware of the nature of their problem. But few seem eager to do something about it. Many scholars propose diagnosis, but few suggest prescriptions. Overall, people seem resigned to the current spiritual situation.

This collective helplessness may be due to two reasons. These are my theories. In the first place, after two world wars, Europeans no longer looked to the church to maintain peace among them. Instead, they looked to another institution. The European Union fit this role. In Eastern Europe, people turned to communism. Both institutions were political and supranational. Politics became an idol. People must ask themselves if the European Union is not a new Tower of Babel for them. In Genesis, the motive of the pre-historic people to build the Tower is explained. People said to one another, "Come, let us build ourselves a city so that we may make a name for ourselves; otherwise we will be scattered over the face of the whole earth" (Gen 11:4). It was more than a big construction project. People's purpose was to build a universal city where they would maintain a common language and unity so that they would not scatter over the face of the earth. The motive behind organizing the European Union was very similar. After suffering two world wars in one century, European nations felt the need to establish a universal city where they would share the collective identity to avoid more conflict. They also wanted to build a common market to compete with the United States. Why was God displeased with the Tower of Babel? Did he favor confusion? No. God knew that the Tower of Babel would replace God in the minds of people. The formation of the European Union coincides with the beginning of the decline of the faith in Europe. It may not be a coincidence. That does not mean that the members of the EU must try to leave the Union like Britain. What has been done has been done. There is no going back now. Europeans must navigate their destiny from where they are.

Another theory is about the guilt of the several centuries of exploitation of the rest of the world. White men committed almost all the bad things that happened in the past several centuries, it seems. It was the white men who enslaved Africans and sold them all over the world, colonized the Global South, decimated the native Indians in North America, and took over their land. It was white men who instituted the Apartheid, the racial segregation policy, in South Africa. It was the white men who made Jim Crow laws in the American South. It was the white men who killed millions of Jews, Romans, homosexuals, and other people deemed "undesirable" to the Third Reich. And it was the white men who made atomic bombs and dropped them on people. It is impossible to talk about all the evils in modern history without mentioning white men's guilt. After all these things, how can the white civilization return to Christianity as if nothing has happened?

It is not surprising that most of the moral leaders in the latter half of the twentieth century were non-white people. Martin Luther King Jr., Malcolm X, Nelson Mandela, and Mahatma Gandhi were all non-whites. They all stood up against the moral failure of white men. Mother Theresa of Calcutta was white but was a woman. She felt indebted to her non-white neighbors.

The future is female. Thousands years of experiment with the male-dominated society have suggested the logic of giving women a chance at leading the world. We will see spiritual leadership passing to women in the future. The reasons are not hard to understand. In the first place, there are fewer and fewer white men who are willing to serve the Lord in the ministry. Already there is a shortage of men in western societies who are willing to be priests, so that priests must be "imported" from the Global South. More women will take up the posts in the absence of available men.

In the second place, men are losing the right to be moral and spiritual leaders in the era of #MeToo, as many men's sexual abuse history is brought to light. God tends to pass over from one person to another when the first person he approaches is unwilling to believe. That is what happened when the gospel went from Jews to gentiles in the first century. When the Jews refused to believe Paul's message, he and Barnabas announced, "We had to speak the word of God to you first. Since you reject it and do not consider yourselves worthy of eternal life, we now turn to the Gentiles" (Acts 13:46). God is neither male nor female. God made human male and female after his image. For the past two thousand years, men have represented the patriarchal aspect of God. Perhaps it is women's turn to represent the maternal aspect of God. The first shall be last, and the last shall be first. If God allows another millennium to humankind, he may allow women to take up the leadership role, not only in the world, but also in the church. We will have to wait and see if it happens.

The religious title of Queen Elizabeth II is the "Defender of the Faith." United Kingdom is still supposed to be a Christian nation. But it is not clear that the Queen has actively performed her duty during her reign. Her primary concern seems to be maintaining the monarchy in Britain. How Prince Charles will fulfill his duty is yet to be seen. Lately, he expressed his desire to be not the titular head of the Church of England but the defender of all religions in Britain.[16] Political correctness will not provide the mandate for keeping the monarchy.

Nonetheless, there are signs of the Christian faith trying to express itself in European society. Angela Merkel, daughter of a Lutheran pastor, has approached the role of Germany and the European Union from a practicing Christian's perspective. Brexit reflected, among many other things, the desire of the British Protestants to recover the Christian identity of Britain. The conservative political movements in Europe harbor the desire to restore the Christian heritage. Hungary's Prime Minister Viktor Orban allegedly vows to defend Christian Europe. Europeans agree that they must do something to restore the identity of Europe, Christianity being part of it. It is probably unlikely that the conservative political movements in Europe will help society to return to their Christian roots. Returning to the roots is not the same thing as Christian renewal. Nonetheless, regardless of merit, there is a growing number of people who are asking questions about the European identity and the role of Christianity in it. At least

---

16. Yedroudj, "Prince Charles' Views."

people will be willing to engage in dialogues about the Christian heritage. That is better than indifference. We can use this situation as an entry point for presenting the gospel again.

Europe did not have the Healing Revivals or the Jesus People movement like America. But Europe has had the Taizé Communauté, and L'Abri. These movements have proved to be more profound and more thoughtful than the American expression of the faith. L'Abri, which means shelter in French, was founded by Francis Schaeffer as a residential resource center for visitors to discuss theological and philosophical topics. The Taizé Communauté is an ecumenical monastic fraternity where young people gather from around the world for prayer, Bible study, and communal work. Europe had dynamic preachers like Charles Spurgeon and Helmut Thielicke before. There is no reason it cannot have such preachers today.

The guilt of the European psyche should not push the gospel away from people. Instead, it should draw them closer to the gospel. Where sin increased, grace abounded even more (Rom 5:20). The sins of the past will not stop Jesus because he did not come to look for the righteous, but sinners. Europeans have a debt to pay to the rest of the world. Apostle Paul said, "Owe no one anything, except to love each other" (Rom 13:8). The practice of love will overcome the sense of guilt and fatigue. Guilty conscience should not make them helpless but more active in service. Instead of feeling superior over others, learn to be the servant of all. This is the debt of love.

Does Jesus Have the Will to Save Europe Again?

The most crucial question in all our discussions about the future of Christianity in Europe is whether Jesus still has the will to save Europe once again. This question is more important than whether European Christians are willing to defend their faith or whether we should try to reintroduce Christianity to Europe. Unless the Lord builds the house, those who build it labor in vain. Unless the Lord watches over the city, the watchman stays awake in vain (Ps 127:1). We know that the Lord can do it, but we want to see if he will do it—like the leper who asked Jesus, "Lord, if you will, you can make me clean" (Matt 8:2). After all the disappointment in Europe, does Jesus want to give Europe another chance? Is the Lord willing to save Europe one more time? What are the modern-day prophets saying about the Lord's intentions toward Europe? Has the Lord himself grown tired of Europe?

It is for such questions that faith is most important than prophecy. The just shall live by faith, not by prophecy. It does not require a new prophecy to know the Lord's will. The Lord already made his intentions clear two thousand years ago. He made his purposes clear. If we do not believe his words, we do not believe him. In the military hierarchy, there is a principle concerning the validity of a standing order. Until a new order is issued, the earlier order is always binding. The famous Japanese officer in the Philippines' jungles who did not know that World War II was over was being faithful to the last order he had received. His last order was to keep his post, and he was not given a new order superseding the previous order. So he kept his post. After outsiders found him and told him that the war was already over, he requested a superior office to come to him and issue an official order. A retired officer went to the Philippines from Japan to deliver an official order to leave the post, after which the officer in question returned home to Japan. This officer was not very sensible, but undoubtedly faithful. It was also significant that the chain of command did not disappear, but there was someone with proper authority to speak to this man.

In the realm of faith, the same principle applies. Jesus commanded his disciples to go and make disciples of all nations, baptizing them, and teaching them to observe all Jesus had commanded. Jesus promised that he would be with his disciples to the end of the age (Matt 28:20). Jesus has not revoked his order. Jesus is still Lord, and the Great Commission still stands. We do not need any additional prophecy to remind us of this fact. When we obey the Lord's command, he will give us more directions. We cannot stay still waiting for further instructions without obeying his command.

With a significant influx of immigrants to Europe from the Global South, God has more reasons to remember Europe. Even though the white Europeans may be indifferent to the gospel, the vast numbers of immigrants are open to it. At least for their sake, Jesus cannot abandon Europe. European people may receive another chance to believe on account of the immigrants in their midst. It does not mean that the Lord is showing favoritism toward the immigrants. If the native Europeans open their hearts to the Lord in the same way as the immigrants, he will grant them the same kind of favor. Though the Lord might have removed the candlestick from the European church, the presence of the immigrants from the Global South in Europe may motivate the Lord to speak his heart more clearly and audibly about his determination to save the continent again. Though Europeans complain about the influx of immigrants for chipping away European identity and being free riders of welfare benefits, the immigrants are a blessing to the native Europeans in ways that they do not fully appreciate. God has chosen those who are poor in the eyes of the world to be rich in faith (Jas 2:5). The immigrants, though poor, have many spiritual riches to contribute to the European society.

The COVID-19 epidemic in Europe, though terrible, may allow the Europeans to be humble before God. They are not as mighty as they might have thought. The bubble of false comfort and denial in which the Europeans have lived has burst.[17] After the COVID-19 epidemic is over, Europeans will feel as if they have come out of a major war. They will realize that the European Union could not protect them during moments of greatest danger. They were more vulnerable and helpless before a major epidemic than they could ever imagine. The social infrastructures could not stand under the weight of the disaster. Life was fragile. Western civilization has not reached the pinnacle of knowledge or accomplishment available to humanity.

The measure of time that we use to determine the act of God is much shorter than the standard of time God uses to do his work. Our memories and knowledge are limited to our lifetime and perhaps several decades previous to our birth. When we compare the current spiritual condition of the world, we compare it to one hundred years ago at best. British Christians, at best, will remember the times of the Welsh Revival or Smith Wigglesworth. French Christians will remember the miraculous healings at Lourdes. Within a short period, the work of God may seem to have waned. Compared to half a century ago, Christianity in the western world seems to have dwindled. But God uses a much longer measure of time to accomplish his work. For God, one day is like a thousand years, and a thousand years are like one day (2 Pet 3:8). He looks at things from a more prolonged and bigger perspective. The events in the past half a century cannot have justly demonstrated what God has in store for the world.

What the Lord will do in Europe can be gleaned from what he has done in other parts of the world. God is not a respecter of persons. He does not discriminate between people and nations. God is capable of doing among Europeans what he has done elsewhere. God desires to say

---

17. Monbiot. "Covid-19 Is Nature's Wake-up Call".

to Europeans the same messages that he has said to other people. Paul did not give different messages to the Ephesians, the Philippians, or the Romans. Though the specifics may have been different, Paul delivered the same gospel message to all the churches that he wrote to. In other words, the Lord does not have a special message tailored for just the Europeans. It is unlikely that the Lord will do something special just for Europe. Thus, if Europeans are not thrilled with what the Lord is doing elsewhere in the world, the Lord has little to offer Europeans. To decline the works of the Lord is to reject the Lord himself. Lord Jesus is the Lord of all his churches all over the world. The Christianity of the Europeans is not different from the Christianity of Asians or Africans. If the Europeans humble themselves before their brothers and sisters in other cultures, they will discover that the Lord will grant the same power and grace to them.

— 7 —

Options for European Christians

Theology Is the Problem

IF EUROPEAN CHRISTIANS WANT to stop Christianity's downward trajectory on their continent, they need clothing that will suit them. David could not wear Saul's armor to fight Goliath. Borrowing the American version of evangelicalism is not necessarily the best option for Europe. The American evangelicalism was the armor that suited the Americans. It was useful while it lasted, but it has done its job and coming to the end of its natural life. Today the term "evangelical" is identified with the Republican political agenda and is avoided even by the evangelicals.

The American version of evangelicalism has some critical shortcomings. While emphasizing salvation, it left out a considerable portion of Jesus's teachings about the kingdom of heaven. Evangelicalism was necessary for avoiding the failure of the mainline denominations; otherwise, Christianity in America would have followed its path toward eventual death. Nonetheless, evangelicalism was only a temporary alternative to mainline Christianity. It does not have the theological breadth on its own to justly represent Christianity. Jesus's teachings cannot be reduced to the assurance of salvation. Billy Graham, great as he was, was an evangelist, not a pastor or teacher. He preached the salvation message only. If evangelicalism is built on the same theology, it is too narrow.

Pentecostalism has become excessively spiritualized and became preoccupied with health and wealth. Not knowing what to do with their spiritual energy, the pentecostals directed their energy toward prosperity and fighting amorphous spiritual battles. The power of the Holy Spirit is for world evangelism (Acts 1:8). When churches are not channeling their spiritual fervor to evangelism, it is bound to go to the side issues. The charismatic leaders in America have long departed from world evangelism; thus, they turned to health and wealth as an alternative. The Vineyard movement was valuable as a new expression of the charismatic movement, focusing on equipping lay Christians for ministry. Unfortunately, after John Wimber's death, there is no one of similar caliber to carry on the torch. The Holy Laughter revival was a hiccup in the charismatic movement. The seeker-sensitive churches could not develop sequels to their excellent Bible skits and music programs. Though great for seekers, seeker services are no longer suitable for making disciples once seekers become believers.

Nonetheless, there are some valuable lessons to learn from the evangelicals. The first lesson is their energy. Old and tired churches do not have the energy to sustain faith. Evangelicalism always has much energy for church services, evangelism, preaching, singing, and diverse programs. The second lesson to be learned is their conviction. Faith is the substance of things hoped for and the evidence of things not seen (Heb 13:1). If one claims to be a believer but lacks conviction, his faith is ineffective to both himself and others. In the name of tolerance, Europeans have lost confidence. A "live-and-let-live" mindset, which permeates society, is responsible for the loss of confidence.[1] The third is spiritual power. What moves people are powerful preaching, powerful prayer, and the demonstration of the Holy Spirit. People should not neglect this dimension. European Christianity has a rich history, exquisite church architecture, music, and liturgy, but lacks spiritual power. It is as if they are shy of spiritual power. The kingdom of God is not in words but in power (1 Cor 4:20). If one had to choose between the two, it is better to have spiritual power over theological sophistication. Spiritual power will revive the church, while theology without power will go nowhere.

The most valuable contribution of evangelicalism is the belief that Christians can be assured of salvation. Until evangelicalism came along, churches did not teach about the assurance of salvation. They did not know how to. The Catholic Church, to this day, does not emphasize personal salvation. Calvinist denominations did not teach the assurance of salvation, either. Calvinism emphasized the sovereignty of God and the total depravity of man. There is little that a man can do to attain salvation.

---

1 Davie, "Europe," 74

It all depends on God. Such a view led to a passive attitude to the matter of salvation. It was evangelicalism with its emphasis on "accepting" Jesus as personal Lord and Savior, which taught that one could be assured of his salvation. The evangelicals were right in their interpretation of scripture. Jesus wanted people to know that they were saved and that their sins were forgiven. He pronounced, "Your faith has healed [saved] you," and "Salvation has come to this house." He healed the paralytic man so that he could know that he had authority on earth to forgive sins (Luke 5:24). It is possible and desirable for people to know that they are saved.

The benefits of this knowledge are immense. When people know that they are children of God, they can use their authority as children of God, they will have peace in their hearts with God, and they will be able to confidently share the gospel with others. The hesitance to share the gospel with others stems from the lack of assurance of one's salvation. Evangelicalism could engage in evangelism and mission actively because of the personal conviction of salvation. Nonevangelicals, who could not be sure of their salvation, on the other hand, had little motivation or power to share the gospel. They cannot give to others what they do not have. The decline of the mainline denominations in the west can be understood in this light. They must replenish their pews through evangelism; otherwise, nothing can stop the emptying of churches due to demographic changes.

The liberal theology of the west is responsible for the loss of faith. Either that or the loss of faith produced liberal theology. Liberal theology has eliminated the reasons to preach the gospel with urgency and conviction. When pastors no longer believe in the divinity of Jesus, or the necessity of conversion, or the exclusivity of the gospel, there is little motivation to preach the gospel. There is no message to preach. When pastors are not able to say confidently, "Believe in the Lord Jesus, and you will be saved—you and your household," they have lost their faith as preachers of the gospel. They have lost their qualification as the custodians of Christianity. The reason for the decline of Christianity in the west is quite understandable. It does not require sophisticated research to discover the cause.

Changes must begin in theological seminaries. If seminaries cannot produce pastors who can preach the gospel with confidence, they have lost their reasons to exist. They are academic institutions but not training grounds for future preachers and pastors. Many seminaries no longer believe in Trinity. Instead of saying Father, Son, and Holy Spirit, they say Creator, Savior, and Sustainer. Instead of evangelizing, they "dialogue." The idea of the Son of God dying for our sin is viewed as "divine child abuse."² After a certain point, it is almost impossible to recognize such theology as Christianity. Such a distorted and diluted form of Christianity cannot appeal to people. Those who formulated such liberal theology may have thought that the public would welcome it as open and tolerant, but they were wrong. The public does not welcome it. Liberal theology fails to indicate what to believe. It gives them little reason to be enthusiastic about anything. It does not answer their profound questions. It is spiritually dissatisfying. Liberal theology neither meets the spiritual demands of people nor supplies the real thing. By making theology so progressive, they have made it unrecognizable. The tragedy is that those who subscribed to such liberal theology thought that the public would like it. Nothing can be further from the truth. Progressive theology kills faith, and it kills churches. There is no Holy Spirit in liberal theology. The condition for the coming of the Holy Spirit was Jesus's glorification (John 7:39). In our present days, the Holy Spirit will not work where the name of Jesus is not lifted up. The Holy Spirit came to glorify Jesus (John 16:14). When theology is not confident about Jesus, we cannot expect the Holy Spirit to be present where such theology is taught. By espousing empty values, liberal theology fails to satisfy the spiritual needs of the sheep.

The split between liberal theological seminaries and evangelical seminaries is quite evident in the United States. We need to ask in what ways some of the oldest and most prominent theological seminaries can still be considered as Christian seminaries. They have turned into schools of religious studies and radical political agenda. If we suppose the theological orientation of such academies reflects the condition of the mainline denominations in the United States, it is not difficult to understand why these denominations are rapidly dying away. They have given up believing in biblical Christianity. They are preoccupied with their agenda instead of trying to meet the needs of their sheep. The congregations need to be fed the word of God, but these liberal seminaries only push progressive political and social agendas such as LGBT+ rights and radical feminism. They are ignoring the basic principle of supply and demand. The sheep vote with their feet. Liberal seminaries are not able to meet the need of the people. It is not surprising that disenchanted sheep leave churches.

The LGBT+ rights and feminism may be important social issues, but not necessarily critical theological issues. Pastors must feed the sheep the word of God, not the radical social agenda. Why do pastors speak to their

---

2. PastorStudy, "Tragedy of Mainline Protestantism," 17:28.

flock those arguments that must be reserved for denominational meetings and seminary classrooms? Poorly fed sheep will not grow well. Some preachers confuse their social agenda with the word of God. Claiming to speak the word of God, they express their opinions. They confuse their vigor with the Holy Spirit. The sheep are not interested in listening to their pastors' personal opinions, regardless of how well educated or socially conscious they are. "My sheep know my voice," said Jesus. When pastors preach the word of the Lord, their congregants will recognize it and keep returning to the church to hear it. Reinhold Niebuhr called on preachers to comfort the afflicted and afflict the comfortable. But liberal seminaries have forgotten how to comfort. They must remember that the purpose of prophecy is to strengthen, encourage, and comfort (1 Cor 14:3).

There is something seriously wrong when people equate biblical scholarship with liberal theology and equate evangelical theology with inferior biblical scholarship. The real problem with western Christianity began at that point. Theology that kills off faith ceases to be Christianity. Theology professors who teach theories that discourage faith must ask themselves why they do what they do. Those who teach unbelief in the name of theology should stop calling themselves Christian theologians.

Biblical scholarship is not a *fait accompli* as some people seem to think. There are still many areas to be explored in biblical scholarship, which can support greater confidence in the Bible's integrity. Biblical criticism does not have to entail the loss of faith in the Bible. Douglas Murray attributes the decline of the faith to higher criticism and Darwinism, but his view is old-fashioned. There is no reason why one cannot reconcile intelligent design with evolution, and no reason why biblical criticism has to lead to the loss of faith in the Bible. Instead, biblical criticism enables a more enlightened understanding of the Bible, which leads to well-balanced faith instead of fanaticism.

Clothing That Suits Europeans

Borrowing the ministry models from America or from elsewhere does not suit Europeans for many reasons. The American version of evangelicalism assumes high voluntary participation of church members, a large talent pool, much money, organizational skill, and much time. In contrast, European churches cannot lean on any of those things.[3]

---

3. Nachtigall, "Why Evangelical Churches Struggle in Europe."

Europeans cannot eat yesterday's manna. The American version of evangelicalism is pragmatic. To Americans, what works is right. This pragmatism applies to their faith, too. Europeans, in contrast, are loyal to their heritage and tradition. Europe has always been the Old World, while America was the New World. As a result, if the Christian expression does not accommodate the rich heritage and tradition, it may look alien and strange, and Europeans would have difficulty recognizing it. When the sheep do not recognize the shepherd's voice, they will run away (John 10:5).

Europeans must work out sustainable and viable expressions and confessions of Christianity from their Christian heritage. Prince William of England heartily sang, "Guide Me, O Thou great Jehovah." at his wedding ceremony. It was the same hymn at Lady Diana's funeral service. He must have picked this hymn because it had left a deep impression. Whatever expression of the faith the Europeans embrace must be recognizable from their experience since Christianity was once an inseparable aspect of their lives.

Thus, what are the options for European Christians? The only answer is to recover the message and spirit of Jesus Christ. After two thousand years, humanity still has not learned how to follow the teachings of Jesus fully. The institutionalized church coopted much of Jesus's message and spirit.

Albert Schweitzer knew what he was doing when he left his career as a theologian and organist in Germany and served as a doctor in Africa. Schweitzer chose to practice his faith without dogmatism, believing that his quiet service would speak louder than any words. The only drawback was that he chose the life of service as an alternative to his earlier attempt to discover the historical Jesus. He despaired of its theological possibility. His choice to go to Africa as a medical doctor was an existential act to take the place of theological research. As a result, Schweitzer, though a good man, is not a good example to follow for other Christians.

What would win the heart of people, especially young people, is the selfless practice of Christian love and an authentic community of faith—a mixture of St. Francis and the Taizé Community. In the film *The Shoes of the Fisherman*, a newly elected Pope, who had served twenty years as a political prisoner in Siberia, proclaims the divesture of the church property to help the starving people of China. It is an old film, and the international situations have changed since then. Nonetheless, the Pope's action in the movie profoundly moves not only the faithful but also the atheistic communists of Russia and China. We no longer make films like this. This film is powerful because it depicts a Christian who has experienced suffering—an element missing in the discourse about Christianity in Europe—and knows how to practice the spirit of Jesus in the contemporary world.

The Suffering Element

Whenever the subject of suffering comes up, most people like to ask why there is suffering in the world if God is a loving God. However, the way the Bible approaches the subject of suffering is that it is beneficial for the human soul. "It was good for me to be afflicted so that I might learn your decrees" (Ps 119:71). People, in general, do not want to think of God until they face hardship. Most people who sought Jesus earnestly during his earthly ministry were sick people or people with desperate problems. It is not the healthy who need a doctor, but the sick. Although most people want to avoid suffering, it is mainly through suffering that people come to faith. One cannot criticize faith as the "crutch" for the weak. If there were no suffering, most people would think that they could live without God. That does not mean that God deliberately allows suffering in people's lives to force them to come to him. Instead, it means that, if suffering permits people to come to the Lord, suffering is not in vain but may even be beneficial. "All things work together for good to them that love God, to them who are the called according to his purpose" (Rom 8:28, KJV). Without faith, it is difficult to see any meaning or purpose in our sufferings, no matter how hard we try.

The experience of suffering tends to make one's faith credible and authentic. In the film *The Shoes of the Fisherman*, Russian Archbishop Kiril was imprisoned in Siberia for twenty years before he is released to Rome. Contrary to everyone's expectation, Kiril is elected as Pope. He is elected to papacy without a secret vote but by the unanimous support of the College of Cardinals. In our theoretical discourse about the fate of Christianity, we often forget that Christ did not conquer the world through theological persuasion but his death and resurrection. Christianity recovers its original power when it is tested in the refining fire. When the doubting Thomas demanded the valid evidence of Jesus's resurrection, Jesus showed him the nail marks on his hands and the lance wound on his side. Thomas kneeled before the evidence of the Master's suffering.

One of the reasons that Christianity proliferated in Korea was the experience of deep poverty and suffering due to the Japanese colonialism and the Korean War. The power to heal was birthed out of the deep pain suffered by Christians, both men and women.

Indeed, blessed are the poor and those who mourn. The fundamental reason for the European church's timidity and lukewarm state may be the absence of such poverty and mourning. How will the Lord bring about a spiritual renewal in Europe without making the European people go through a season of poverty and mourning?

The message to the Laodicean Church applies to us today. We say that we are rich and lack nothing, but we do not know our real poverty, blindness, and nakedness (Rev 3:17). Christ's command to the Laodiceans was to be earnest and repent. Out of one's realization of real spiritual poverty comes earnestness and repentance.

The Laodicean Church bears the closest resemblance to the contemporary age that boasts of economic progress and prosperity. When people become prosperous, they have less motivation to seek the Lord earnestly. They do not necessarily abandon faith but lose humility and zeal. Man shall not live by bread alone but by every word that comes out of the mouth of God (Matt 4:4). Economic prosperity is the inverse of spiritual poverty. It would be better if prosperity and spirituality would go hand and hand, but they hardly do. Such is the meaning of "Blessed are the poor, for theirs is the kingdom of God."

Remember that Job was a rich man, but he went through an extreme refinement by fire. Only after he had endured the troubles did God give a double portion of what he had had before. The more God blesses us with prosperity, the poorer in spirit we need to be. The problem with Europe is not new. There is nothing new under the sun. Knowing this fact can help the pastors to feel less intimidated and to know how to deal with the situation with faith and wisdom.

"Why Do You Go to Church So Diligently?"

One of my congregants told me that, while her family lived in Germany, her German neighbor asked her, "Why do Koreans go to church every Sunday?" This German neighbor went to church herself, but once a month was enough for her. She suggested that perhaps their Korean neighbors went to church so often because they were lonely.

If someone asked me the same question, I would reply as follows: "I go to church every Sunday because I want to." It is the most obvious answer to which no one can object. And I would turn the table around: "Why don't you want to go to church every Sunday?" Instead of considering themselves as the norm, Germans should consider their neighbors to be a new norm. It should occur to them that perhaps the immigrant Christians have something in them that the native Europeans do not.

Faith must arise from within the inner person. It cannot be enforced from the outside. It is never the right answer to say, "I go to church every Sunday because I have to," or "I go to church every Sunday to receive a blessing," or "I go to church every Sunday because God will punish me otherwise." None of these answers is right for this postmodern society. The only convincing reason for going to church is one's desire to go. And this desire must arise from within.

Jesus said that he would give living water to those who believe (John 4:10). Living water for the ancient people meant running water, as opposed to stagnant water. Though we take running water for granted today, in the desert climate, running water was a highly rare and precious resource. Jesus likened the Holy Spirit to living water. The Holy Spirit continually motivates a believer from within. From this living water come energy and desire to serve Christ. A Spirit-filled Christian does not practice faith out of obligation or duty, but out of inner motivation.

Therefore, if a person does not desire to go to church every week, there is no other force that can motivate him. The same principle applies to every other aspect of Christian life—prayer, worship, service, ministry, and charity.

The power of spiritual renewal in Europe must come from the same source—the Holy Spirit. Nothing else is strong enough to bring about renewal. Europe has valuable traditions and legacy of Christianity, but they are not enough to motivate people today. Maintaining Christian identity is also a worthy goal, but where will people receive the power to do so?

Church Members Vote with Their Feet

The above title speaks for itself. People vote with their feet. If they like what they experience at a church, they will come back; if they do not, they will stay away. It is obviously more complicated than that, but this is the gist of the principle. In the streets of Seoul, Korea, foreign tourists will discover that there are many, many churches in every neighborhood.

In one city block, they might find five or six churches. Sometimes, they will find two churches in the same building! One church may be on the fifth floor, and the other church, in the basement. There are over a hundred denominations and fifty thousand churches in Korea. True religious diversity exists in Korea. Such plurality of Protestant churches in Korea draws much criticism from Koreans—Christians and non-Christians alike. Churches seem to run on the same free-market principle as coffee shops and convenience stores. Some people point to this situation as evidence of the fractured state of Protestantism. Until sociologists discovered the supply side theory of religion, everyone thought of such plurality of churches as a problem.

Despite the cluttered religious landscape, the plurality of churches gives the public a variety of choices. Europeans may find it odd that people can pick and choose churches, but that is the reality in Korea and America. People vote with their feet. They will congregate at churches that seem to meet their needs the best. Megachurches were born as a result. They are more successful in meeting the needs of a high number of people.

People's needs are not always spiritual. Often, they congregate in churches where they feel socially comfortable. The so-called homogeneous unit principle is real. There are churches for blue-collar workers, yuppies, students, artists, ex-pats, and other demographical categories. Birds of a feather flock together. People will gather at churches where they find cultural similarities. It is a sociological and psychological phenomenon, not spiritual. Demanding that all people in one geographical area attend the same church is tyrannical and impractical. They will go where they feel comfortable. When a person feels uncomfortable at a church, there are no effective means of keeping him there, to the chagrin of a well-meaning pastor.

When church members leave a church, the chances are that they will move to another church. The horizontal movement of church members is very high in Korea. The official membership rosters are unreliable because the same people are counted multiple times due to horizontal transfers. From an individual church's perspective, losing a member is a loss, but from he collective perspective, there is no real loss. It is a good thing that the plurality of churches exists in Korea.

The demand-side model of the Secularization Hypothesis suggests that the diversity of religion will reduce religious participation because it makes people doubt the correctness of their own religion. However, research has shown that, in societies with high levels of income, more democratic institutions, and high levels of education, religious diversity has a more positive effect than a negative effect on religious participation.[4] In less developed countries, establishing new churches may shake the belief in the existing churches, reducing people's overall religious participation. In contrast, in the more developed countries with a higher level of secularization, people are freer to switch denominations in search of churches to their liking.[5] In developed countries, there is a more consumer mentality of looking for churches that offer the highest quality of ministry.

Based on the above theory, it is not difficult to diagnose the problems of European churches. When dominant churches rely on state support, they constitute a religious monopoly. Religious monopoly reduces the competitiveness of churches. Religious liberty entails the ability to leave one church and join another. When people do not have this freedom, they end up not going to any church. Human beings are very complicated creatures. Anyone who has pastored a church understands this fact. It is not easy to meet everyone's needs. No one church can meet all the needs of people. Even Apostle Paul could not satisfy everyone. Some Christians at Corinth preferred Apollos or Peter to Paul. Paul was not impressive in speech (2 Cor 10:10) compared to Apollos in particular (Acts 18:25). The Lord gives diverse gifts to church is so that various people and churches can meet people's different needs. The competition between churches, which makes pastors very uncomfortable, could be the Lord's method of keeping his churches vital and alert. Ministers must always keep in mind that they serve at the pleasure of the Lord Jesus. Jesus did not come to be served, but to serve. Likewise, ministers must always remember that their ministry is not for their personal satisfaction or glory. Pastors of megachurches will not receive greater rewards from the Lord on Judgment Day than pastors of smaller churches. Our rewards in heaven will not be in proportion to the amount of outward success on earth. Our rewards come from the Lord for being good and faithful in his sight.

---

4. Opfinger, "Two Sides of the Medal"
5. Opfinger, "Two Sides of the Medal"

— 8 —

Recovering of the Gospel

God Is Christian

THE TRUEST AND THE complete revelation of God took place through Jesus Christ. Jesus is the only way of knowing God truly. This view does not limit the concept of God to the narrow confines of Christianity. Instead, it celebrates the fullest revelation of God made available by Christ. We must remember that God was once the God whose name could not be spoken. He was distant and fearsome. He dwelled on top of a mountain surrounded by thunder and clouds. Anyone trying to approach died. Christ made it possible for sinners to approach God boldly and call him "Abba, Father." No other revelation of God is as powerful and revolutionary as this. Not only did Christ make God known to men, but also he gave men the power to become children of God. Jesus not only revealed God but also reconciled man to God.

God has always defined the unique rules that people had to follow to worship him and serve him. From the beginning, God did not accept all the religious initiatives of men. In Genesis chapter 4, he accepted Abel's offering but not Cain's. Man is free to serve God in any way he chooses, but God is not obliged to receive all such services. There was one definite way to serve God, which he accepted and approved; he disapproved and rejected all the rest. Cain was angry that God did not accept his offering while God accepted Abel's, but Cain's anger was not just. Instead of repenting, Cain murdered Abel and became a wanderer upon the earth.

The same situation exists in our times. Many are angry that there is only one way to God. They demand that there should be multiple ways to God. Nevertheless, a man may not make demands on God. Cain could not change God; he had to change himself. People fallaciously demand that God must change the rules. Instead, people should change their thinking. The fairness of God does not mean that he equally accepts every man's religion.

The magicians of the Pharaoh performed miracles similar to Moses, but Moses' serpent devoured the magicians' serpents. Amid the plurality of gods and religions, there was only one true servant and prophet of God. The others were false prophets. Elijah's spiritual contest with the prophets of Baal on Mount Carmel typifies the folly of religious pluralism. God did not honor the prayers of the prophets of Baal. He only accepted Elijah's prayer. Baal was not a true god. The worship of Baal was not a true religion.

It takes God's initiative and revelation for man to know him. God is beyond man's ability to know. He is wholly other. The fundamental difference between Christianity and other religions is that Christianity is based on God's self-revelation. The holiness of God does not refer to God's moral qualities, but his complete otherness from man. If man can discover God on their initiative, God is man's imagination. Freud interpreted the idea of God as the Super-Ego within man's psychology. Freud would have been right if God were the product of man's imaginations. However, God is holy. Not all roads lead to God, and not all searches inevitably lead to God. God cannot be responsible for some human-made theology based on man's imaginations and wishful thinking. What does it mean to say that God can be known truly and sufficiently through Christ?

God the Father Is Forever Committed to His Son

Christianity is the result of God's self-revelation as testified by the Law, prophets, and fulfilled by Jesus Christ. Christianity was the continuation and fulfillment of God's plan to save humanity. God's first reference to the coming Savior of the world was in Genesis 3:15, where he prophesied about the seed of the woman bruising the head of the serpent while the serpent bruises the heel of the seed of the woman.

Noah's ark was a type of Christianity in that those who were in the ark were saved from the judgment while those outside were destroyed. It was not the personal moral status that determined their fate, but whether they were in or out of the ark. The seven blessings God gave to Abraham in Genesis chapter 12 were the foreshadowing of the salvation of the world, which would come from the seed of Abraham—Jesus Christ. The descendants as numerous as the stars in heaven refer to those who would become God's children through Jesus Christ. In that sense, calling Jesus the son of Abraham was tantamount to calling him the Messiah.

King David was a type of the anointed servant of God who would save the people of Israel; Jesus came through the bloodline of David. As a result, calling Jesus "the Son of David" was also equal to calling him the Messiah.

John wrote his gospel partly to explain the relationship between the Father and the Son. One question that drove John was the relationship between the Father and the Son—whether Jesus made up his own religion or he was obeying the instructions of the Father, how much the Father and Son agreed with each other, how much the Son revealed the Father, and how much the Son obeyed the Father. All these were not only important theological and Christological questions but also confirmations of God's commitment to Christ.

God the Father is committed to his Son Jesus Christ. God's commitment is based on the covenant that he made with Christ. God proved his acceptance of Jesus's sacrifice by raising him from the dead. From this covenant, we have the word "New Testament." The Father's commitment to the Son means that the Father will not bypass Jesus in his dealings with humanity. Jesus represents humanity before the Father. That is the meaning of the high priesthood of Jesus.

Jesus constituted the last and complete revelation of the Father. Jesus said, "Whoever looks at me is seeing the one who sent me" (John 12:45). He also said, "I am the way, the truth, and the life. No one can come to the Father except through me" (John 14:6). These statements, and many others like them, show that Jesus was the way that God provided by which humanity may know him and go to him. Anyone who wants to know God and go to God must go through this path that God established.

No one can willfully bypass Jesus and complain that God is exclusive. Why would anyone complain that God is narrowminded after ignoring the definite and clear way that God personally established? Such willfulness borders on rebelliousness to God and dismissal of God. Some people take Jesus's teachings on inclusivity and use them to discredit his teachings about hell and judgment. Jesus never intended his inclusivity or mercy to be used to negate his teachings. He said, "Anyone who hears my words and does not put them to practice is like a foolish man who builds his house on sand" (Matt 7:26).

Anyone who disagrees with the Christian Bible is free to ignore it or dismiss it. But instead of doing that, many try to distort the meaning of the Bible to suit their thinking. Some people take certain segments out of the Bible to argue that Christianity cannot be the only way of salvation, which is tantamount to distorting the whole counsel of the Bible. If anyone is trying to take Jesus's words and use them to deny Jesus, his argument is circular and untrustworthy.

God Revealed Himself Finally and Sufficiently through Jesus

The finality of Christian revelation does not necessarily mean that the end is imminent. It means that there will be no more revelation after it. The frequent use of "the last days" in the New Testament refers to this fact. To call Jesus the "Last Adam" means that Jesus is the last and greatest representative of humanity before God the Father.

The complete revelation of God means that all that needs to be revealed about God has been revealed through Jesus Christ. Being complete does not mean being exhaustive. God has revealed enough about himself for humanity to believe and trust him. The Book of Mormon added strange and dangerous ideas about God, which are clearly at odds with the Bible, such as the blasphemous theory that God has a body and a spouse. The idea of God always attracts curiosity and imagination by man. But all that must be revealed about God has been revealed by Jesus Christ and the New Testament. God does not add extrabiblical revelation through other channels. People fall into error by seeking extrabiblical revelations.

When we talk about various religions, we use such words as "Christian God" and "Muslim God." Usually, people are hesitant to define God as belonging exclusively to one religion. Defining God's religious affiliation looks like treating him with disrespect. However, if we presume that God is consistent and true in his words, not all the religious doctrines about God can be right. God cannot say one thing in one religion and then contradict himself in another. If God has permitted multiple religions to disclose him, God is inconsistent and inaccurate, and thus unreliable.

Inclusivity is a big trap for those who are trying to understand God. By inappropriately attributing an inclusive nature to God, they dilute the biblical revelation of God and turn him into someone that he is not. People can experience God insofar as they seek him within the confines of the biblical revelation. When people leave these confines, they are making up their own God. It becomes even more presumptuous when people add their requirements to the concept of God. This is the trap of trying to build a politically correct theology.

Nadab and Abihu lit strange fires before God and died as a result (Lev 10:1–3). What was particularly offensive to God about the Israelites' worship of the golden calf in the desert was that they wrongly ascribed to the golden calf God's act of delivering the Israelites (Exod 32:4). Religious inclusivity leads to syncretism, which the Lord hates the most. The Lord even prohibited sowing fields with two kinds of seed or wearing a garment of cloth made of two types of material (Lev 19:19). Such restrictions do not show God's bias, but his utmost holiness. Whether man worships God or not is up to him, but as long as he worships God, it has to be according to God's strict demands. It is better not to worship God than to worship him in an unholy way.

Man Experiences God Most Definitely through the Holy Spirit

Jesus Christ sent the Holy Spirit to abide with believers. The most potent way in which one can experience God is through the Holy Spirit. The further one moves away from the Holy Spirit, the more unclear and uncertain God becomes. The closer one approaches the Holy Spirit, the clearer and more definite God is. The Holy Spirit has been sent to the world to testify to the Lordship of Jesus Christ. The Holy Spirit presents the most explicit and powerful way of experiencing Christ and God the Father.

Many of the liberal theologians have neglected the person of the Holy Spirit. The Holy Spirit cannot be known apart from the personal experience of his presence and power. The reason that God is so remote and abstract to so many cultural Christians is that they have not experienced the Holy Spirit. Instead of a personal experience of the Spirit of God, many philosophers turned the Spirit into an impersonal spiritual force like Zeitgeist or the force in Star Wars. Hegel described history as the self-expression of the Spirit. Such abstract philosophizing is undoubtedly impressive but far removed from the biblical definition of the Holy Spirit. The role of the Holy Spirit is very spiritual. Nevertheless, the western philosophers and theologians have turned him into a historical force. They will never be able to make sense of Jesus's words that casting out demons by the Holy Spirit demonstrates the kingdom of God in our midst, or that the Holy Spirit came upon all who were listening to Peter, making them speak in tongues and prophesy. The pentecostal and charismatic movements have made invaluable contributions to Christianity by demonstrating the reality of the Holy Spirit, not as a theological concept, but as a spiritual reality that people could experience. Reviving Christianity in Europe will have to include personal experiences of the Holy Spirit.

It is possible for pastors to lose faith in God if they do not keep up a real relationship with the Holy Spirit. Without the Holy Spirit, the idea of God is only a theological proposition. A theological proposition cannot replace God, and it will succumb to the trials and temptations that inevitably come to us. In the face of intense trials and temptations, our faith in God will be tested. Even pastors can drift further and further away from the living God unless they maintain an active fellowship with the Holy Spirit through fervent prayer and worship. Smith Wigglesworth, the famous British evangelist, said that he read the Bible every fifteen minutes and prayed every thirty minutes. How many contemporary ministers have this kind of spiritual discipline? And we are curious why we do not have the kind of spiritual power that the men of God of old used to have.

Charismatic Christianity does not have the monopoly on the Holy Spirit. The person and ministry of the Holy Spirit are available to all Christians. No one can say, "Jesus is Lord," except by the Holy Spirit (1 Cor 12:3). The Holy Spirit plays a crucial role in the faith of every Christian, whether he realizes it or not. The Pentecostals emphasize the second experience of the baptism of the Holy Spirit while the evangelicals stress that believers already have the Holy Spirit. There is a never-ending debate between the two camps over this topic. A theological compromise is possible between the Pentecostals and non-Pentecostals: the potential for the fullness of the Holy Spirit exists for all believers. Those who are baptized in the Holy Spirit have realized that potential while those who have not received such baptism have not fully realized the potential. God is not a respecter of persons, and he is willing to give the Holy Spirit to those who asks him (Luke 11:13).

Not only does the Holy Spirit play a crucial role in someone becoming a Christian, but also in his fellowship with the Father and the Son. "God is a Spirit, and they that worship him must worship him in spirit and truth" (John 4:24). Jesus's intent in John 4:24 was to emphasize the spiritual nature of God and the necessity of worshiping God spiritually. More specifically, worshipers must worship God through the aid of the Holy Spirit.

Worship services that are devoid of the Holy Spirit's touch will fail to engage the hearts of the congregation. In contrast, when the congregation experiences the Holy Spirit's presence and power during worship, they will feel the reality of the existence of God. What meets the spiritual needs of the congregation is the Holy Spirit. A pastor cannot make a worship service successful and satisfying apart from the help of the Holy Spirit.

Attempting to experience the existence of God without the Holy Spirit is formless and indefinite. Anyone who claims that God can be known apart from Christianity enters a world with no rules, no clear guidance, and no protection. It is like Nadab and Abihu who lit up a strange fire, which had them killed. The world is full of people who try to look for God through random methods. Some have even tried hallucinogenic drugs. It is very dangerous to dabble with the spiritual world. Recall that Satan tempted Jesus in the wilderness. Anyone dabbling with the spiritual world without the protection of Jesus exposes himself to dangerous spiritual deception. God has disclosed himself most fully and finally through his Son Jesus Christ. And Jesus has sent the Holy Spirit so that people can believe in Jesus and worship the Father. Any religious attempt outside this boundary is aimless and indefinite. Any willful attempt outside the edge of Christianity amounts to unbelief and rebellion.

The Ever-Present Pitfall of the Law

What Christianity has to offer the world is always the message of the gospel. Jesus Christ has expressed himself most completely in the gospel. One must know the gospel to know Christ. If someone thinks that he loves Jesus without knowing the gospel, his love is incomplete. A Christian is a person who has heard the gospel and assented to it. There is a pedagogical element in conversion as well as a relational element. Reintroducing Christianity to a post-Christian society, therefore, requires confirming the gospel message.

Many times throughout the history of Christianity the gospel was distorted or mistaken. When people were offended and turned off by the church, it was mostly because the church failed to truthfully present the gospel. By failing to preach the true gospel, the church failed to properly present Jesus.

Often what is preached from the pulpit is not the gospel but the law. How does it happen? It happens because the preacher himself is not acquainted with the gospel or because he is tempted to motivate his congregation through other means than the gospel. Apostle Paul rebuked the church at Galatia for succumbing to the "false gospel" of trying to meet righteousness through the works of the law. As the early church was susceptible to the distortion of the gospel, churches in every age are vulnerable to the false gospel. The Reformation was an effort to recover the truth of the gospel. The Protestant Reformation was not a revival movement in the sense of improving religious zeal. The pre-Reformation society was religiously zealous. Religious intensity was so high that people focused their devotion on wrong things that could not save them, like relics, pilgrimages, and indulgences. It amply proves that religious zeal alone cannot bring about a genuine conversion. Likewise, in this age, Christian renewal in Europe requires the recovery of the gospel

Knowingly motivating the flock by means other than the gospel is a common pitfall for many pastors. After many attempts to lead the congregation by love, pastors get hurt and disappointed by the congregation's hardened hearts. As a result, pastors are tempted to resort to those methods which promise quicker results, such as criticism and legalism. Instead of gently exhorting the congregation, they rain down fire and brimstone from the pulpit. Such a method works for a while, but the sheep are bruised and intimidated. More importantly, the love of God feels distant to them. Gradually the sheep are led astray from the truth of the gospel.

The prosperity gospel is one example of distorting the true gospel. It is an attempt to make a financial deal with God. A deal necessarily involves a give-and-take. It is conditional. The prosperity gospel emphasizes giving to God as a condition for receiving material blessings from him. God indeed rewards faithful tithes and offerings. There are many Bible verses to support this fact.

Nonetheless, when churches emphasize this teaching, they push the gospel aside and dwell on righteousness by works. Those who believe they have received rewards for their faithful giving boast of their righteous deeds. In contrast, those who have not received such rewards are considered to have failed in their dealings with God. Until the prosperity gospel came into existence, people never knew that God was so conscious about dollars and cents. The prosperity gospel is greed disguised as faith.

Sometimes legalism is practiced in more subtle ways. Although preachers may preach the gospel from the pulpit, they resort to legalistic rules in the church life. Every church is a community of people. As a community of people, each church has specific rules for organizing itself. Whenever there are several people in the same community, there are rules for determining the hierarchy among them. The most faithful application of the gospel to social hierarchy is allowing no authority except what is necessary for upholding God's truth and order in the church. Apostle Paul gives specific rules to support in church, but all these rules presuppose common sense. Paul says, "The elders who direct the affairs of the church are well worthy of double honor, especially those whose work is preaching and teaching" (1 Tim 5:17). The author of Hebrews says, "Have confidence in your leaders and submit to their authority, because they keep watch over you as those who must give an account. Do this so that their work will be a joy, not a burden, for that would be of no benefit to you" (Heb 13:17). But these instructions are following the standard rules of courtesy. Common rules of social etiquette are clear: "Do not rebuke an older man harshly, but exhort him as if he were your father. Treat younger men as brothers, older women as mothers, and younger women as sisters, with absolute purity" (1 Tim 5:1).

Many times, however, certain people in the church receive VIP treatments contrary to the guidelines of the New Testament. In some circumstances, senior pastors reign over their flock like kings. The more spiritual power they display, the more they are tempted to lord over the congregation. Martin Luther tried to escape from the clerical tyranny of the Roman Catholic hierarchy, but Protestant churches have developed their own regime. In some church circles, the senior pastor and his family are called "the First Family." Such abuse of clergy authority sometimes leads to financial mismanagement or other forms of abuse. Peter instructed pastors not to lord over their flock but to be examples (1 Pet 5:3). Paul said he does not want to lord over the faith of the sheep (2 Cor 1:24). Jesus was the King of kings and Lord of lords, and yet he served humbly by dying on the cross. Jesus's humble service is the message of the gospel. It means that God demonstrated his love for sinful humanity through the death of his Son. God showed his love through the suffering and weakness of his Son. If the clergy chooses to lord over the flock, they violate the very spirit of the cross. Often religious communities turned into cults not because of false theology but because of spiritual abuse.

It is not only the clergy who receive the VIP treatment in church communities. Pastors often grant other members a higher status than the rest because of their "contribution" to the church. It is like George Orwell's *Animal Farm*: "All animals are equal, but some animals are more equal." Though all Christians are equal before God, some Christians receive greater "equality" in church communities. Their higher status is due to the amount of money they donate to the church, the amount of faith they are supposed to have, or the amount of influence they wield over the congregation. Often pastors and elders wrestle with each other for the hegemony over the church. In the film *Chocolat*, the head elder of the church writes the sermons for the young priest, drawing satisfaction from listening to his own sermons from the pulpit.[1]

James admonished the churches for showing favoritism to people based on their appearance (Jas 2:1–3). If we believe that we are all sinners justified solely by the grace of Jesus, we are fundamentally equal before him. We cannot claim any intrinsic hierarchy in the church apart from what is necessary to keep order in the church. The Jerusalem church needed a hierarchy for establishing order in the church. However, the first martyr was Stephen, one of the seven deacons, and the second martyr was Apostle James. None of the VIPs claimed their special status for personal gain. Instead, they were the first people to suffer for the gospel of Jesus Christ. The greatest in the kingdom of God must be the servant of all.

When legalism governs the the church, it uses bullying and coercion in the name of faith. Abuse is more deadly at church because it is practiced in the name of God. When church leaders try to elicit obedience from the flock not by the persuasion of the Spirit, but by coercion and threatening, they are unfaithful to the spirit of the gospel. If God had wanted to coerce people to believe and obey him, he would have done it a long time ago. The reason he sent his Son was that the world could not be saved through force. Humanity would not return to God by threats of hell, judgment, or punishment. If such methods could work on humanity, Jesus would not have had to come to the world.

When communists and totalitarians tried such methods, those times were the darkest periods in the history of the world. The Spanish Inquisition hoped to eradicate unbelief and apostasy from the Christendom

---

1. Hallström, *Chocolat*.

through torture and every sort of cruelty. Nothing could be further from the spirit and method of Jesus Christ. God chose to save humanity by sending his Son to the cross, which was foolishness to the Greeks and weakness to the Jews, but to us who are being saved it was the power of God (1 Cor 1:18, 23). God chose to show his power through the weakness of the cross. This irony is the central truth of the gospel, but Christians have often had a difficult time grasping it and practicing it. Whenever they departed from it, Christianity fell into profound error.

Jesus leads his sheep, not through the display of force, but love and grace. He does not drive the flock like herds of cattle. Instead, he goes ahead of them, and his sheep follow him because they know his voice (John 10: 4). He is a good shepherd who lays d his life for the sheep (John 10:11). When he confronts us, he does not condemn us, even though he has the right to. To the woman caught in the act of adultery, Jesus said, "Neither do I condemn you. Go and sin no more." Jesus deals with all of us in this way. There is no condemnation for those who are in Christ (Rom 8:1).

For many people, condemnation is a powerful tool of coercion. Jesus could condemn us if he wanted, but he bore our sins upon himself instead. The most famous instance of a penitent person who adored Christ in the New Testament was the sinful woman who washed Jesus's feet with her tears. Jesus said that this woman loved him much because her sin was forgiven much (Luke 7:47). Even Jesus's disciples had a hard time understanding what Jesus meant at that time. After his resurrection, Jesus visited Peter and asked him only one question: "Simon, son of John, do you love me?" And then Jesus commanded him, "Feed my sheep." The only motivation that Jesus was looking for in Peter was love. Jesus wanted Peter to serve him out of love, not guilt or obligation.

Jesus deals with us in the same way. He can force us to do many things if he wanted to, but that is not his way. If that had been his intention, he would not have had to die for us. Jesus loves us wholeheartedly and hopes that this love will move us to obey him and serve him. He said, "If you love me, keep my commands" (John 14:15). The proper motive to keep his commands is the love for him. If anyone thinks that he does not love Jesus enough to keep his commands, he is free not to. If anyone is shocked to hear it, it proves how much we are used to thinking contrary to the gospel's truth. We still have difficulty understanding the methods that God chose to save the world. He took a big gamble because humanity may choose to reject God's love. Good took that risk. He would not have done it unless he was confident that his method would succeed. The success of God's method will lead to the triumph of Christianity. The success of Christianity is the success of God's love. Love never fails (1 Cor 13:8). Therefore, God will never fail.

The reason that Christians have such a tough time appropriating the truth of the gospel is that the law appeals to the flesh better than the gospel. The law makes more sense to the flesh than the gospel. It is easier to hit back than to turn the other cheek. Hitting back makes more sense to the flesh. "An eye for an eye, and a tooth for a tooth" is the typical principle of the law. From the very beginning of Christianity, the ever-present temptation to go back to the law persisted. Jesus pointed out the temptation to display one's righteousness before people through ostentatious prayer, outlandish offering, and visible practice of religion. The temptation to receive rewards before men was often greater than the desire to earn rewards from God. The moment that Peter baptized the house of Cornelius, there was an immediate outcry from the leadership in Jerusalem about Peter's fraternizing with gentiles. Despite Jesus's many predictions about the gentiles coming to the household of God, the disciples were slow to understand them or believe them. After the first gentile church came into existence in Antioch, false teaching began to sneak in, calling for the need to be circumcised to be saved. The First Jerusalem Council was convened to discuss this matter. After that, someone made another attempt to spread a false gospel to the church at Galatia. Against this event, Apostle Paul wrote his most angry letter to the Galatians.

Paul called man's attempt to be justified by the works of the law "means of the flesh" (Gal 3:3, 6:12). The works of the law appeal to the flesh, as opposed to the Spirit. Though saved by grace, Christians are easily tempted to seek justification by works. The law sounds reasonable to the flesh. The moment churches turn to the principle of the law, people can feel it. Instead of finding Jesus, they find something else in the church. The reason many people say that they love Jesus but not the church is because they have not found Jesus in the church. Churches depart from the power and presence of Jesus when they depart from the truth of the gospel. This is the most frequent and costly mistake that churches can make.

To bring people back to the faith and the church, churches must recover the truth of the gospel. It does not require specific techniques or know-hows but being faithful to the message of the gospel. Some pastors may be under the impression that they need to receive the great power of the Holy Spirit to make their churches grow. But spiritual power based not on the truth of the gospel will be just another manifestation of the flesh. Many cults and false prophets started like this. Anyone building his ministry on the law is making his own disciples instead of Jesus's disciples.

Church historians must search the history of Christianity in Europe to discover when the churches departed from the truth of the gospel. Such moments were probably the beginning of the decline of the churches. This realization should sound alarms because many churches depart from the gospel, not during lean times, but during fat times. Churches that are enjoying growth and prosperity must be careful not to sow the seeds of their decline by leaving the gospel. Why would any church be tempted to do that? It is because they seek popularity, praise, earthly glory, and to show how great they are instead of how great God is. The seeds of the current decline were probably sown during the times of past revival and growth. But we should not lose heart because the lean lean times will make us seek God's grace again, and it will prepare the ground for renewal and revival in the future.

The Authentic Motivation of a Believer

The law of Moses permitted Hebrew servants to get freedom in the seventh year of servitude. This was the right of all Hebrew servants. But the law provided an exception: if a servant declared, "I love my master and do not want to go free," then his master would pierce his servant's ear with an awl, and then the servant would be his master's for life (Exod 21:1–6). Though legally free, a servant could choose to serve his master out of love. In an age when freedom is valued more highly than anything else, the servant's choice to stay with his master may seem foolish. This arrangement may even seem politically incorrect. All servitude is considered bad and must be rejected. Servitude may be a thing of the past, but service is not. Serving one another in love is the highest virtue we can practice. Freedom is most precious when it enables us to love more fully.

Western civilization has come to a place in history where it can assert freedom from all its past obligations. In the past, people owed loyalty to the monarchs, the nobles, and the church. Religious identity accompanied national identity. Those days are gone. Christianity no longer controls people by political means. Among the diverse kinds of freedom given to modern western people, religious freedom is one of them. It is the result of centuries of social and political evolution of the western world—a truly remarkable accomplishment. The chessboard has been cleared of all kings, queens, knights, and bishops. Never in history has humanity possessed this much freedom. Europeans are still learning what this freedom means to them. We are living in the seventh year. Those who were under servitude can go free. Nothing holds them back institutionally or legally. The critical question is, now that we are free, what possible reason do we have for serving Jesus Christ? Having just come out from the rule of religion, why should we not go forward to enjoy the newly found freedom? What makes us stay with the faith? Is it the fear of punishment? Fear of hell?

There is only one reason left for European people to stay with Jesus—love for the master. No one is forcing people to come to church or to observe any religious duties. One is free to go away if he wishes. But if he loves the Lord and does not want to go free, he can stay with the Lord and serve him. Faith is no longer a sacred canopy enforced by the state or social opinion, but a private and voluntary activity. Jesus asked Peter only one question after the resurrection: "Simon, son of John, do you love me?" (John 21:15–17). Jesus asked for only one motive. Only one would be enough.

The Meaning of Freedom

Hegel defined history as the self-actualization of Spirit toward freedom. He said that in old times only a king was free, but in modern times all people are free. History progresses towards freedom, said he. To define freedom thus is, however, too abstract and vague. Jean-Jacque Rousseau claimed that man is born free but is everywhere in chains. His idea of the natural freedom of man was only hypothetical; he could not prove it historically.

There is no natural state of freedom to which humanity can return. History moves forward, and going back is neither possible nor desirable. Secularists believed that religion deprived man of freedom. A cursory look at religion confirms that view: religion always tells people what not to do, what not to eat, and what not to drink. God appears to exist only to meddle with men's freedom. Taking off the cloak of religion, therefore, seemed natural to obtain freedom. But this kind of reasoning also applies to governments. Governments not only tell people what to do but also lock people up for not paying taxes. But few people advocate eliminating governments to obtain freedom. Such an anarchist option is too costly for people. In a chaotic state, only the physically strong would be free, while the weak lose all freedom.

Freedom does not exist in a vacuum. The absence of restraint does not mean freedom. Real freedom is created by consensus. When there are many family members and only one bathroom, they need an agreement concerning who will use the bathroom at what time. This way, family members will be able to use the bathroom with maximum freedom. When many cars are trying to enter intersections at once, they need traffic lights to help them take turns crossing intersections. Traffic rules are the mutual agreements concerning road usage by drivers and pedestrians which, if observed, maximize their freedom instead of curtailing it. Laws of the state are social contracts that, if kept, create freedom.

God never imposed his will on people at whim. Instead, God always made promises to people as rewards for obedience. This has been the distinctive way he has dealt with Israel in the Bible. Faith is based on God's promises. Abraham believed God because God made a promise to him. The covenants that God instituted created new definitions of human liberty. This principle was akin to the social contract theory. God's covenants defined the obligations of people, but also created their freedom.

To the first murderer in the Bible, Cain, God did not just condemn him. When Cain complained that whoever finds him would kill him, God placed a mark on Cain to protect him. Even with a murderer, God made a promise by which Cain would have a certain amount of liberty. When God confronted David for his sin, though God was angry with him, he made specific promises not to go beyond a certain level of punishment. What is remarkable about God was that he conversed with David even when dealing with his sin. Who says that God is a tyrant who does whatever he wants to do?

When God laid down rules for humanity to follow, the rules created freedom for humanity instead of restricting it. When God told Adam and Eve not to eat the fruit of the tree of knowledge, he said they were *free* to eat from any other tree in the garden (Gen 2:16). This passage was the first time the term "freedom" was used in the Bible. As long as Adam and Eve stayed away from the forbidden fruit, they enjoyed an enormous amount of liberty—any other tree in the garden!

The law of Moses is often regarded as restricting humanity's freedom. Compared to the gospel, the law certainly has such a characteristic. Nonetheless, God's purpose for giving the law to Israel was not to deprive them of freedom. On the contrary, God's goal was to turn Israel into an autonomous people. The Preamble to the Ten Commandments states God's purpose for giving the Commandments to Israel: "I am the Lord your God, who brought you out of Egypt, out of the land of slavery" (Exod 20:2). If God aimed to turn them back to being slaves, he would not have said these words. Instead, the law would turn Israel into a free and autonomous people who would be responsible for their own destiny. When they were slaves, they had no such rules to guide their lives but did as slave drivers told them. Now that they have become free people, the law would guide them like traffic rules so that they can live as free people.

The First Commandment, which forbade having other gods before Yahweh, greatly expanded the spiritual freedom of Israel. Modern people have difficulty understanding this fact. Ancient people lived in a pantheon of gods. There were gods everywhere, and people were always fearful of offending them. The First Commandment liberated Israel from the fear of the false gods. As long as they are faithful to Yahweh, they do not have to worry about all the other "gods."

The Second Commandment, which forbade making idols and worshiping them, liberated Israel from the primitive fear of nature as a divine entity. Primitive people suffered from the tyranny of nature disguised as gods. Some worshiped animals; others worshiped trees and mountains. By forbidding the making and worshiping of idols of any creature in nature, God liberated people from the superstitious fear of the creatures. Only Yahweh is the Creator, and all other things are creatures.

The Fourth Commandment, which commanded the keeping of the Sabbath, freed the working class from the tyranny of their masters. Not only were the masters forbidden from working on the seventh day, but also their children, servants, aliens, and even animals were forbidden to work. This commandment promised to be liberation for the working class. Without this commandment, slaves, children, aliens, and animals would have worked to death. In that sense, the Fourth Commandment was the first pro-labor provision in history.

All the other commandments offered protection and safety of life, property, marriage, and justice in society instead of restricting them. Without these commandments, no one could be sure of keeping their lives, property, spouse, and justice in the world.

Though God intended the law to be of good purpose, people turned it to wrong uses. Hence, the Pharisees criticized Jesus for healing the sick on the Sabbath. Although the Sabbath's purpose was to benefit man, not to injure him, the Pharisees used the law for the purposes that God did not intend. The law became a heavy yoke upon people's shoulders. Instead of presenting God's love for people, the law was used to condemn and accuse people. The only time people quoted the law was when they wanted to throw stones at a sinner. The law became a tool of condemnation and death.

Even if Jesus had not come into the world, God had already done much to expand the amount of freedom and dignity of humanity. But God sent his Son to the world to perfect his plan of salvation. With the coming of Jesus Christ, grace and truth replaced the law of Moses. Under grace, man is no longer obliged to achieve righteousness by keeping the law. Instead, man is justified by the gift of God's grace through his Son. Righteousness is not the result of our religious work. Instead, we serve and obey the Lord out of our love and appreciation for him. This covenant was called the New Testament.

The new covenant is a revolutionary transformation in religion. All other religions impose heavy burdens upon the shoulders of believers. Religious people are like slaves under the domination of the priestly class. Threats of punishment and hell go with these burdens. One must follow religious precepts to avoid doom. The psychological motivation for religious practice is fear. Instead of loving God, people fear him. Adam and Eve were afraid of God and hid from him on their accord because they had sinned. Fear has to do with punishment (Gal 2:16; 3:11; Rom 3:22, 28). Fear became the underlying religious motive not by God's original intention, but by the fall of man.

Jesus said to the disciples toward the end of his earthly ministry, "I longer call you servants, but friends" (John 15:15). His statement was not a populist attempt. It was a revolutionary turnabout in the relationship between God and man. Jesus did not come to be served but to serve. This intention does not only apply to his sacrificial death on the cross but also to his relationship with people. Jesus's intention is not to force believers to serve him out of fear of punishment but to move them to follow him out of love. This was not Jesus's independent attempt but the plan of God the Father: "In this is love, not that we have loved God but that he loved us and sent his Son to be the propitiation for our sins" (1 John 4:10).

Jesus demonstrated this design in his cleansing of ten lepers. Jesus cleansed all ten of the lepers. But out of the ten, only one came back to Jesus, throwing himself at his feet and thanking him. Jesus asked him, "Were not all ten cleansed? Where are the other nine?" Jesus's feelings must have been hurt. He would have much preferred if all ten had come to thank him. But he accepted the situation as given. Though he was disappointed, he did not blame the nine who did not come back. Jesus did not let leprosy return to those nine people. Healing was irrevocable.

This incident aptly reflects Jesus's way of dealing with humanity. He does not want to force people, even those who have received his favor, to come and serve him. Ten is the number of wholeness; we have ten fingers in total. The fact that Jesus cleansed ten lepers suggests that his salvific power is potentially available to all people. But not all of them come to Jesus. Jesus did not make serving him the condition for their healing. Leprosy did not return to those who went away. The one leper who came back to Jesus and thanked him did so voluntarily out of love for him. Love cannot be coerced. It presupposes freedom. Hence, love is based on freedom. One who loves is a free person. One exercises his freedom to the utmost when he loves. Christ has set humanity free, permitting them to serve out of love and not out of compulsion.

This is the basis of the freedom that Christians enjoy. One may ask, "Is not the threat of hell still real? Are not those who refuse to believe condemned to hell?" That is true. But the last thing Jesus expects from us is to believe him out of the fear of hell. Jesus's gospel is good news, not a threat. It is not an ultimatum. Never did Jesus or the apostles preach by saying, "Belief or else!" This is where human reasoning hits its limitations. We tend to focus on the alternative scenario. The Bible says, "God so loved the world that he gave his only begotten Son so that whoever believes in him shall not perish but have eternal life." We just need to take God at his word. Why do we have to imagine the alternative? Instead of appreciating God's generosity, why do we make him out to be exclusive? Instead of believing in his love, why do we conjecture him as an angry God? Instead of adoring God's existence, why do men wish that he did not exist? It is the perversion of the fallen nature which twists good news into the news. It is like winning a lottery and, instead of being grateful, complaining about the taxes owed. Would it have been better if one had not won the lottery? Would it not have been better if God had not sent his Son?

Freedom is at the basis of God's grace. God intends men and women to be free and responsible beings. Such freedom would fulfill the image of God in man. God's love for the world does not include compulsion. People are free to leave church if they want. They are even free to leave Jesus—psychologically, geographically, and intellectually. Many did, even during Jesus's public ministry, and Jesus did not stop them. Their freedom is God's gift. God takes the responsibility for what he has granted people.

The story of humanity with God is not like *Waiting for Godot*. In Samuel Beckett's *Waiting for Godot*, the protagonist waits and waits for a person named Godot who never comes. The nine lepers did not wait in vain for Jesus to cleanse them. Jesus came to them and granted their request. They left after they were cleansed. Leaving Jesus became a possibility only after they had received their healing. If they left Jesus without being cleansed, their going would not be an issue. It would be meaningless even to use the word "leave" because the nine lepers did not have any meaningful relationship with Jesus. There would be nothing to leave from. Samuel Backett's thesis represents the modern man who has lost his faith. It is not God who never comes even if man waits for him. The fact that man waits demonstrates that God will come. In agnostic religions like Buddhism, there is no concept of waiting because there is no one to wait for. The Bible is the narrative of the believing people who wait for God's promises. The Old Testament people waited for the Messiah, and their waiting was rewarded by the coming of Jesus Christ. The disciples waited for the coming of the Holy Spirit, which was rewarded on the Day of Pentecost. And Christians wait for the second coming of Jesus, which will be rewarded some day. The fact that Christians wait means that God has made promises to them. Without the promises, there would be no need to wait. If a person loses his faith, he would lose his reason for waiting. And his soul would fall into despair.

Did Jesus take a big risk by giving man freedom? Yes, he did. Love always assumes risk. When you do not love someone, you do not care for him. Not caring is convenient because it does not involve any emotional obligation. But the moment you love a person, you are emotionally involved with him so that everything he does or says greatly matters to you. Pain comes into existence when one falls in love with someone. There is always a possibility that the person he loves may not love him back. There is no assurance of reciprocal love. Despite this risk, loving someone is much better than not loving anyone at all.

The law involves compulsion and compensation. These two features are two sides of the same coin. One obeys the law out of necessity and duty. Those who are under the law are its servants. They are subject to the demands of the law. The law commands them what to do and what not to do, what to eat and what not to eat. Those who are under the law must live by the law (Rom 10:5). It is like an unhappy marriage from which there is no escape.

Also, those living by the law are motivated by compensation and reward. To a person who works, his wages are not counted as a gift but as his due (Rom 4:4). Paul likened the law to Hagar, the slave concubine of Abraham (Rom 4:24). Figuratively, a slave serves the master under compulsion expecting compensation. In contrast, Sarah was a free woman. Even if Hagar and Sarah did the same things for Abraham, they did them out of different motives and for different purposes. Hagar did those things out of obligation in anticipation of a reward because she was a servant. Sarah, on the other hand, did them because she loves her husband. Even if they did the same things, they were moved by different motives. Hagar would draw no joy from her work because she was compelled to do it, whereas Sarah could draw joy from it because she did it out of love. Hagar would work expecting compensation, while Sarah would do the same things without reward. This is Paul's figurative comparison between the law and grace. The reward in this metaphor is righteousness. Those who are under the law must earn their righteousness through their deeds, while those who are under grace are already declared righteous. Any service they render is out of love, not compulsion.

The Old Covenant of the law put a man in a slave's position before God. It was not a coincidence that the Hebrew people had been slaves in Egypt before entering into a covenant with God. They would not have understood God's intentions towards them unless they experienced liberation from slavery. After coming out of Egypt, they had not yet learned how to manage their affairs like autonomous people. They had not learned to be responsible for their destiny. The only thing they understood was a display of force—at first by their slave masters, and next by God. This is how their relationship with God began.

In return for people's obedience, God offered rewards. The biggest reward was the promised land, the symbolic object of the Israelites' faith. If people obeyed God, they would receive the promised land. If they did not, they would lose it. The Israelites' relationship with God was based on a straightforward deal of give-and-take. Deuteronomy 28 outlines this deal in detail. If Israelites obey, they would be blessed, and if not, they would be cursed.

Nevertheless, God was not content to leave humanity in that kind of childish state. Hence the Son of God came to redeem humanity from the curse of the law (Gal 3:13). Many Christians think that Jesus redeemed people from sin, but that is not correct. Jesus redeemed them from the curse of the law. How can the law be a curse? If a man is under the law, he remains in that childish state of fear and recompense. What brings man out of that childish state? It is the grace of the Lord Jesus that provides righteousness not by acts of the law, but by faith. God demonstrated his love to us by Christ's dying for us while we were sinners. Through Christ, man comes to believe that God loves him, and thus he does not have to merit God's love by trying to please him. The earnest need to achieve righteousness through deeds disappears. This vanishing of the law liberates man.

Henceforth, man can serve and obey the Lord, not out of fear of punishment, but out of love and gratitude. This was the original intention of God towards man until the first Adam hid from God out of fear and shame. For the first time, man can be mature. When he was a child, he talked like a child, thought like a child, and reasoned like a child. But when he became mature, he put childish ways behind him. What characterizes the mature man is love (1 Cor 13:10–13).

Through Christ, God intended to bring humanity to maturity. Christianity is the vehicle by which God brings humanity to the mature status of man. Humanity has come a long way, and Christianity has played a significant part in it. Jesus compared the kingdom of heaven to a man sowing seed in his field. Seed refers to a word or an idea placed in the hearts of people. Despite all the errors and wickedness of men, the seed never loses its life-giving power. Herein we find the enormous contribution of Christianity to the progress of humanity. What the destiny of man's progress will be is not known to us. What we shall be has not yet been made known (1 John 3:2). The future of humanity coincides with the eschatological hope.

The Role of Personal Choice and Faith

When Abraham's servant asked Laban if he could take Rebekah, Laban's younger sister, to Canaan to marry Isaac, Laban did something that one would hardly expect from any Middle Eastern man in ancient times. He asked Rebekah what she wanted to do. When she said yes, Laban respected her decision and sent her along to Canaan. This incident in Genesis 24 demonstrates what a significant role each person's choice plays in his or her destiny. We tend to think that God imposes his will on us. In Islam,

"Inshallah" is a famous confession that if God wills, something will happen. In the case of Rebekah, though, her choice and decision worked together with God's providence to shape her future. This fact demonstrates how much potential freedom exists for everyone, whether male or female, old or young, Jew or Gentile, and slave or free.

When Jesus was on earth, he never exercised tyrannical authority over anyone. Even when he desired to heal sick people, he asked for their consent. He asked the blind Bartimaeus, "What do you want me to do for you?" (Mark 10:51). It was not as if Jesus did not know what Bartimaeus needed. Anyone can guess what a blind man's greatest wish must be. Nonetheless, Jesus was not presumptuous. He wanted to hear Bartimaeus' wish. Jesus wanted to hear Bartimaeus's confession of faith. He asked the invalid man at Bethesda, "Do you want to get well?" Jesus had the power to heal him, but he did not want to impose his power on him. He wanted to hear and respect the man's wishes. We tend to think that the critical question is whether the Lord wants to heal us. But Jesus turned the table around and asked the sick man if he wanted to get well. Perhaps we have been asking the wrong question all along.

The same principle applies to the matter of salvation. In original Greek, the same word σῴζω can be translated as either "heal" or "save." Thus, when Jesus asked, "Do you want to be healed?" he was also asking, "Do you want to be saved?" Debating between Calvinism and Arminianism is not necessary. One's choice and faith play as much role in his salvation as God's will.

Faith is the most meaningful expression of one's free will. The greatest thing that Jesus wanted to see in every person was his or her faith. Faith as small as a mustard seed can move mountains. Whenever a person demonstrated genuine faith, Jesus recognized it and honored it, regardless of who that person was. Jesus was not impressed by anyone's riches or status, but people's faith often marveled him. "Great is your faith" was the highest compliment coming from Jesus.

We are aware of the Calvinist position on God's sovereignty and man's total depravity. But Jesus never steamrolled anyone he met. Jesus respected and honored anyone's wish. He asked them, "Do you believe that I am able to do this?" (Matt 9:28). If genuine faith was present, Jesus never ignored or despised anyone's wish. Jesus allowed the request of one of the robbers crucified next to him to remember him when he comes into his kingdom. No other religion accommodates personal choice and faith like Christianity. Not even Christians fully comprehend this freedom;

how much less would non-Christians understand the freedom in Christ? Much of the criticism directed at Christianity is due to an incomplete understanding of faith and freedom. Throughout the history of Christianity, we cannot say with confidence when the churches properly presented the liberating message of the gospel. The prejudice that the world has toward Christianity reveals that the world has never really understood the liberty in Christ. It is another reason that Christianity must be reintroduced to the oldest Christian civilization.

The Maturing of Humanity

The fall of humanity did not defeat God's intentions for humanity. Total depravity did not destroy God's purpose for man. The Dispensationalist School of eschatology mistook the purpose of God for man. According to the Dispensationalists, the plan of God has failed, and the world is doomed. Only the last remnant of Christians is to be rescued from the earth, like the Vietnamese refugees on the top of the US Embassy in Saigon waiting for helicopters to save them. Is the history of the world going to end up like that? How can a scenario like that glorify God?

Apostle Paul explained the role of grace in historical terms. In Galatians 4:1–7, he compared the progress of humanity to a child heir who grows into adulthood. While the heir is a child, he is subject to guardians and managers even though he is the heir. When he becomes an adult, though, he can come into the full possession of his inheritance, free from the guardians and managers. Likewise, humanity was under the law while they were children. When the fullness of time came, Jesus redeemed man from the law. With the coming of the Son of God, humanity grew into "mature manhood" (Eph 4:13). This fullness of time arrived with the Son of God so that true worshipers could worship the Father in Spirit and truth (John 4:23).

Christianity presupposes the maturing of humanity. The law was our guardian until Jesus came. Now that Jesus has come, we have become adults (Gal 3:23–25). The maturing of humanity took place throughout history. During the two millennia of Christianity, humanity accomplished tremendous progress. Jürgen Habermas, the German philosopher, attributed the accomplishments of western civilization to Christianity: "Christianity, and nothing else, is the ultimate foundation of liberty, conscience, human rights, and democracy."[2] Sometimes the church stood in the way of this progress by not fully understanding the liberating potential of Christianity. Whenever the church kept people in superstition, ignorance, and fear of freedom, the church stood in the way of progress. Nonetheless, maturing has taken place. Humanity is learning to handle the rights and duties of adulthood. The rights of adulthood are the freedom from the law. The duties of adulthood are the law of love. A mature human being is free to love. That is the image of a mature Christian.

The maturing of humanity does not mean that we will become perfect on earth. It means that God treats us not as children but as adults. The passage of John 9:21 applies to all of us: "Ask him, he is a mature adult. He will speak for himself" (NET).

The freedom that man enjoys is the result of God's design. God deals with man as an adult. What a man will do with his adult status is up to him. It is in this context that we need to talk about Christian faith in the post-Christian era.

What about the Threats of Hell and Punishment?

During the financial crisis of 2008, the US Government adopted a highly socialist policy to save capitalism. This incident sounds like a contradiction in terms, but it is true. Henry Paulson, the Treasury Secretary of the US Government, was a staunch champion of the free market. It would be unthinkable for him to do anything that would negate the principle of the free market. But the threat to the US financial system was so massive and urgent that, unless the US Government bailed out the Wall Street banks right away, all of the Main Street banks would go bankrupt, wiping out all the savings of mom-and-pop stores and average citizens in the streets. Such an event would be a catastrophe not just for America but also for the whole world. As a result, the US Government bought major shares in Wall Street banks, almost nationalizing them—to save capitalism. The Government restricted freedom temporarily to save freedom.

Free societies sometimes must restrict freedom to protect freedom. In emergencies like wars, natural disasters, or social unrest, governments limit certain civil liberties for a limited duration to save the country from collapsing. During wars, for example, many countries issue commodity

2. Allen. "Christianity under siege."

coupons to conserve economic resources for the war effort. During a power failure, authorities impose curfews to prevent looting.

Democracy supposedly contains the seeds of its destruction. Abusing the freedom given to them, some people engage in destructive and anarchic behavior—so much so that society begins to demand the restriction of freedom, which results in the demise of democracy. How to preserve society without damaging democratic values is a big challenge to any society.

God also reserves the right to suspend man's freedom in exigent circumstances to preserve his purpose on earth. Not all people honor the freedom God grants them to love and live responsibly. They take advantage of God's mercy and grace. If God permits them to continue doing destructive things, his purpose for humanity runs the risk of being damaged. In such cases, God takes exceptional measures to uphold his goals. One such example is the judgment of Ananias and Sapphira at the hand of Apostle Peter. We do not fully understand why such drastic judgment was necessary and what "lying to the Holy Spirit" constitutes. Even though God loves humanity, he sometimes has to resort to extreme measures to protect the holiness of his church. It is his prerogative.

We need to pray that such exigent circumstances will not arise. After all, God is God, and he reserves the right to do what he wants. Even though he gives us freedom, he does not owe it to us. What he does, he does out of the goodness of his heart. Therefore, we ought to honor him. This is simply common sense.

For democracy to prosper, people have to have a certain maturity of character by demonstrating respect for law and order, consideration for other people, and a certain amount of faith in the democratic process. If drivers voluntarily make way for ambulances and emergency vehicles without anyone forcing them, they are mature citizens. But if the opposite is the case, they are not yet ready for a free society.

Christianity works in similar ways. God's grace presupposes certain maturity of character on the part of believers. When a person is mature, he can accept God's love as love and respect it. If not, he will mistake God's love as permissiveness or lawlessness, acting in ways contrary to God's purpose. He would take advantage of God's goodness. Paul warned against receiving God's grace in vain (2 Cor 6:1). This is precisely the reason that the maturing of humanity goes hand in hand with Christianity. The values of a mature and free society agree with the purposes of God for humanity. Western civilization, therefore, should not depart from Christianity. Jesus is the perfect partner for the mature human race. If western civilization pushes Christianity away, it no longer has the foundation of its values.

The Radical Equality of Men before God

All people are equally sinful before God. At the same time, all who believe are made equally righteous by the grace of God. No one is so sinful that he is beyond the saving grace of God, and no one is so righteous that he does not need Jesus the Savior. All are sinful but are equally made righteousness by faith.

This inherent equality of man before God negates all discrimination on the grounds of religious merit, gender, social status, and birth. There are no VIPs in the kingdom of God. The only person worthy of glory is Jesus Christ. The only thing worthy of boasting is the grace of God. Apostle Paul said that he was ahead of his contemporaries in terms of the observance of the Law and religious zeal. But he counted all his gains as loss for the sake of Christ (Phil 3:4–11). Because righteousness comes from God and not from the law, we have nothing to boast about. Jesus said a poor widow who donated two copper coins gave more than a rich person. Tax collectors and prostitutes enter the kingdom of God ahead of the Pharisees. Jesus complimented the Roman centurion for having faith the kind of which Jesus had not seen Israel. The only leper who returned to Jesus after being cleansed was a Samaritan.

Jesus did not bring about institutional changes to establish equality in the world. Such changes would require a long time to arrive. What Christianity initially provided was the ideas, beliefs, and spiritual basis. These ideas of religious equality formed the basis of all other kinds of equality. It broke down the wall between Jews and Gentiles. Everyone is made righteous by faith, whether Jew or Gentile. Jews have no exceptional merit over Gentiles. It broke down the wall between men and women. God poured his Holy Spirit on all flesh—both sons and daughters, both male servants and female servants (Acts 2:17–18). Women could prophesy just like men (1 Cor 11:2–16). "There is neither Jew nor Greek, there is neither slave nor free, there is no male and female, for you are all one in Christ Jesus" (Gal 3:28).

Not everyone was ready to accept such radical equality—even to this day. Many people in the religious establishment resisted Jesus's teachings. Jewish religious leaders resented Jesus's eating together with tax collectors and allowing a sinful woman to touch his feet. Proud of their religious standing, Jewish leaders were not willing to accept Jesus's teachings. Even after the birth of the church, apostles and elders were upset when Peter went to the gentile Cornelius' household and ate with them. Peter had to resort to hypocrisy for fear of the Jews when they saw him eating with gentiles in Antioch (Gal 2:11–14). It took much discussion and evidence of the grace of God upon gentiles to persuade the apostles and elders at Jerusalem to agree that God had granted the gentiles repentance leading to life.

The equality of women in the early church was evident in many events. The first witnesses of the resurrected Jesus were women, not men. All the gospels recorded that fact. By disclosing his resurrection to women first, Jesus demonstrated that he did not discriminate against women. Mary Magdalene's status in the early church was equivalent to the status of the apostles.[3] It was only later that the church leadership demoted the status of Mary Magdalene by staining her reputation.[4] For more than a millennium, women's position in Christendom was kept lower than men—not out of the Lord's will, but out of man's inability to keep up with the Lord's radical equality.

The radical equality of all human beings is based on the grace of Jesus Christ. Because righteousness is given to all people as a gift, all the things that human beings boast to assert their superior status are counted as nothing. God chose the foolish, the weak, the lowly, and the despised people of the world to shame the wise, the strong, and the rich (1 Cor 1:26–31). The kingdom of God is more revolutionary than any earthly movements.

The fact that people still find it challenging to adopt Jesus's radical equality fully highlights Jesus's unique contribution to the progress of the human spirit. These values could not have developed on their own, apart from Jesus's contribution. How much impact Jesus has had on the progress of human rights and democratic values in history, only God knows. Although we take them for granted, humanism owes itself to Christianity. Humanism is the product of Christianity without its religious attributes.[5] Non-Christians have only picked out the ethical teachings of Jesus without

---

3. King, "Women in Ancient Christianity," paras. 7–13.
4. King, "Women in Ancient Christianity," para. 30.
5. Libby, "Christianity Provided a Foundation." 7.

believing him as the Son of God. Even if people take Jesus's moral values without believing him religiously, Jesus has had more impact on the world than any other teachers or philosophers combined. The care for the sick, the poor, the gentiles, women, and the marginal members of society sprang from Jesus. He did not merely make rooms for them, but laid the foundation for sacrificial love for such marginal members. If the Christian foundation of human rights disappeared, the entire western civilization would fall.[6] We have waited two thousand years since the time of Jesus, and we have not encountered one teacher who can even come close to Jesus in his ability to help us love the unlovable.

Jesus not only taught the virtue of loving one's neighbor as oneself, but also provided the power to do so. When one looks to the cross, he obtains the strength to forgive those who have wronged him. "At the cross, at the cross where I first saw the light, and the burden of my heart rolled away." It is unlikely that we will ever have another teacher who can tell us the kind of love that Jesus taught us and put it to practice as Jesus did. All the theories of morality for the past two thousand years are just footnotes to the spirit of Jesus.

Christians have always had difficulty fully incorporating Jesus's principles into their lives. Those who criticize Christian civilization for its moral failure in the past should realize that Jesus set the standard of righteousness very high for any persons. This fact proves that Christianity indeed came from God and not from man. As Karl Barth pointed out, one of the essential characteristics of God is his "otherness." Without the otherness of God, we can always suspect that God might have been created in man's image. Jesus's teachings demonstrated this otherness of God. It is almost inconceivable for man to come up with the radical ethics of Jesus such as "turn the other cheek," "blessed are the poor," "give to those who ask," "lusting is the same as adultery," "saying you fool is the same as murdering," and many other challenging teachings. If Christianity were from men, it would have taught reasonable and doable ethics concerning money, sexuality, and power. Even though Christians are made righteous by God's grace and not by their deeds, Jesus made no compromise concerning the ethics of the kingdom of God. The fact that Jesus's ethical teachings are inordinately difficult to practice demonstrates that his teachings came from God and not from men.

---

6. Pera, *Why We Should Call Ourselves Christians*, 4.

— 9 —

Major Issues of Christianity in the Twenty-first Century

The Exclusive Claims of Christianity

ONE OF THE MOST common criticisms of Christianity is that it is exclusive. In this age of pluralism, it is unpopular for anything to claim its absolute status. But we have to remember that religion, by its nature, makes total claims. Unlike academics, religion does not propose hypotheses and theories. It makes absolute claims about ultimate questions. Otherwise, it is not religion. If Moses had said, "I give you the Ten Helpful Suggestions," would the Israelites have taken him seriously? If Jesus said, "I am one of many prophets," would you believe him?

Therefore, those who preach Christianity must believe in its truth if he wants to be taken seriously. If someone does not believe in what he preaches, he has no business being a preacher. The sheep lose faith when they listen to half-hearted and hesitant preachers.

We see the same principle in politics. What the public expects to see in a political candidate is an unshakable conviction that he offers a better alternative to his opponent. Anyone who wants to win must present a convincing case that he provides a better choice than his opponent. If a candidate lacks this certainty, he loses credibility and, hence, voters have no reason to vote for him. Such a candidate should not run. Real leadership is not based on acting, but true belief. If a political leader truly believes in what he says, people will trust him.

Voters vote with their ballots, but believers vote with their feet. Despite their best intentions, religions compete for the hearts of people in the world. It is natural for a religion to assert that it offers the best truth to the world. Without such a conviction, it is better to close down. Religions, by their nature, will not cede their high ground to other religions out of the goodness of their hearts. Exercising religious virtue does not mean that one must compromise his beliefs out of consideration for other religions. Even the godliest person in the world has to stand his ground to practice his beliefs. A soldier at war must believe that his country's causes are just, and the opposing country is unjust. If he does not believe that, the war is as good as lost. Contemporary history is full of wars with murky moral justifications. When a nation engages in a morally unjust war, it sells its soul.

Believing in the truth of one's religion does not mean opposing or combating other faiths. It means being aware of how one's beliefs differ from other religions. When a person believes in monotheism, for example, he cannot agree with polytheism like Hinduism or Shintoism. When a person believes in the existence of a personal God, he cannot consent to the Buddhist philosophy that attaches little significance God's existence. When a person believes that Jesus Christ is the Son of God and the Savior, he cannot give credence to the submission to Allah as the condition for salvation. Understanding other religions does not lead to inclusivity. Instead, it clarifies the reasons for believing in one's faith.

If the world accuses a person of dogmatism because he is faithful to his religion, does the world expect him to compromise his faith and sell his soul for the sake of political correctness and inclusivity? Christians will not make such a demand on others. The world should not make such a demand on Christians, either. Warriors at war respect the enemy combatants who are loyal to their duty and country. Though they are opponents, they pay tribute to a valiant and loyal warrior and wish that such a warrior was on their side. Athletes at sports events compete with one another fiercely according to the rules, but give respect to the worthy players of opposing teams. But we do not see such manners in religious affairs. Instead, people accuse and antagonize those who hold to different views. That is why it is difficult to have civil conversations on religious topics. Christians are often guilty of this error, but non-believers are guilty of the same mistake, too. It seems, however, that criticism flows mainly in one direction—against devout Christians. Instead of crediting faithful Christians for their sincerity, critics blame them for exclusivity.

If a college student confesses his wish to stay chaste until marriage on account of his Christian convictions, fellow students should respect him for his integrity. The chances are that more young people will ridicule such a student than respect him. If this is the true picture of society, we can only say that the criticisms directed at Christians arise from prejudice and ill will instead of a wish for inclusivity and tolerance. Those who accuse Christians of being intolerant should consider if they are not being prejudiced, too.

When Tokugawa persecuted the Catholics in Japan, the persecutors put a cross on the ground and demanded that Catholics step on it. When they stepped on it, they lived; when they refused, they were killed. This kind of persecution is evil regardless of its motive. The persecutors were demanding that believers renounce their conscience. If the goal of the persecution was to eliminate Catholicism from Japan, the persecutors should have either killed or jailed Catholics. However, requiring them to step on a cross achieved their goal in the most perverse way. Even if Tokugawa succeeded in removing Catholics from his land, it was not a moral victory. It was, instead, an expression of extreme hatred and prejudice.

If those who accuse Christians of being intolerant are desirous of eliciting tolerance from Christians, they should invite them to frank dialogues and discussions. If they engage in name-calling and vilifications, instead, their motives are not tolerance but hatred and prejudice. Those who blame Christians for being intolerant are themselves intolerant.

Being a faithful Christian in a pluralist world means that he is dedicated to his beliefs without depriving others' right to be truthful to their beliefs. We can agree to disagree. It is the only way that people can coexist in a pluralistic society. However, that does not mean one must give up his belief in the unique status of his religion. That would be neither desirable nor necessary. A McDonald's and Burger King can exist in the same neighborhood. Each respects the other, but both do their best to make the best hamburgers. What is wrong with that? Must we criticize McDonald's or Burger King for believing that they are the best? Will we go and eat at a restaurant that openly confesses that the other restaurant next door is probably better? We buy not only its product but also its spirit. Nobody wants to board a leaky ship. According to American sociologist Rodney Stark, it is a religion with the most unambiguous boundaries and the highest demands of members that flourishes, while low-tension religions dissolve "into the cauldron of secularism." That does not mean that a believer must act in order to be credible. It just means that one must believe in the justice of his cause.[1]

Science and Religion

It is no longer in fashion to reject religion for scientific reasons. There were times in the past when religion, especially Christianity, seemed threatened by scientific progress. That was because neither scientists nor Christians knew enough about their respective fields. With more knowledge and reflection, Christian thinkers are now more comfortable with the claims of science, and more scientists have room for religion in their scientific worldview. NASA seems to think that discovering extraterrestrial life will put an end to Christianity. Why does anyone think that finding evidence of life will lead to the denial of God, who is the source of life? The real quest of scientific inquiry should not be why there is no life in space, but why there is such richness of life on earth.

The ongoing clash between Christianity and science is regarding creation versus evolution. Neither side witnessed the event that it teaches. No Christian saw God creating the heavens and the earth. Similarly, no scientist observed the evolutionary process taking place before his eyes. Why, then, do they consider each other as mortal enemies? Both are holding on to claims that require a certain amount of belief.

There were times when humanity ascribed to God those things in nature that they could not understand. When the sky thundered, people thought God was angry. When there was a plague or a famine, they thought God was punishing them. Nonetheless, the origin of Judeo-Christianity was not man's attempt to explain the universe. The author of Genesis did not make up religious doctrines to explain the natural phenomena that he could not comprehend. The constant quest of Judeo-Christianity was the cause of being, such as why the universe existed and why human beings existed, not how things came to be in the world. The fundamental quest of Judeo-Christianity was philosophical and spiritual, not cosmological.

It was not the goal of the Bible to explain natural phenomena in religious ways. The writers of the Bible never considered nature as a mystical entity fraught with spiritual meaning. Instead, the Bible begins with the bold statement that, in the beginning, God created the heavens and the

---

1. Allen, "Christianity under Siege," 6.

earth. Christians believed in Creator God who stood above nature, not in nature itself. It was this knowledge that nature was a creation which encouraged the progress of science and exploration.

The evolutionary theory does not necessarily deny the biblical account of creation. After all, Genesis only states that God made man, not how he made him. It is more reasonable to interpret the first several chapters of Genesis as parabolic accounts of complex and profound events in prehistoric times than to interpret them literally. Those who say that they cannot believe Genesis on scientific grounds must be reading the Genesis accounts very literally. They are approaching biblical interpretation with more piety than many Christians.

Religion and science do not have to consider each other as opponents. The church did not have to try Galileo for heresy, for instance. It was a rash decision. Christians did not have to treat Charles Darwin as the devil. Likewise, scientists should not treat Christians as opponents of reason and progress. The relationship between science and religion is like the relationship between oriental medicine and western medicine. These two medical traditions make different presuppositions about the human body. Patients can benefit from oriental medicine in different ways than from western medicine. They complement each other. If the relationship between science and religion had been more cordial from the start, we would not have had such rancorous debates between the two.

Mutual exclusivity between science and religion is predominantly a western phenomenon. We do not find Buddhist scientists disavowing religion over science. Nor do Hindu believers renounce scientific theories on the ground of their religious beliefs. Most Muslims do not think that an inherent conflict exists between religion and science.[2] In contrast, western civilization held on to the either-or mentality: Man is either a creature of God or an evolutionary product. Why can we not think that man can be both? God does not oppose science; instead, God encompasses science. God is much bigger than our thoughts and knowledge. He has much more at his disposal than we can ever imagine. Instead of denying God, science unveils the wisdom of God. Although Christians cannot force secular scientists to acknowledge the Bible, Christians can accommodate scientific claims within their theology.

---

2. "World's Muslims: Religion, Politics, and Society," 130.

Intellect and Faith

When even a well-meaning believer learns of an intellectual theory that challenges his faith, doubt arises in his mind. He is like an automobile without a bumper. When another vehicle hits it, it directly injures the driver. There is no protection between the driver and the outside forces.

Such a person has only a unitary system of faith within him. Doubt affects the person directly. That is why every believer must have a dual system of belief. The dual system means that a person has digested his faith in his mind and his spirit. The mind is the mental and intellectual faculty, while the spirit is the more intuitive inner being. God is Spirit, and one must worship him in spirit and truth (John 4:24). The experience of God must take place both in our minds and spirits. Each faculty supports the other. When our mind is challenged, the spirit helps the mind. On the other hand, the mind absorbs knowledge and understanding, clarifying the intuitive aspect of the faith.

Thus, if a believer's faith is challenged intellectually, he does not fall into doubt right away because he has experienced God spiritually. It is like an aircraft with redundant computers on board. Even if one computer is down, other computers keep the aircraft flying. Likewise, while the mind is reeling from a challenge to his faith, the spirit sustains the faith. If he did not have his spirit developed, his faith would crash from a severe intellectual question.

When I was a college freshman, reading Nietzsche for a freshman philosophy course challenged my faith with such an impact that I doubted God's existence for several months. I do not blame Nietzsche because my doubt was due to my own unresolved questions and not his intention. It was my psychological weakness that made me vulnerable. At that time, I did not have a spiritual side to my faith. It was after that event that I developed the spiritual side. This experience was beneficial to me in the end because my faith became more robust and resourceful.

What should you do if the spiritual aspect of the faith, as opposed to the intellectual, suffers a challenge? This is a different topic. Spiritual challenge is more dangerous than intellectual challenge. The devil's temptation of Jesus was spiritual in nature. Jesus was able to overcome the temptations because his heart was in the right place. His quotation of the word of God demonstrated that his heart was right. On the other hand, when Peter was tempted, he was not strong enough to overcome the temptation. Hence, he denied knowing Jesus three times. It took the prayer and special grace of Jesus to restore Peter.

Spiritual temptation comes from the source that is well acquainted with Christianity, looking for hidden weaknesses in a man such as secret doubts and unresolved trauma. A person must experience God's love which is greater than any moral condemnation. A secret guilt makes a person vulnerable. Although Peter recovered his faith after denying Jesus, Judas Iscariot lost his soul after betraying Jesus. Judas' spiritual temptation overcame him. The Bible does not elaborate on what Judas' reasons might have been. We do not need to know why someone fails spiritually. One thing is clear: even someone close to Jesus is not immune to spiritual temptations.

Intellectual doubts are more straightforward than spiritual doubts. One becomes intellectually doubtful not because he knows too much but because he does not know enough. All those who think that they cannot believe the Bible because of evolution or psychoanalysis or any other conflicting theories must further study their subjects. If they look for the truth, they will eventually arrive at God because God is the source of all truth.

It is partial knowledge that is dangerous.

Likewise, Christians should not consider intellect as the opponent of faith. It is natural for people to want to understand what they believe. Believing something without understanding it can go only so far. We must remember that God said, "Come, let us reason together." That does not mean that every Christian must study apologetics. It just means that introducing Christ to people in the postmodern era cannot dispense with sound reasoning and understanding. When boy Jesus was sitting among the teachers in the temple, Jesus was listening to them and asking them questions. It is proper for Christians to ask questions, sometimes difficult questions. Unquestioning faith is unstable. Jesus commanded us to love God not just with all our hearts, but also with all our minds. The intellect, therefore, is an integral part of our faith.

God and Money

Christianity's view of money has developed on two levels in modern times. The first level is the priority of the spiritual over the material. "Man shall not live by bread alone, but by every word that comes out of the mouth of God" (Matt 4:4). The second level is the criticism of the capitalist culture. For seventy years, communism was the most potent check on capitalism. Now that communism is gone, there are few means of checking on the excesses of capitalism—except Christianity. In the past, it was difficult to distinguish between the anti-capitalist rhetoric of communism and the Christian criticism of capitalism. Christian critics got a free ride on the backs of left-wing ideology. But they cannot do that anymore because communism has collapsed. As a result, Christians need to develop a new critique of capitalism, especially in this age of the widening gap between the rich and poor.

The church's role to care for the poor has been largely taken over by governments in modern times. It does not mean that the governments have embraced socialism, but that welfare has become an integral aspect of advanced societies. For some reason, conservative Christians equate Christianity with capitalism. It is unclear where they got that idea. Capitalism might include some biblical principles, such as hard work, responsibility, and faithful stewardship. But there is no biblical basis for equating Christianity with capitalism. Assigning the role of welfare management to the state is the product of many centuries of experience. Christians are entitled to be conservative or liberal regarding the role of the government, but calling for capitalistic policies in the name of Christianity is misusing the name of Christianity. It is a far better idea for governments to collect taxes from the rich and use it for welfare than for the churches to do it. It is more efficient, stable, and neutral. When state welfare was not well developed, churches were the only institutions to care for the poor. Such is not the case anymore. Modern times have witnessed the shifting division of roles between governments and churches. Governments should do their duties, and churches should do their duties. The shift in the roles of churches benefits the churches by helping churches to focus on their central responsibilities. Deconstructing Christianity is inevitable in post-Christian societies. States collect taxes from citizens to help the poor. In modern welfare states, taxpayers should receive a certain amount of credit. Jesus said, "Give to Caesar what belongs to Caesar, and give to God what belongs to God" (Mark 12:17). But in modern welfare states, what is given to Caesar is sometimes used for God. Church offerings are not necessarily more virtuous than paying income taxes since the money is going to be used for the poor either way. In fact, in an age when the income tax rate is as high as 50 percent, we must ask if the biblical concept of tithing is not outdated.

In the age where governments have taken over many of the churches' previous tasks, what lessons can churches teach people about money? Jesus's warning that one cannot serve God and money is still valid. There is a difference between needing money and worshiping it. Although it is sometimes a slippery slope, there is a difference between a person owning money and money owning a person. Without firm faith in God as the source of our life and purpose, there is nothing that can stop money from turning into an idol for us.

Warning about the danger of worshiping money is not the only lesson that Christianity has to teach about money and wealth in the contemporary world. The economic reality of society in Jesus's times was vastly different from the current times. Money was a zero-sum game in those times. If somebody was rich, somebody else had to be poor because there was only a fixed amount of wealth in society. In the modern market economy, money is not a zero-sum game. Wealth can be increased through business enterprise and innovation. Let us take an elementary example. An apple sells for 50 cents. But if you make an apple salad, it will sell for $5.00. If you derive medicinal substances from an apple and turn them into an FDA-approved drug, it will sell for $50.00. By turning a raw apple into a more advanced form of product, you can increase its value a hundredfold. This is how wealth can be created.

Because money is not a zero-sum game, being a rich man is not necessarily a sin in the market economy. In the past, being rich was synonymous with being sinful. Now rich people can make invaluable contributions to society by creating wealth and jobs. Nothing solves poverty better than job creation. Jesus empathized with the poor but did not propose ways of solving poverty. His teachings on money were not complete. Humanity needed more time to come to a fuller understanding of money. At the time of Jesus, society was not sufficiently advanced to discover ways in which wealth could be used for the greater good. Perhaps Jesus did not go into more teachings about money because he believed there was not enough time.

Even though Jesus said, "Blessed are the poor," he did not equate poverty with a blessing. His purpose on earth was not to improve the social welfare of Israel. He did not do anything to improve the livelihood of the poor while on the earth. The economic condition of the world was not Jesus's concern.[3] Thus we cannot apply Jesus's teachings about money

---

3. Bauman. *The Sermon on the Mount.* p. 79.

verbatim to economic principles. We have the liberty to develop our principles about money and wealth.

The delay in eschatology has given humanity more time to develop a more complete perspective on money. God has placed on earth infinite ways by which humanity can enrich his life. God has given man the ability to produce wealth (Deut 8:18). God did not create a poor world. Even though the earth sometimes produces thorns and briars, man can find ways to get one hundredfold return on his labor through the sweat of his brow. As long as Christians uphold poverty as the utmost spiritual virtue, they will never make use of the full potential God had given the earth. Teaching our descendants the virtue of poverty, as the medieval monasteries did, will not be a proper representation of the abundance of God's creation.

There is something about man's desire to possess things that coincides with the principle of faith. Faith is the substance of things hoped for. If one does not hope to have anything, he does not need faith. Jacob's secret know-how to increase his share of sheep and goats resembled modern-day innovation. The virtues of diligence, faithfulness, and prudence in the Proverbs match the Protestant work ethic. Most of the men of faith in the Old Testament were rich men, including Abraham, Isaac, Jacob, Joseph, Solomon, and even Job. After Job's sufferings were over, God doubled Job's possessions. In the New Testament, Jesus taught the importance of giving up privileges. At the same time, he said, "everyone who has left houses or brothers or sisters or father or mother or wife or children or fields for my sake will receive a hundred times as much and will inherit eternal life" (Matt 19:29). He said, "Give and it will be given to you. A good measure, pressed down, shaken together and running over, will be poured into your lap" (Luke 6:38). Jesus said that the master will take one talent from the lazy servant and give it to the servant who made five talents, hinting that a more efficient person should be given greater roles in the production of wealth. There are principles of increasing wealth in the principles of the kingdom of God.

The church can no longer teach obscure and ambivalent values about money to its flock while vaguely hoping that church revenues will increase. This is duplicity. This is also a lack of faith. This does not mean that the prosperity gospel is right. Instead, there are valuable principles in the Bible that we can apply to create wealth for all people for the common benefit. Anything less than that would deprive us of God's best.

Christianity and Sex

The Uneasy Relationship

Christianity has had an uneasy relationship with human sexuality. This phenomenon is unique to Christianity. The same kind of troubled relationship did not exist in the Old Testament times. The sexual ethics taught in the Old Testament were not highly strict, but according to common sense that all cultures may find familiar. In the New Testament times, in contrast, Jesus lived a celibate life and commanded his disciples to imitate him. He demanded the near-impossible standard of sexual ethics by announcing that whoever looks at a woman lustfully has already committed adultery with her in his heart. The first gentile to be baptized was an Ethiopian eunuch, and this fact might not have been a coincidence, but have a symbolic meaning. Chastity and self-restraint were always considered the highest virtue in the area of sexual mores. On the other hand, Jesus defended the woman caught in adultery from the condemnation of religious men. Considering how important sexuality is to human beings, the New Testament seems to have left us insufficient material upon which to build sustainable sexual ethics.

Those who try to construct Christian sexual morality run into a wall. Surprisingly, Christianity has sustained this uneasy relationship with human sexuality for so long. But it can continue no longer. By staying in this state, Christianity will only invite ridicule from the world. The satire Christianity attracts from the world is not necessarily due to the world's unbelief and irreverence, but due to the almost impossible moral standard that Christianity has imposed on people. Instead of eliciting faith and obedience, Christian morality evokes suspicion of hypocrisy and lack of empathy. Unbelievers do not expect that believers abide by the same standard that they espouse.

People suspect hypocrisy because they consider it undoable. Those who require it on others know how challenging it is. The harder they require it, the more they hide their secret struggles. When Christians lack credibility, they invite ridicule. From that point on, people will not listen to Christians.

People also perceive a lack of empathy on the part of Christian moralists who always seem angry. During the height of the evangelist Jimmy Swaggart's ministry, viewers of his telecast often indicated how angry

Swaggart seemed while preaching against sin. Little did they know that he was struggling with the same sins that he preached against.

The more conservative preachers are, the more they single out sexual sins as the target of their condemnations. It sometimes looks as if sexuality is the only thing evangelical moralists are preoccupied with. They are not only angry with sin, but also with sinners. Their anger fails to persuade people. After preaching that the grace of God saves us, they preach against the basic human instinct. They are angry with youthful energy. Sometimes it is difficult to separate actual godliness from prudishness. They are fighting a losing fight. Anyone who tries to fight human instinct will lose. Even if they win, it does not bring much joy. Human instinct is like an untamed horse. It is better not to fight it, but to tame it so that you can ride it.

In western societies, those who pioneered the sexual revolution had, at one point, adhered to Christian ethics—at least on the surface. Hugh Hefner, the founder of the *Playboy* magazine, was a virgin until he left the military service. He was not a playboy as a young man. Bob Guccione, the founder of the *Penthouse* magazine, was once a seminary student before going into publishing. Neither of these publishers would have enjoyed success unless they provided guilty pleasures to western men who had grown up in Christian culture. Reading those magazines was fascinating because it felt like cheating.

Both those who led the sexual revolution and those who advocated strict Christian sexual ethics had wrong assumptions about God's demands. God is not opposed to human sexuality. It was God who invented sex. God created Eve to be Adam's helpmate, and Adam joyfully called Eve the bone of his bones, and the flesh of his flesh. The sexual instinct of humanity starts from the command of God to be fruitful and multiply. The instinct to be fruitful and multiply drives men and women. There is something wrong when a person is ashamed of his instinct. Likewise, there is something wrong when a person accuses others of being dirty for being honest about their instinct. It is ironic that those who observe the same human instinct vehemently oppose each other because they interpret it from the opposite points of view. Adamant Christian moralists turned away many people who would have otherwise believed in Jesus Christ. We cannot demand people to clean themselves up before they come to Jesus. Once they come to Jesus, Jesus will help them to clean up.

The fundamental rule of human sexuality is that sex must be shared between a husband and a wife. This is a reasonable rule but built on unstable ground. The satisfaction of this moral requirement depends on the success of something else: marriage. It presupposes a successful marriage to be a virtuous Christian. It can only work when marriage works well. A virtuous Christian must be a master at maintaining a successful marriage. It is hard enough following the ethical rules, but Christians must also make their marriages work. It is unclear if this rule is trying to achieve moral purity or to protect marriage. It tries to catch two birds with one stone. That is the reason for the unstable ground.

The Christian sexual ethics, as traditionally taught by the church, makes no provisions for those who are single, too young to be married, unable to get married, unhappily married, separated, divorced, and widowed. Also it makes no provisions for the fundamental need for love, companionship, sexual curiosity, and basic instinct. It is sinful to be honest with one's desires. One must be untruthful to even himself. When a young man happens upon a nude picture of a woman, he must tell himself that he did not look at it intentionally or derived any pleasure from it. This is plainly absurd. This kind of ethics cannot stand. Christianity is teaching legalism as long as it teaches human instinct as sinful.

The standard rule for permissible human sexuality is tyrannical and incomplete. It is tyrannical because it imposes the institution of marriage to fulfill human instinct. It is like Microsoft requiring the Window users to also use the Internet Explorer, which was ruled by the court to be a monopoly. Marriage is a tough proposition. It seems to get more difficult as times go by. The average age of marriage is getting older all over the world, and the number of people who remain unmarried is increasing. Young people entering puberty begin to be interested in sex. How many years do they have to wait until they are married? If it is a sin to engage in sexual activity until one is married, how many years does a young person have to live with unfulfilled desires? Is it some kind of an abstinence test? In many cultures, a man cannot get a bride until he acquires economic means to support a wife. What happens to men who cannot afford a wife? Men and women who are physically or mentally impaired cannot hope to get married, although they have the same sexual desires as everybody else. Some people are unsuccessful at finding a spouse despite their best intentions. Must all those who cannot get married deny their sexuality for the rest of their lives? This is more than just a matter of sexual ethics but human rights. The fact that few Christians discuss these issues candidly demonstrates a logical gap in the traditional Christian sexual ethics.

The proof that the standard rule for acceptable human sexuality does not work is visible all around us. Teenagers find their ways to ease sexual urges. Young people cohabitate instead of getting married. Cohabitation has far fewer requirements than marriage. Acknowledging the changing times, the evangelicals have quietly dropped premarital sex and divorce from their list of cardinal sins in the past couple of decades. As the average life expectancy increases, married couples face the possibility of staying married for much longer than ever before. More and more people are attracted to the idea of renewing marriages like renewing driver's licenses. Requiring people to live with the same spouse for such a long time seems overbearing for a growing number of people. At the time of this writing, Jimmy and Rosalyn Carter celebrated the seventy-third anniversary of their wedding. The Carters are truly faithful Christian people, worthy of admiration. But not everyone can be like the Carters.

The institution of marriage is worth protecting and preserving. Nonetheless, tying sexual ethics to the institution of marriage is unreasonable and unworkable. Those who strongly advocate traditional Christian sexual ethics are perhaps driven by the fear that the institution of marriage might otherwise collapse. They seem more concerned about preserving the social structure of marriage than Christian ethics. To them, sexuality is like a beast that threatens the sanctity of marriage. In their concern for maintaining a marriage, conservative Christian moralists forget that Jesus did not attach much significance to marriage and family. Ironically, conservative Christians consider marriage to be the most important institution, while Jesus did not. This is an irony. Although Jesus talked about many things, he did not talk about how to preserve a marriage or how to improve one's marital life. For that matter, Jesus did not talk about how to raise children well. Family matters were not Jesus's priorities. The middle-class evangelical Christians who focus on family more than anything else must remember this fact. Jesus was not anti-family, but he was almost post-family. Jesus taught radical departure from man's daily concerns in order to dedicate himself to the kingdom of God. Evangelical Christianity has not explored this aspect of Jesus's teachings, and it deserves further inquiry and discussion.

Then what are the most important principles for Christian sexual ethics? The following are some of the basic principles to consider for sexual ethics.

Sex Must Be between Two Consenting Adults

In this age of the MeToo movement, the necessity of consent requires no further explanation. People, young and old, need to learn how to express consent and how to verify it. Furthermore, people need to learn how to act like adults. Adolescents used to peek into adult material, but even as adults, they still act as if they were adolescents. In matters related to sexuality, people are still embarrassed and ashamed. They make one another feel that way. Unless accompanied with guilt, pleasure does not feel like pleasure. Human beings are never at peace with their honest instinct.

Respecting Marriage

Marriage deserves the utmost respect. People should receive congratulations not just for getting married, but also for staying married. What God has joined together, let no man separate. But maintaining marriage cannot be the highest moral goal for Christians. Some will sidestep the institution of marriage so as not to break the rule. In *Le retour de Martin Guerre*, a man who claims to be Martin Guerre returns home after two decades of military service.[4] His wife knows that this man is not her true husband, but receives him regardless because having a false husband is better than having no husband. This couple appears to remain within the institution of marriage when, in fact, they are not. This film showed how it is possible to hide behind the institution of marriage to commit immorality.

Polygamy is forbidden in most cultures. But people practice serial polygamy by divorcing one spouse and getting remarried to another one. Instead of faithfully following the rules of marriage, people use the institution of marriage to fulfill their desires. They think that, if sexual acts occur within the confines of marriage, they are legitimate.

Some marriages are in name only. A divorce is an unacceptable option for many. As a sign of failure, divorce brings much pain and shame to all the members of the family. Rather than face a painful breakup of the family, they choose to remain in an unhappy marriage. As a result, such people are neither bound nor free. They neither faithfully fulfill marital obligations nor achieve the freedom of celibacy. Instead of wishing they were divorced, they wish their spouses were dead. When reporters asked Ruth Graham, the wife of Billy Graham, if she had ever considered

---

4. Vigne, *Le Retour de Martin Guerre*.

divorce, she jokingly replied, "No, but I have considered murder." This statement represents the sentiment of many married people. Imposing the yoke of marriage too forcefully can tempt some to consider committing a greater sin than divorce.

Jesus permitted divorce in case of adultery. That means that there are exceptions to the rule. If Jesus had come in the twenty-first century, he might have added other exceptional circumstances than adultery—such as physical abuse, addiction, and nominal marriages. Maintaining a marriage is not the highest goal of Christianity; loving God and loving one another is.

Love Has to Go with Sex

Sex without love can leave deep hurts. Sex without love treats a person as an object. It degrades a human being into a thing. Usually, it is women who expect to be loved by men that they are intimate with, while men tend to think that they can engage in casual sex—until they hear a loud knock on their door by an angry father or brother. Sometimes the table is turned around, and men find themselves used by women for pleasure. Then they understand the meaning of abandonment. When a man is jilted, he will not only be hurt but turn vengeful. In the 1993 TV movie *Between Love and Hate*, a college boy working at a country club for the summer is seduced by a wealthy housewife. She does it one boy at a time each summer, but this college boy, who falls in love with her, does not know that. When he is dumped at the end of the summer, his love turns into a jealous rage with tragic results.[5] Playing with someone's affection is not only immoral but also dangerous. Remember that a jealous husband started the Trojan War.

Nonetheless, in the heat of passion, it is difficult to tell if one is motivated by love or lust. Human beings tend to act first and think later. One is more clear-headed after the act than before. Many couples are driven to marriage as the only right option after a sexual act. Although they do not love each other, duty motivates them. If they could do it all over again, they would reconsider before jumping into bed. It seems that the only available choice for people is between pleasure and regret.

---

5. Hardy, *Between Love and Hate*.

Follow Moderation and Self-Control

In 1991, Magic Johnson announced that he had tested positive for HIV. Although he did not know how he contracted HIV, Magic acknowledged that he had had innumerable sex partners during his basketball career. It was not unusual for famous sports stars or rock stars to have female fans lining up behind the stage after each game or performance. Some just could not resist the temptations. Costly consequences usually followed immoderation.

One does not have to be religious to realize the importance of self-control. Any kind of immoderation carries enormous risks of various sorts. One who cannot control food is bound to develop serious health problems. One who cannot handle drinking is in deep trouble. The same rule applies to substance abuse and gambling. Too little of something can cause pain, but too much of anything can cause pain also.

Psychologists believe that the inability to control sexual urges may originate from the lack of affection during childhood. A person whose need for love was not met in his early years is likely to feel the need to compensate later. This theory has some merit but does not explain all people. Some people just want more and more. It has nothing to do with childhood affection deprivation. We should not try to blame childhood experiences for every problem in a person's life. Some people are like a child in a candy store. They just cannot control themselves. Blessed are those whose life situations are not like a candy store.

There was a rich man who owned many houses. He had a young son whom he spoiled so much that he sold a couple of houses to buy candies for his son. What happened as a result? The boy lost all his teeth. It would have been better if the father were not so rich. The ability to satisfy one's desires without the strength to control them leads to disasters.

It is a good thing that people do not possess the power to satisfy all their desires. It is God's way of protecting us. It keeps us humble. Sometimes "whoever gathered much had nothing left over, and whoever gathered little had no lack" (2 Cor 8:15). Those who seem to have less than others do not really lack. On the contrary, those who seem to have much end up having little. Johnny Fontane, a celebrated singer in Mario Puzo's *The Godfather*, is a playboy who can have any women he wants in Hollywood. But his wife, also a star, taunts him by being unfaithful and imprudent. On some evenings, as a result, Johnny has to beg his ex-wife to let him into her house so that he can feel some affection and warmth.[6] Though Johnny seems to have much love on the surface, he has little in reality. This is God's way of evening things out. God is righteous. We have to remember this truth and always stay humble.

Christianity and LGBT+

How I Came to Understand Homosexual Brothers and Sisters

God created people male and female. The only permissible sex takes place between a man and a woman in marriage. Stating this basic principle does not end the discussion but starts it.

How Christians should approach homosexuals is the most heated point of contention in our time. Perhaps it was better in the old days when this issue did not come out of the closet. But now that the cat is out of the bag, no Christian can ignore the issue of LGBT+ in the contemporary society. Some people will automatically jump into heated arguments from either side. Such people will always argue, no matter what. We cannot talk reasonably to such people. If people are not willing to engage in respectful dialogues, this chapter is not for them.

In the twenty-first century, the LGBT+ issue will be the most controversial and divisive issue for Christianity. Perhaps the most prudent course of action is "Ask not and tell not." But such a course of action assumes that the issue can hide in the closet all the time. For those people who come out of the closet, Christianity must offer more choices than "Accept this or leave." The amount of hurt this will cause upon people, and the amount of resistance and anger this can create, is beyond imagination. Many of the harshest critics of Christianity are homosexuals who were once hurt at church.

When I was a newly arrived immigrant in Toronto in the mid-1970s, a couple of rascals in my class gave me an unpleasant experience one day by bluntly asking me, "Hey, are you gay?" I knew this was a trick question, but I did not know what the trick was. They were preying on my lack of English skills to get a cheap laugh out of me. The only definition of "gay" that I knew was "happy." The other rascal assured me, "Don't worry. Gay means happy." So, I replied, "Yes." This was what they were looking

---

6. Puzo, *Godfather*.

for, and I fell into their trap. Later I found out that this was a favorite routine to which these rascals subjected all newly arrived immigrant boys.

That was the first time that I experienced the world of homophobia. When one has a couple of unpleasant experiences like that, he develops high sensitivity to the LGBT+ issue. In my teenage years, gay people were sort of rarities. My friends would snicker over The Eagles' album cover, where a couple of men were in an intimate posture. It was not until I went to college that I realized there are more homosexuals in the world than I had known. Not only was there a campus organization for LGBT+, but also there were many closet gays around me.

What surprised me was that there were gay Christian brothers. It was still a guessing stage at that time. Very few men came out, but there were suspects. It was a confusing time. There were reports of AIDS coming out of San Francisco, but few people paid any attention. The church I was attending then adopted a very conservative and belligerent attitude toward homosexuality. The pastor announced that gay men could be "delivered" and even announced a sample case. One poor young man had to stand up before the congregation and confess that he had been delivered from his gay orientation. I had no way of knowing the veracity of this claim.

When I went to study in New York City in the mid-1980s, it was at the height of the promiscuous gay culture. My friends told me about a notorious parking lot on the west side of Manhattan, where gay men were supposed to be cruising. Somebody pointed out to me how gay men walk differently from straight men. Their peculiar gait was supposedly due to anal intercourse. When the AIDS epidemic began to hit the front pages of newspapers, conservative Christians called it a punishment from God. Even youngsters were sure of this fact. In the mid-1980s, everybody was afraid of AIDS and blamed gays for the international health scare. I once saw an AIDS patient whose pale, emaciated face filled me with horror.

What caused me to think differently about homosexuality was getting to know several brothers and sisters at my church who were terrific people and devout Christians. Despite their genuine faith, God did not change their sexuality. Some of them confessed to their constant struggles, frequent failures, and excessive amount of guilt. I hit a wall every time I tried to make sense of it.

As more time passed, I discovered more and more people who were gay and yet faithful servants of the Lord. The best example was Lonnie Frisbee. Since a documentary film about his life and faith was publicly released,[7] I think we can discuss him openly. Lonnie Frisbee, often called the Hippie Preacher, was the legend of the Jesus People movement. He was instrumental in the revival of the Calvary Chapel and played a pivotal role in the rise of the Vineyard Christian Fellowship. It was not John Wimber but Lonnie Frisbee who coined the famous phrase "Come, Holy Spirit!" One cannot get to know the history of the Vineyard movement without hearing about Lonnie Frisbee—a true legend. However, before dying of AIDS in 1993, he confessed to being gay.

At Frisbee's funeral, Pastor Chuck Smith compared Frisbee to Samson, a man of tremendous anointing and power, and yet with a critical flaw. It was true that Frisbee was a man of immense anointing and power. But I am not sure if his homosexuality was a critical flaw. Perhaps his immoderate lifestyle was a critical flaw, because Frisbee was known to party wildly on Saturday nights and still do wonderful ministry on Sunday mornings.

When there are so many wonderful brothers and sisters in the body of Christ who are homosexuals, accusing them of sin hurts us all. Those who want to know what it is like for a devout Christian mother to have a gay son, I recommend *Prayers for Bobby*,[8] a TV movie featuring Sigourney Weaver. Bobby grew up in a Christian home, convinced that homosexuality was a sin, struggling with guilt, only to throw himself from an overpass. His grief-stricken mother was once a diehard believer in Leviticus 20:13 and Romans 1:27.

There are some theories proposed by Christians about the "healing" of homosexuals. John and Paula Sandford assert that the gender identity created within a person can be restored through confession, prayer, and inner healing.[9] "Healing" of homosexuals is met with angry protests. Nonetheless, if a person desires to talk to a Christian counselor about his sexuality, it is his undeniable right. The effectiveness of such counseling is open to question. I have never met a person whose orientation changed from homosexuality to heterosexuality. That means that they were no longer attracted to the same sex but to the opposite sex. Abstention does not qualify. We may never know the full story. People are never completely honest about their sexuality

---

7. *Frisbee: The Life and Death of a Hippie Preacher* Directed by Di Sabatino.
8. Mulcahy, *Prayers for Bobby*.
9. Sandford and Sandford, *Transformation of the Inner Man*, 310–15.

Is homosexuality innate or learned? Can a person change his orientation later in life? These are two critical questions to which I do not have any answers. But shifting results of research should not determine our attitude toward our brothers and sisters. Even if homosexuality is learned and not innate, that does not mean that they deserve blame. One standard which we should apply is, if our child were homosexual, how would we treat him or her? Once we know the answer to this hypothesis, we know how to act toward everyone.

Reading the Relevant Scripture Passages Again

Three primary Bible verses address homosexuality. One is Leviticus 20:13, the second is Romans 1:27, and the third is Jude 1:7.

Leviticus 20:13, the first prohibition of homosexual acts in the Bible, is understandable. Leviticus was the first detailed written moral code about human sexuality in recorded history. It is understandable why Leviticus forbade homosexual acts. After all, God created Adam and Eve, not Adam and Steve. Nature plainly suggests that the homosexual act is against nature and the procreative purpose of sex. The Israelites probably did not need any in-depth discussions about the matter. Forbidding homosexual behavior would not have surprised them. The kind of serious discussions we now have probably did not exist then.

The Leviticus author intended to forbid the acts of homosexuality, not to do away with homosexuals. The passage prohibits the act of homosexuality without mentioning homosexuality as an orientation. Society at that time could not have understood homosexual people as well as we do today. There were no society-wide discussions. Ancient people were not familiar with an inherent sexual orientation.[10]

The second reference to homosexuality in Romans 1:27 is a little out of place: "In the same way the men also abandoned natural relations with women and were inflamed with lust for one another. Men committed shameful acts with other men, and received in themselves the due penalty for their error." Paul was theologically establishing the original sinful condition of humanity from a historical perspective. In Calvinist terms, Paul was discussing the total depravity of man. In the middle of the passage, Paul suddenly mentions men committing shameless acts with men. This passage does not go well with the context. There are many

---

10. Smith, "Ancient Bisexuality," 225.

more wicked and severe things that humanity can do other than homosexuality. If Paul's purpose was to establish the universal sin of humanity, he did not have to mention homosexuality. Even if he wanted to say it, he could do it elsewhere. That is why this passage seems out of place. When we read the rest of Paul's letters, we do not find any evidence that he was opposed to homosexuality as particularly sinful. Why he had to mention it the way he did in Romans 1:27 is mysterious. Some scholars argue that Paul was referring to the ancient Greco-Roman practice of older men taking advantage of young boys and, hence, not the modern way of mutually consenting adult homosexual relationships.[11] Even so, Paul was quite emotional about it for reasons we do not understand. Mentioning pederasty in the middle of depicting the spiritual degeneration of humanity sounds like a non sequitur. Was he critiquing the corrupt Roman culture at this point? Was he not carried away by emotions? If Paul had known that his letter would be read by billions of Christians afterward, would he have said the same things?

We, therefore, need to put this Romans verse in a freezer for separate analysis at later times. It is not a natural passage to apply to the issue of homosexuality. Paul mentions, "Men likewise gave up natural relations with women" (Rom 1:27). Does it mean that Paul was advocating man's natural relations with women? Paul was not a champion of heterosexual relationships. He recommended his celibate lifestyle to other people (1 Cor 7:7). It is difficult to imagine that Paul, who advocated celibacy, was in favor of men's natural relations with women while opposing men's unnatural relations with men. Romans 1:27 requires a separate attention on its own and is inappropriate for proof-texting to condemn homosexuality.

The third reference in Jude 1:7 must be considered with the actual situations at Sodom when the angels of the Lord visited the city. The wickedness of Sodomites was not only homosexual activity but sexual debauchery, including gang rape, violence, and murder. The residents of Sodom surrounded Lot's house, demanding the release of the angels of the Lord so that they could rape them. Sodom must have been like federal penitentiaries where inmates commit predatory acts to one another. The men of Sodom were violent and dangerous perverts who were willing to commit sexual assault and murder.

Homosexuality was not the primary sin of Sodom. In Ezekiel 16:49, the guilt of Sodom is defined as arrogance, being overfed and

---

11. Smith, "Ancient Bisexuality," 226.

unconcerned about the poor and needy. To interpret Jude 1:7, one must correctly understand the condition of Sodom. Using Jude 1:7 as a proof text for condemning homosexuality seems to be a bad theology.

The Task Falls on Us Now

Analysis of the three most prominent Bible verses regarding homosexuality suggests that all these verses refer to the act of homosexuality but not its orientation. These verses do not demonstrate that there was any widespread pastoral discussion or investigation regarding homosexual orientation at the time they were written. Furthermore, the Bible omits any mention of lesbianism. Although all scripture is inspired by God, the writers do not seem to have reached a reasonable conclusion about this issue at the time they wrote scripture. Therefore, the task falls on us now. This case is by no means closed. Churches should not assume that the Bible provides comprehensive rules about how to regard homosexuals. Churches should at least demonstrate a willingness to talk about the issue openheartedly. We should remember that all people are lost sheep that Jesus came to seek. Allowing this issue to divide the church will accomplish little for the kingdom of God.

On the other hand, heartily celebrating LGBT+ is a different matter. Some denominations are more interested in pursuing their radical social agenda than seeking the edification of the church. LGBT+ is currently the most controversial and toxic issue dividing the church. Everybody must tread on it carefully. If this issue results in the split of denominations, it is a better result than imposing an unpleasant decision that member churches cannot accept in good conscience. Any denomination that pushes this controversial issue to the forefront is committing spiritual suicide. There are far more critical tasks for churches and denominations than forcing uncomfortable decisions on the LGBT+ issue.

Jesus did not discuss this issue during his ministry. We should not assume that it was because homosexuality did not exist at that time. Some matters are best not treated forthrightly. Jesus demanded his disciples to renounce themselves and take up their cross. Every disciple of Christ must deny something. In this context, discussing people's sexual preferences could not be a vital issue for any of the disciples. If we must place all our wishes and desires below Christ, we will not have to make homosexuality the central issue of Christianity.

Christianity and Islam

In the global context, Islam is a rival religion of Christianity. But so are Buddhism, Hinduism, and secularism. In the European context, Islam is not just a religion but a sociological and cultural force. When Europeans protest that the influx of Muslims is threatening Europe's Christian heritage, they must specify whether they are talking about religion or culture. If they are so concerned about their Christian heritage, they should have acted sooner. Christianity was disappearing from Europe long before the Muslim immigrants began to arrive on their shores. If European Christians are genuinely concerned about the state of Christianity, they must not blame anyone. They only need to take their faith seriously.

When the German conservatives complained that the influx of Muslims into Germany threatens its Christian identity, Angela Merkel retorted that Islam does not pose a threat to Christianity. Her remark was correct. Only a thoughtful Christian can make such a statement. The actual danger to faith comes from within, not from outside. Christianity endured far more severe persecutions in the past and survived. What corrupted Christianity was the wealth and prosperity that it enjoyed after Constantine. It is a refreshing turn of events that Europeans are starting to be concerned about their Christian heritage. They should not worry about external threats. What matters is the inward condition of the European people.

How the religious landscape of the world will change in the twenty-first century is hard to predict. Many Christians worry about the massive migration of Muslims to Europe and what it can do to Europe's religious identity. People point out that the most popular first name for newly born boys in Britain is Muhammad. Be that as it may, it is not Christian people migrating to Muslim countries, but the other way around. Though we cannot go to the mountain, the mountain is coming to us. If anyone is going to be affected, it is the Muslims. After all, they are choosing to live in the western world. Germany is the most favorite destination for migrants from the Middle East and Africa. The most apparent reason for the mass migration is the availability of employment and a better future. But another not-so-obvious reason is the allure of western society—its openness, freedom, and tolerance. Muslims will have to adapt to the western environment. There is a small but growing number of Muslims becoming Christian Democrats in Germany. The center-right parties of Europe may become the natural home of the Muslim middle class because the traditional morality and a strong role for religion in public life appeal to them.[12] If such an event happens, Muslims and conservative Christians will be allies, not adversaries, in European politics.

God of our Lord Jesus Christ has permitted Islam to grow into a world religion alongside Christianity for some unknown reason. Perhaps God did not want Christianity to have a monopoly in the world. Such status would inevitably have led to corruption and pride. Absolute power corrupts absolutely, and religion is no exception. We tend to think that the kingdom of God would come on earth if all people convert to Christianity. Nothing could be further from the truth. The number of Christians in the world, though important, does not in itself translate into the kingdom of God. Israel of the Old Testament was a theocratic society. The entire nation believed that Yahweh was their God. They had made a covenant with God. Nonetheless, God was not happy with them. Jews in captivity, who were minorities among Gentiles, were more faithful to Yahweh than the Jews back home who had constituted the majority in their land.

Christians have no right to blame Muslims for any trouble that Christians perceive—especially in exercising their faith. Aside from terrorism that is perpetrated by a small band of radical Muslims, ordinary Muslims are just living their lives. They are trying to make sense of the rapidly changing world like everyone else. In the 2015 film *Fatima*, Fatima is the name of a divorced Muslim woman trying to support two daughters in France by working at odd jobs as a cleaner. Fatima speaks French poorly and is always frustrated by her interactions with her daughters. Not being able to share her troubles with anyone, she writes down her diaries in Arabic.[13] Muslims living in Europe have the same concerns as everyone else. If Christians suspect that the Muslims are trying to take over Christian Europe, they are paranoid.

Islam and Christianity have coexisted in the world for more than fifteen centuries. Any conflict that exists between them is not new. If there is anything new, it is the fact that the world is growing smaller than before, so that the two religions run into each other more often. Nonetheless, this affects Muslims as much as Christians.

Until 9/11 occurred, no one around the world paid much attention to the Islamic world. September 11th, 2001 was a tragic turn of events for both Christians and Muslims because each camp began to view the

---

12. Allen, "Christianity under Siege," 6.
13. Faucon, *Fatima*.

other with suspicion and hostility. We should not view the war and conflicts that resulted from 9/11 as confrontations between the two religions. Islam did not attack Christianity. Al-Qaeda attacked the United States. There is a difference. Perhaps the terrorists hoped that their attack would trigger a worldwide religious war. Such intention comes from the devil, which both Christians and Muslims must resist.

The conflict between the Muslim world and the western world is not over religion but culture. Muslims who are critical of the Christian civilization seem to believe that the west's moral corruption is somehow due to Christianity. Sayyid Qutb, who provided the ideological basis for Al-Qaeda, was spending two years in the United States as a teacher when he was shocked by the apparent lax morality among Christians. From his experience, Qutb established a radical religious theory that viewed anything non-Islamic as evil and corrupt.[14] The radical Muslims' worldview is similar to the Japanese military leaders' view on America before attacking Pearl Harbor. The Japanese military leaders were under the impression that America was morally corrupt and weak, and the Japanese could easily beat America. Iran's Islamic revolution was also based on a similar worldview: America was corrupting Iranian society's moral values. This suspicion worsened after the United States granted asylum to the Shah. Hence Iranians rejected America drastically. Ayatollah Khomeini called America the devil. Remember that his criticism was directed against one country and not the western world as a whole. We must remember that Khomeini had lived in France during exile.

Whether they are right or wrong is beside the point. Muslims fear what the rapidly changing world can do to their religious values and, consequently, they are trying to protect their religion and culture. On the other hand, Christians in the west fear that the growing Muslim population in the west may try to turn their society into Islam. This is more than just a religious concern but political and cultural. One word of caution is needed: Europe's changing demographics demonstrate the secularizing tendencies among westernized Muslims and also the migration of highly active Christians from the southern hemisphere.[15] Among the twenty-four million migrants in the European Union in 2003, 48.5 percent belonged to Christianity, and 30.95 percent belonged to Islam.[16]

---

14. Curtis, *Power of Nightmares*.
15. Clements, "Christian Faith in Europe," 4.
16. Clements, "Christian Faith in Europe," 5.

Christians have to ask themselves this question: since when is religion determined by number? Do they think that Europe will turn to Islam just because Muslims make up the majority? Whatever happened to the freedom of religion? If Europeans worry that Muslims can take their country away from Christianity, should Europeans not begin to take their faith more seriously? One fights an idea with another idea, not with laws or prohibition. The wars fought between the Catholics and Protestants were silly and misdirected. Why did it never occur to either Catholics or Protestants that they should compete for the minds of people instead? What led them to think that eliminating the other was the best way to protect their faith? Did they have so little faith in the power of God? Did not Jesus promise that, when the Holy Spirit comes on us, we will receive power to be his witnesses to the ends of the earth? Since when do we trust the laws of the state more than the Holy Spirit?

We sincerely hope that no one is harboring a thought in his heart that eliminating Muslims is the means of preserving Christianity in the western world. We also hope that no Muslims are holding the idea in their hearts that removing Christians is the means of protecting Islam. Neither idea does justice to the true religion.

Religious Pluralism

Neither Christians in the west nor Muslims in the Middle East seem to be used to a religiously pluralistic society. In contrast, Koreans are used to religious pluralism, except that they do not use that concept. Protestantism makes up about 20 percent, Catholicism makes up about 15 percent, Buddhism makes about 30 percent, and other religions and no religion make up the rest in Korea. Even though there are rivalries and suspicion, religious differences do not lead to wars, murders, terrorism, or political strife. The competition takes place mainly in the marketplace of ideas. Sometimes Buddhism appeals to the masses; sometimes, Catholicism appeals to the masses. Recently the Catholic Church was best able to empathize with the public grief over the sinking of a ferry carrying more than two hundred high school students. As a result, many people converted to Catholicism. The Protestant churches of Korea have seen a decline in membership lately. But no one blames other religions for such changes. If they blame anybody, they blame themselves for not doing their job well. Koreans consider religious differences an inconvenience, but never a social problem that should be remedied through coercive means.

No one tries to push religious plurality in Korean society. Everyone takes it for granted. Religious issues never come up when Koreans try to reach political or cultural consensus. People know implicitly that religious beliefs are private. They practice their faith within their religious circles and expect others to do the same. Single people, especially women, want their spouses to be of the same religion, but they also know that practical considerations often outweigh religious ones. And quite often, husbands follow their wives' religion after many tumultuous years of marriage.

Not many people in Korea are concerned about the big religious issues covered in this book. People, by and large, are busy just trying to survive. Most people feel a need for religious faith, but they will not think of going to war over it. The religious history of the west and the Middle East seems alien to many Asians. Koreans do not believe that they have inherited a religious identity from the past. One's identity is what one makes of it. If a tradition is difficult to maintain any more, perhaps it is not worth preserving.

The reason that Koreans do not even use the term "religious pluralism" is that Korea is a very homogeneous society. There are more factors that unite them than divide them. There are obvious political differences and divisions, but ethnic and cultural unity provides social and psychological stability. Koreans do not feel the need to think in terms of religious plurality because there exists an overarching homogeneity in society.

This fact suggests that the heated debate over religious pluralism in the west is not really over religion but other things. The true nature of the confrontation has not shown its face. Western society is already so fragmented that people blame religious differences as the culprit of the fragmentation. People blame religion for the problems that have other causes. Religious people should not fall into this trap.

— 10 —

Restoration of Christianity in Post-Christian Europe

Understanding Post-Christian Christianity

Although "post-Christian Christianity" sounds like a new phenomenon, its principle is not new. Instead, the same principle existed from the beginning. Christianity began as a "Post-Christ" event. When Christianity was birthed, Christ was already gone. We believe in his resurrection and ascension. Nonetheless, it does not change the fact that Christ was absent on earth when Christianity began. Jesus planned it that way. He stated, "it is to your advantage that I go away" (John 16:7). How was it to the advantage of the disciples that Jesus went away? It is because the Holy Spirit would not come unless he went away: "If I do not go away, the Helper will not come to you. But if I go, I will send him to you" (John 16:7). The Helper refers to the Holy Spirit. Despite the enormous role Jesus played on the earth, Jesus's departure was necessary so that the Holy Spirit could come. In place of Jesus, the Holy Spirit would guide and direct Christians. Thus, it was not Jesus but the Holy Spirit and the apostles who started Christianity. Jesus laid the foundation on which Christianity could be built. But Jesus left it to the Holy Spirit and the apostles to build Christianity on that foundation. Therefore, post-Christian Christianity is only an extension of post-Christ Christianity. The word "post-Christian" should not scare Christians.

Apostle Peter's first sermon displayed a post-Christ theology. Jesus did not begin the church himself but left it to his disciples. The sermon that launched Christianity was not Jesus's sermon, but Peter's sermon. The apostles' witness of the death and resurrection of Jesus and their faith confession became the foundation of the Christian faith. Thus, it is not an overstatement to say that Christianity was a post-Christ event.

Apostle Paul was the first post-Christ Christian because he received his apostleship after Christ had left the earth. Though he had not met Jesus during Jesus's earthly ministry, Paul was able to confidently talk about "the gospel I preached" (Gal 1:11) and "my gospel" (Rom 2:16, 2 Tim 2:8). How could Paul be so confident about his gospel? It was because it was revealed to him from Jesus Christ without any human agency (Gal 1:11–12). Paul was the first example of a post-Christ Christian. He was the first proof that a person is blessed when he believes in Jesus without seen him (John 20:29).

At the beginning of Christianity, the first converts were all Jews. After the Jewish leaders denounced Christians, however, the two groups were torn apart. This schism must have been traumatic for Christians because they were forcibly uprooted from Judaism. The gospel of John addressed this sentiment. Nonetheless, this event enabled Christianity to grow into a world religion instead of remaining a small branch of Judaism. If it had remained within Judaism, gentile Christians would have to convert to Judaism to be Christians. By losing the cradle from which it began, Christianity could independently grow into a world religion.

There is a remarkable similarity between the experience of Abraham and the experiences of the early Christians. Abraham left behind the familiar world to follow the word of the Lord. The only thing guiding Abraham's life was the word of the Lord (Gen 12:4). Likewise, the Holy Spirit's leading was so sure and powerful that the early Christians risked losing everything else to follow the Holy Spirit. The Lord leads the church in the same way in the twenty-first century. One thing that will lead the church is the word of the Lord, not anything else. It takes the loss of everything else to return to the fundamental principle of following the Holy Spirit wholeheartedly. Having lost its dominant place in the world, post-Christian Christianity can return to its original spirit.

The early Christians had to adapt to new situations continually in a rapidly changing hostile world. After Apostle James' martyrdom, a terrible persecution occurred in Jerusalem, which scattered all Christians except the apostles (Acts 8:1). To those who remembered the glorious days of the church of Jerusalem, this event must have seemed apocalyptic. The Jerusalem church was the legendary church that was birthed on the day of Pentecost. Its membership had, at one point, risen to five thousand people. It was the model for all other churches to emulate. Nevertheless, one fateful day, it all ended with deadly persecution. The apostles remained in Jerusalem, but all the members were scattered.

However, the scattering of the members of the Jerusalem church had a beneficial effect on Christianity. The scattered Christians preached the gospel wherever they went. It was not their plan, but the Lord used the occasion to spread Christianity to gentiles. It was at this time that Philip, one of the seven deacons, went down to Samaria to evangelize it. He also baptized the Ethiopian eunuch, who was the first gentile to be baptized. The Jerusalem church's loss was the gospel's gain. Severed from the mother church at Jerusalem, Christianity grew beyond the borders in unexpected ways.

The same pattern repeated in the following ages. After the Roman Empire embraced the Christian faith, Christians thought that the kingdom of heaven had arrived. Instead, the barbarians began to invade from the north and eventually crushed the empire. Utterly shocked, Saint Augustine wrestled with the question of how God could permit the fall of a Christian kingdom. The conclusion Saint Augustine drew was that even though the kingdoms of men fall, the kingdom of God is established. What Saint Augustine looked forward to was a form of post-Christian Christianity—Christianity independent of its earthly glory. What is happening in Europe now is very similar to what occurred in the Christian Roman Empire. The familiar world that Christians could depend on is disappearing, leaving little for them to lean on, except the grace of God. This is a blessing in disguise.

Christianity always works best in a position of weakness. In the New Testament, Christians were in such a position. Nonetheless, God chose the weak things of the world to shame the strong (1 Cor 1:27). God's power is perfected in man's weakness (2 Cor 12:9). This has always been God's method. Christians erred when they tried to depend on earthly power—whether in terms of number, wealth, or political protection. Christians were able to preserve their spiritual purity while they were under persecution. Once persecution stopped, and Christianity began to enjoy political patronage and privilege, Christianity began to lose its innocence. The Edict of Milan, by which Emperor Constantine legalized the practice of Christianity in the Roman Empire, was therefore both good news and bad news. It was good news in the sense that Christians could practice their faith without fearing persecution. But it was bad news in the sense that they now depended on the Emperor instead of God.

The Age of Faith was the period when the church's power was at its peak. This age is the benchmark against which scholars measure modern secularization.[1] But this thinking is more of a myth than a fact. The church, in medieval times, was corrupt and steeped in superstition. The public did not go to church frequently, did not know the basics of Christian faith, and could not distinguish between superstition and Christianity. The film *Kingdom of Heaven* well depicts the spiritual condition of Europe and the Holy Land during the Crusade. The church was powerful enough to send Christians to fight in the Holy Land in return for the salvation of souls, but what the Crusaders discovered in the Holy Land was anything but the salvation of souls or the kingdom of heaven. The 1986 film *The Name of the Rose* depicted life within a monastery during the middle ages. There is very little that we can admire about the lives of either laypeople or monks since they were all steeped in superstition and ignorance. By putting poison on the pages of forbidden books, the church implicitly encouraged ignorance for the sake of protecting the faith.

The Protestant Reformation protested, among other things, the obese power of the church. The Catholic Church claimed unbiblical power to absolve sins regardless of the genuine faith of the penitent. It was an abuse of spiritual power to dispense absolution in that way. The Protestant Reformation propelled the world into a post-Christian era. Paving the way for modernity, the Protestant Reformation took Christianity away from its dependence on the powerful church. The Reformation credo that the just shall live by faith alone made it theoretically possible for people to be Christians independent of the church. Robinson Crusoe, who landed on an uninhabited island with only a Bible in his hand, characterized the quintessential Protestant who can exercise faith independent of church.

The Protestant Reformation was the first time that Christianity was distinguished from the church. The prosperity of the church was not necessarily the same as the prosperity of Christianity. This issue, first pointed out by the Reformers, stands on the forefront of the theological discussions of our time. We must ask if the waning of Christianity in Europe is the problem of Christianity itself or the problem of the church. We have to make the basic assumption that the public still has a place for Christ in

---

1. Stark, "Supply-side Reinterpretation," 241.

their hearts although they do not go to church. Is our priority renewing the church or Christianity? The answer will affect the strategies of missionaries and evangelists.

The United States of America was the first nation on earth to stipulate the separation of the church and state in its Constitution. This stipulation was the deliberate design of the framers of the Constitution to create a secular state. The purpose of the separation of the church and state was not to take away the church's privileges, but to prevent the kind of trouble that existed in the Old World. Separating the church and state would enable the church to operate freely without the meddling of the state, they believed. This established the foundation for a secular society, which in reality benefited Christianity rather than damaged it.

Religious freedom has been at the basis of American Christianity. The churches were going to get people to join them by the power of persuasion and not coercion. In the Old World, people were de facto members of the church, whether they believed or not. But in America, diverse churches and denominations had to compete for the souls of people. Those churches that were effective at winning people's souls grew, while those which were ineffective dwindled. Churches and denominations did not only compete with one another but also with opposing philosophies and ideologies. For example, churches had to actively teach creationism in repudiation of evolutionism to win young people's minds. Billy Graham sent a team of sociologists in advance to the cities where he would hold crusades to study people's felt needs so that he could tailor his messages. Those who hoped to win people's hearts did not presume that the Christian heritage or culture would automatically lead people to church. Churches had to be true fishers of men. The emphasis placed on the born-again experience was the post-Christian mindset in its presupposition that those born into a Christian society are not necessarily believers. Each person has to decide for Christ. People could be outside of salvation even though they have lived in Christian communities all their lives. American evangelical Christianity has been effective because it unwittingly assumed this post-Christian mindset.

But American evangelicalism has fallen into error by taking advantage of its majority status for political purposes. This error has given them a bad reputation around the world. Constituting the majority in certain parts of America, as the term "Moral Majority" implied, they felt justified in pushing conservative political and social agenda. The rest of the world is probably perplexed by the identification of the evangelical voice with the Republican agenda. As a result, those who object to the Republican politics must also object to the evangelical agenda.

By their action, the American evangelical Christians repudiated the separation of the church and state, the very foundation of religious liberty in America. They seemed to believe that, by organizing a Christian lobby, they can usher in the kingdom of God in America. By bringing back the Bible to public school education, they seem to think that they can win young people's minds. By outlawing abortion and gay marriage, they seem to believe that they can establish God's righteousness in America. This thought is pride and error. The law of the civil state cannot establish the kingdom and his righteousness. Such a method had been tried in Europe in the past and failed. Instead of accomplishing the intended religious purposes, the conservative evangelicals are only dividing America—between the Blue States and the Red States. They are also driving people away from Christianity. They will cancel out, by the loss of an untold number of people from church, the gains they hope to get by outlawing abortion and gay marriage.

The evangelicals' error in America is believing they can, and must, go back to the pre-post-Christian society. But such a society does not exist. The New England colonies were religiously organized. But such organizations ended with the foundation of the United States. The evangelicals' attempt to use their number and political power to push their religious agenda is ineffective and counterproductive. It is an attempt to use the power of the flesh, instead of the power of the Spirit. Coupled with the post-9.11 patriotism, American right-wing evangelicals' zeal seems to border on fanaticism. This form of Christianity does not provide a viable alternative to post-Christian Europe.

Can a Person Be a Christian without Going to Church?

Can Christianity exist without the church? No one would ask this question in the past when Christianity and the church were considered one and the same. But in present-day Europe, where the average church attendance is below 5 percent of the population, we must ask whether Christianity can survive without the church. Christianity does not equal the church, and the church does not equal Christianity. Christianity is bigger than the churches. We cannot correctly estimate the number of Christians in society just from the number of regular church attendees.

Not attending church does not automatically make a person an unbeliever. Between Christianity and church, which is having a tougher time in the western world?

General Douglas MacArthur was supposedly a devout Christian, even though he did not attend church. After he became the Consul of Japan, he hoped that Japan would become a Christian country believing that Christian principles gave moral force to the defeat of Japan and were the key to Allied policies.[2] What is interesting was that he did not consider attending church as a requirement of faith for him. Was it a coincidence that the non-church movement gained popularity in Japan?

Why someone does not want to go to church even though he is a believer is not difficult to imagine.[3] Churches cannot measure up to what people expect from Jesus Christ. It is an unfortunate fact. All churches are gatherings of imperfect people. One can be hurt by pastors or people in the pews. Unless a person has a stable relationship with Jesus on his own, he will be disappointed by the imperfect representation of Jesus's love by church-goers.

The gap between those who profess faith and those who attend church is wide. Let us take the example of Germany. As of December 2018, the Evangelische Kirche in Deutschland had 22.2 million members. Of this number, 3.2 percent of the members, approximately 684,000, went to church, according to the latest EKD report.[4] The Roman Catholics of Germany fare better, with about 9.3 percent of them attending the Sunday mass.[5] The statistics of other western European nations vary, but compared to the number of people who consider themselves believing Christians, the number of those regularly attending church is significantly low in western Europe as a whole.

Only God knows who true believers are. True faith does not necessarily translate into church attendance. While Christianity includes church, church is not Christianity by itself. Before Barnabas took Paul to Antioch, Paul practiced his faith without church attendance during his self-imposed exile in Tarsus. There was no church at Tarsus, to begin with. Christianity had not been spread to even Antioch yet. Paul probably spent a significant period of time praying, meditating, and studying on

---

2. Chadwick, *Christian Church in the Cold War*, 4.
3. Jackson, *Loving God when You Don't Love the Church*.
4. "More Than 220,000 People Left the Protestant Church of Germany," para. 7.
5. "More Than 220,000 People Left the Protestant Church of Germany," para. 11.

his own without being involved with church activities. Only at Antioch, Paul began to be involved with local church ministry actively.

Attending church is not like getting a job or going to school. One can work anywhere to make a living. One can go to any school to pursue his studies. But attending a church requires more than just necessity and opportunity. It involves the sense of belonging and a personal touch. People do not like to go to church where they do not know anyone. Church is like a home. Unless one has family living with him, he does not call his place of residence home.

As a result, many young people stop going to church once they move out of home. In university towns, there are hundreds, and even thousands of young people who used to go to church when they were living at home, but now that they are away from home, do not go to church anymore. That does not mean that they stopped believing. It just means that they have not connected meaningfully with a new church in new surroundings. Church affiliation and attendance were more secure and stable when people were living in pre-modern times. The concept of parish does not apply when schooling, employment, and urbanization frequently move people from one place to another. The number of church-goers is lower in big cities like New York City because many residents are transitioning.

It is with good reason that Jesus said that whoever does the will of God was his brother, sister, and mother (Matt 12:50). Unless someone cares for an unchurched person like a brother or a sister, he will not consider attending that church. A person can attend a Christian conference or a revival meeting alone if it is for a short duration. But making a church one's home requires a long-term commitment, which is impossible without a warm human connection. It is especially difficult for young single people to make that kind of relationship. A young woman can be kind to a young man only up to a certain extent, and vice versa, whereas married couples can express kindness to other couples more naturally.

Going to church is not just a spiritual endeavor, but a sociological and psychological act. Certain conditions must be met for people to attend church for a long duration. Even those who attend church for a long time need changes from time to time. From my thirty years of experience as a pastor, I have observed that people do not stay in the same church indefinitely. Like natural seasons, church involvement seems to have various seasons. Some churches have a quicker metabolism than others. No one church can meet all the needs of the seasons. The traditional parish system is ineffective in dealing with this fact. People move from one church to another, and sometimes move from church attendance to non-attendance and vice versa. Marriage and family seem to play a significant role in church attendance as young people get married and have families. The need to teach religious values to children is a significant factor in choosing a church. When a person gets divorced, it affects church attendance almost immediately. The death of a wife affects the widower's church involvement, whereas the death of a husband does not seem to affect the widow's church involvement. Abrupt changes in financial situation also affect church attendance. Most people stop going to church when unfortunate events occur in their personal or family lives. That is not because they stop believing, but because they are uncomfortable disclosing their private affairs to others.

Occasionally people have unhappy experiences at church. There are myriads of possible things that can hurt people's feelings. Sometimes it is the pastor's fault. Other times it is someone else's fault. And sometimes, it is the immaturity and unreasonable expectations of the victim. As long as human beings attend churches, there will always be possibilities of unhappy experiences. But churches are not the only places where people can be hurt. Families can hurt people, too. Although nothing can replace family, even homes can be dangerous places for people. Therefore, blaming the church is not always fair.

When Christians make horizontal moves from one church to another, it is because they had some unhappy experiences in previous churches. Trouble arises when people do not make horizontal moves but stop going to church. The benefit of megachurches is that people can become anonymous in the crowd. People want to go to church without exposing their personal lives. Caring for newcomers does not require interrogations about their personal lives—especially about their marital status and prior church attendance.

In many cases, newcomers are not necessarily new Christians. Requiring newcomers to go through a new believer's course is not a good idea. Helping them to adapt to the new church community is necessary, but one should not presume that they are new believers.

Bringing unchurched people to church is always a priority of the church's ministry. But keeping the people who are already there is just as important. Who is responsible when a church member stops coming to church? Is it the member's fault, or the pastor's responsibility? One cannot blame a person for not wanting to go to church. A church is a voluntary organization. A person must like to attend. It is the responsibility of the pastor to help people want to keep attending church. How can he do that? He can do that by making church attendance useful and beneficial. There is no other way. That does not mean that the pastor must make worship services entertaining. The world provides far more entertaining events. Churches cannot compete with the world for a better entertainment value. What people look for in a church is not entertainment. What people look for in a church is a glimpse of God. If a pastor can help people catch a glimpse of God during a worship service, he is successful at his task.

The popularity of charismatic churches stems from people's expectation that the gifts of the Holy Spirit will offer the proof of God. The gifts of the Holy Spirit can certainly help. But there are certain limitations. First, it is up to God to decide what gifts he will make available. A church's charismatic orientation does not guarantee signs and wonders. The Holy Spirit is shy of publicity. There is a Korean proverb that says, "Famous banquets have few worthwhile dishes." When public attention focuses on a particular movement, the Holy Spirit seems to quietly exit the stage. Having a reputation for spiritual power tends to force ministers to shout louder and try harder to prove that they have the Holy Spirit. Nevertheless, human zeal cannot substitute for the Holy Spirit.

The second limitation is that, contrary to many people's impression, catching a glimpse of God does not require glitzy signs and wonders. God is not stingy, nor is he a respecter of persons. God does not favor certain denominations or ministry styles over others. Christ loves all his church. All denominations, traditions, and forms of ministry can help people catch a glimpse of God.

In Germany, the most popular Christian events are church music concerts. In one year alone, Germans held more than sixty-five thousand Christian concerts. The second most popular Christian events are theological lectures and seminars—more than thirty-two thousand events a year. These statistics show that German people feel religious inspirations from music the most, and then from theological discourse.

A low church attendance rate, therefore, does not necessarily indicate a low interest in Christianity. This is a fact whether we like it or not. Those who want to serve Christ in this post-Christian society must learn to work with that. As stated above, Christianity includes the church, but the church is not Christianity by itself. Christianity is larger than the church. Those who hope to preach the gospel must work both in and out of the local church. Jesus wants the church to be an instrument of the kingdom of God, not a hindrance. If our efforts to touch the world with the gospel end at the level of local churches, we are not taking full advantage of the potential of the gospel.

Nonetheless, Christianity cannot continue without churches. When Apostle Paul went to Caesarea during his third missionary journey, he greeted the church (Acts 18:22). Many readers of the Bible miss the significance of such a passage. It means more than a casual greeting. Paul was genuinely concerned about the condition of the church there. He did not inquire into the state of Christianity, but the church. Inquiring into the condition of Christianity is too vague. It is amorphous. The state of the church demonstrates the state of Christianity. To know how Christianity is doing, one has to look into how churches are doing. Wherever churches prosper, Christianity prospers. Wherever churches are doing poorly, Christianity is weak. Jesus does not build Christianity, but church. He said, "I will build my church." Without the success of local churches, no country can expect the Christian faith to prosper there. Though many people are critical of churches, they cannot do without them. Instead of being critical of churches, they must try to build better churches.

Some people say that they love Christianity, but not the church. It is understandable why they would feel that way. However, we cannot build the Christian faith without building churches. The Holy Spirit works with churches to spread the faith in society. The key to resurrecting Christianity in Europe is to strengthen and revitalize local churches. To restore our faith in Christianity, we need to recover our faith in the value and mission of the church.

Should Christianity Be Reinvented in the Postmodern Era?

Some people think that Christianity must be reinvented in the post-Christian era to become more relevant and appealing. Such an idea is not new. Many attempts have been made to reinvent Christianity in the past.

Thomas Jefferson, one of the Founding Fathers of America, published his own version of the Bible. Conservative Christians criticize Jefferson for reducing the Bible to a book of ethics, but his intention was to make the Bible relevant and credible to the Enlightenment man. He felt that the miracle stories in the Bible kept the Enlightenment man away from the Bible. To reintroduce the Bible to the modern man, he collected only the ethical teachings of Jesus, believing that those teachings would be more relevant to people. But the Jefferson Bible failed to accomplish its purpose. Once a man begins to decide what is and is not credible in the Bible, man becomes his judge of the word of God. In trying to make the Bible more credible, Thomas Jefferson ended up making it more incredible.

Universalism/Unitarianism was another attempt at reinventing Christianity. Universalists tried to remove controversial elements from Christianity and make it appealing to all people. They thought that doctrines like hell and the judgment kept people away from Christianity. For this reason, they removed all exclusive claims in the Bible and taught that everyone would ultimately be saved. This was a noble attempt, except that it turned Christianity into a very tasteless, colorless, and bland religion with little appeal to any. Espousing empty doctrines could not meet people's spiritual needs. Also, if anyone is going to be saved regardless, why bother attending Universalist/Unitarian churches?

The monastic movement in the middle ages was another attempt to reinvent Christianity by returning to the original spirit of poverty, chastity, and humility. Pope Innocent III dreamt of a mendicant who was buttressing the collapsing wall of the church, and the man in his dream was Saint Francis. The debt that the Catholic Church owes to the monastic orders is enormous.

The Protestant Reformation was a major effort to reinvent Christianity by restoring the doctrinal truth of the gospel. As Saint Francis buttressed the collapsing church, saving it from collapse, the Reformation also bolstered the collapsing Christianity. The spirit of Reformation is still alive in Christendom.

Evangelicalism was an attempt to reinvent Christianity in the twentieth century. It has indeed saved Christianity from degenerating into liberalism. But its emphasis on personal salvation shifted the focus of Christianity away from the teachings and spirit of Jesus Christ.

The Jesus People movement was another recent attempt to reinvent Christianity. It was in defiance to the bourgeois Christianity as depicted pejoratively in the film *The Graduate* and Simon and Garfunkel's song *Mrs. Robinson*. The counterculture movement of American young people in pursuit of peace and love found their hero in the person of Jesus Christ. Jesus was the most counter-establishment personification of peace and love with immense appeal to young people. Those who became Christians during this youth revival were called Jesus People. They believed in returning to the life of simplicity and community. This movement had a powerful impact on evangelical Christianity worldwide but gradually disappeared as the Jesus people grew old and mainstream.

The non-church movement of Japan was another attempt at reinventing Christian practice away from the obese institutionalized churches. By making Christianity lean and unfettered, the followers of the non-church movement tried to offer an alternative to the churches' excesses. The shortcoming of the non-church movement was that it reduced the visibility of Christianity in a society where the presence of Christianity was already small. It does not fit well with cultures with a large presence of churches like the US The majority of Christians are not independent-minded but are instead dependent on powerful ministers and institutions. Nonetheless, the non-church movement may be effective in societies with high resistance to Christianity like Muslim countries and China.

Sometimes, attempts to reinvent Christianity resulted in false religions and cults. Mormonism claimed to be God's alternative to the existing churches that had fallen into apostasy, but Mormonism itself was a great apostasy and heresy.

No religion in the world has been adopted, experimented with, and reinterpreted more than Christianity. This fact alone shows the depth of resourcefulness of Christianity. No other religion would have survived the kind of scrutiny and experiment to which Christianity has been subjected.

No man has the authority to reinvent Christianity. It would be like trying to reinvent the wheel. It is redundant. No one can invent a program to renew Christianity because the program already exists.[6] Anyone who claims to have reinvented Christianity is either a false prophet or a heretic. Jesus accomplished the task of saving humanity, and no one can either add to it or subtract from it.

Has Christianity Outlived Its Usefulness?

Some people may compare Christianity to the fuel tank of a rocket booster. After propelling a rocket to a certain height, the fuel tank has outlived its purpose and is ejected. Likewise, some people argue that Christianity has contributed to lifting the western civilization to a certain height. Now that it has done its job, it is no longer needed—so they say. This argument assumes two things. First, it assumes that Christianity played an

---

6. Sarah and Diat, *Day Is Now Far Spent*.

essential role in bringing western civilization to a certain height. Second, it assumes that western civilization knows where it is going from hereon and how it will get there. An important question would be what aspect of Christianity played the role of the rocket booster. If Christianity was powerful enough to bring the west to this point, does it not prove its truth and validity?

The argument that Christianity has outlived its usefulness is similar to the nine lepers' thinking that they did not need Jesus anymore since they were healed. When they were ill, Jesus was of great use to them, but now that they became healthy, they can do without him. In theory, this reasoning is correct—if leprosy is the only thing to worry about. But there are other problems in life. If Jesus could heal them from leprosy, he can heal them from other illness in the future.

When a person was a sinner, Jesus was of great help to him, but now that he has been forgiven, he can do without Jesus. This reasoning may be correct in theory but is entirely devoid of any affection, gratitude, and loyalty. In *Kingdom of Heaven*,[7] a Crusader knight fights off a belligerent Arab warrior in the desert, killing him in a duel. As a result, the Arab warrior's slave obtains freedom. The slave owes his freedom to the Crusader knight and vows to serve him. But the knight does not need a slave and so lets him go. It turns out that the slave was, in reality, a nobleman and a confidant of Saladin, and many years hence, he pays back his debt to the Crusader knight by saving his life from danger. In this film narrative, we find the model of a true master and a faithful servant. The master does not lord over the servant whom he has freed. Nor does the servant insist on his freedom. They respect each other implicitly. In them, we discover archetypes of truly mature and noble human beings.

Anyone has a right to leave the person who has won him freedom. The right to leave is an integral part of freedom. If one cannot leave, one is not free. But the purpose of human existence is not only to be free, but to live as a decent human being. The purpose of freedom is not to do whatever one wants. That is closer to licentiousness than freedom. The goal of freedom is to be able to love genuinely. Christ freed us from the law not so that we can live after the flesh but so that we can serve one another in love (Gal. 5:13). Love is the supreme achievement of freedom. Sometimes love enables a person to sacrifice himself. There is no greater love than to lay down one's life for one's friends (John 15:13). Such an act of sacrifice

---

7. Scott, *Kingdom of Heaven*.

is not obligatory but voluntary. Humanity admires such a display of love as noble and praiseworthy.

Ecclesiology in the Post-Christian Era

The book of Revelation is not an obvious place for people to look for ecclesiological ideas. But there is a helpful insight into ecclesiology in the messages to the seven churches. The Holy Spirit warns that, unless churches repent, he will take away their golden lampstands (Rev 2:5). What do the golden lampstands represent, and what does it mean that the Holy Spirit will take them away? It must represent the life and power of the church. If the Lord takes them away, it means that the churches will lose their life and power. The external institution may remain, but the life and power will be gone. The danger of losing the lampstand exists today.

Christianity cannot be reinvented, but churches can. Although Jesus Christ is the same yesterday, today, and forever, the church can improve its representation of Christ to the current generation. When churches can adapt, they prosper. When they do not, they dwindle. If the church's tradition and history stand in the way of innovation, they are excess baggage. Christianity's truth and power reside in the word of God and the Holy Spirit, not in the tradition and history. When the disciples called Jesus's attention to the grand buildings of the temple of Jerusalem, Jesus was not impressed. He bluntly replied that not one stone would be left on another, and every one would be thrown down (Matt 24:1-2). If Jesus was not impressed with the tradition of Judaism at that time, he is not impressed with the tradition of Christianity at this time. What matters is the grace of God for each moment. The Israelites gathered the manna for each day; the Lord gave them bread for every day. They could not eat manna from even a day before because it would spoil. Likewise, God's grace is new every morning. We cannot depend on yesterday's manna. We must pray for bread for this day.

Church members vote with their feet. This is truer among Protestant churches than Catholic churches. When members like what they see and hear at church, they will keep coming. But if they do not like it, they will leave. This freedom of movement looks selfish to the clergy, but it is a fact of life. If a person likes what the church must give him, there is nothing that will keep him away. On the other hand, if a person does not feel that he is getting anything, there is nothing that will make him come back. People say that three things lead to church growth. First, people should not fall asleep during sermons. Second, they must come back the following Sunday. And third, they should bring their friends.

It is easier said than done. The crisis of Christianity in Europe, though, is not as complicated as we fear. What is the exact nature of the problem? Are people who drift away from churches also drifting away from Christianity? Or are they drifting away primarily from local churches? This is the crucial question that we have to answer.

Return to the Original Priority

The priority of the early church ministry was preaching the gospel. That is what the apostles did. The apostles appointed the seven deacons so that they could devote themselves to the ministry of the word and prayer (Acts 6:3–4). Staring churches was almost an afterthought to the apostles. Preaching the gospel had absolute priority. On the day of Pentecost, Peter preached the gospel, and the Jerusalem church came into being as a result. At Cornelius's house, Peter preached the gospel, and Cornelius's household turned into a church. Paul preached the gospel to Lydia, and her home became the church of Philippi. In all these instances, staring a church was an afterthought. The apostles preached the word of God and churches came into existence as a consequence. That is the reason that preaching has priority in Christian ministry.

Even though many Christians consider themselves servants of the Lord, not many consider themselves servants of the gospel. It is a strange phenomenon that not all those who claim to serve the Lord also serve the gospel. Apostle Paul called himself both. He referred to himself as "a servant of Christ Jesus, called to be an apostle and set apart for the gospel of God" (Rom 1:1). How many ministers today can confidently say that they have been set apart for the gospel? The reason that many churches have lost spiritual conviction is understandable: servants of the Lord lost confidence in their calling for the gospel. Preaching the gospel constitutes the central part of serving Jesus.

It is unfortunate that we must distinguish evangelical churches from non-evangelical churches. Why should "evangelical" be a separate label? All churches must be evangelical; they must emphasize the salvation of souls through the gospel. Otherwise, they are not faithful to Jesus Christ.

Many pastors possess this evangelistic zeal when they start their careers but lose it somewhere along the line. They must go back and find it.

When churches reverse the priorities, they lose power. According to Hendrikus Berkhof, the missionary task of the church was given a low priority in favor of the pastoral and traditional character of the church.[8] Scholars argue that the rise of the Constantinian church eclipsed the missionary purpose that had been the intention of Jesus.[9] After Emperor Constantine adopted Christianity, the church and state formed an alliance. As institutions of the state religion, the church became part of the status quo. As the institution of the state religion, the church became part of the status quo. In the process, the church lost its missionary drive in the world.[10] The Protestant Reformation did not correct this error of the church. Assuming that Europe was already a Christian civilization, the Protestant churches engaged in missionary activities only outside the European territory.[11]

Preaching constitutes the first responsibility of a pastor. No other function can take the place of preaching. Those who protest, "Love is more important than speaking in the tongues of men and angels," are confusing the scripture. Paul was not proposing love as an alternative to preaching. A minister is not exempted from the duty of preaching if he practices love. Paul preached harder than anyone else. A minister's most important place of service is his pulpit. He should expect the Holy Spirit to work most strongly from the pulpit.

If he does that, everything else will fall into place. Church members will be blessed, leading to the growth of faith, more participation, more offerings, and service. If a pastor tries to motivate greater participation and service from his congregation while neglecting the ministry of the word, it will not work. There is little grace of God where the word of God is neglected. We must remember that faith comes from hearing the word of God.

Ministers Should Be Faithful to Their Gifts and Calling

The priesthood of all believers does not negate special gifts and calling from God. Releasing the laity for ministry does not mean that anyone

---

8. Shenk, "New Wineskins for New Wine," 73.
9. Shenk, "New Wineskins for New Wine," 73.
10. Shenk, "New Wineskins for New Wine," 74.
11. Shenk, "New Wineskins for New Wine," 74.

can do the works of the ministry. One does not choose to serve Jesus, but Jesus chooses his servants (John 15:16). In that sense, the kingdom of God is not a democracy. Theologians who advocate a more democratic form of ecclesiology must clarify their motives: do they want the democratization of the church or the revival of the church?

Leonard Boff points out the "oppressive" nature of the traditional priest-episcopal-papal structure where a church community is divided between rulers and the governed, celebrants and onlookers, producers, and consumers of sacraments.[12] He reminds us that the Early Church was based on grassroots movements empowered by the Holy Spirit. Boff's analysis is correct. And it is significant because it comes from a Catholic theologian. Many Christians have raised the same point regarding church structure. Many of the vibrant churches employ the laity's active participation in leading small groups and praying for one another.

But Boff cannot deny that the rapidly growing churches in North America, Asia, South America, and Africa have certain firm hierarchies within their church structure. One undeniable factor in the growth of churches is the presence of gifted and capable pastors. The priesthood of all believers cannot replace competent leaders. The Holy Spirit gives each one gifts as he determines, but he does not distribute gifts equally. The callings of God are not equal for all people, either. Not all people are apostles, prophets, or teachers. The priesthood of all believers cannot negate this fact. Those who want to do new ecclesiology cannot work against this fact.

Furthermore, not every Christian is equally dedicated to the kingdom of God. The Pareto Principle seems to apply to church congregations: twenty percent of the people do that 80 percent of the work. Not all church members are willing to participate in the ministry of a local church beyond the role of onlookers and consumers. It is not always their fault. Some preachers have exceptional abilities for ministry and are in big demand. If gifted people can perform exceptional work, what reason do we have to refuse them? Moses, Elijah, and Elisha all exercised charismatic leadership. So did Peter and Paul in the New Testament. Peter's spiritual authority was so strong that sick people hoped even Peter's shadow would fall on them so that they could get well. Handkerchiefs and aprons were taken from Paul's body and laid on sick people to heal

---

12. Boff, *Ecclesiogenesis*.

them. God did not remove the role of powerfully gifted people in the New Testament.

We believe in discipleship and equipping the saints. But long experience tells us that gifted and capable people are rare. They seem to be born rather than made. Though we emphasize nurture, we cannot deny nature. Many churches try to teach spiritual gifts and ministry skills to the congregation in the hope that many people will rise to fill spiritual leadership positions. But the progress is slow.

The priesthood of all believers is on the right track. Democratic principles must apply to church polity so that church finance can be transparent to the congregation. Without a system of responsible accountability, churches fall into financial and doctrinal errors with no one to stop them. If Catholic churches had the lay oversight of priests, the clergy malpractice problems would have stopped long ago.

Accountability and transparency are necessary, but so is the need for powerful ministers. European theologians examining the immigrant pentecostal churches in Europe often point out the pastors' authoritarianism. Those theologians have a point. We must remember, however, that Christianity began with the tremendous spiritual authority of the apostles and deacons. It was necessary to establish the Christian faith on a firm foundation and protect it from heresy and false prophets.

Some aspects of the apostles' spiritual authority offend our modern sensibilities. How would we respond if the Ananias and Sapphira incident happened today instead of two thousand years ago? What about Apostle Paul speaking to Elymas the magician so sternly that Elymas became blind in front of him? If strong spiritual leadership was necessary then, it is still necessary today. Apostle Paul earnestly admonished Timothy to be a strong and effective leader. He reminded him that we did not receive the spirit of fear, but of power, love, and sound mind. A leader is not a leader unless he or she exercises leadership. There are many styles of leadership, such as equipping leadership and servant leadership. People hope that these versions are alternatives to authoritarian leadership. There is a difference between authoritarian leadership and authoritative leadership. We cannot throw the baby out with the bathwater. Reforming the church cannot do away with the authoritative leadership of pastors. Soldiers in trenches need strong leadership. Otherwise, they die. The same principle applies to churches.

Lay Participation in the Ministry Does Not Do Away with Competent Clergy

The priesthood of all believers is overrated and too vague to tell us how it works in reality. It states that the laity can be turned from a passive to an active role, from being spectators to participants, from being consumers to servants in the local church's ministry. In the New Testament churches, the concept of discipleship comes closest to the idea of the priesthood of all believers. Jesus made disciples and commanded them to make more disciples. A disciple is a person who is can do the same work as his mentor. Jesus summed up this principle in the following words: "Whoever believes in me will also do the works that I do" (John 14:12). A true disciple is theoretically able to take the place of his teacher.

But true disciples are few. Though Elijah had many student prophets under him, only Elisha inherited his mentor's cloak and spiritual authority. The rest of the prophets only wanted from across the river. Jesus had twelve disciples, but the Acts records the ministry of only a few of them—Peter, James, and John. As for the rest, Acts does not mention where they went and what they did. Instead, Acts introduces new persons who seemed to have played more significant roles than the unmentioned apostles in the early church, such as Stephen, Philip, Paul, Barnabas, Silas, and Timothy. Singlehandedly evangelizing Samaria and baptizing the first gentile believer, Philip was like an apostle even though he was a deacon.

Apostle Paul trained many people during his missionary journeys, but often he said that all had left, and only a few were staying with him (2 Tim 4:11). Many are invited, but few are chosen (Matt 22:14). The harvest is plentiful, but the workers are few (Luke 10:2). The priesthood of all believers does not mean that all believers can equally share the work of the ministry. Using this slogan does not magically increase the number of faithful volunteers.

Protestants consider the priesthood of all believers as a badge of Protestantism. But the more Protestant churches enjoy church growth, the more they depend on a small number of highly gifted pastors. Large Protestant churches all tend to center around a few charismatic pastors. The charismatic role of the pastor is vital for church growth.[13] In that sense, it is difficult for laypeople to participate in the actual ministry of the church because they can hardly match the pastors in terms of spiritual giftedness and power.

---

13. Wagner, *Your Spiritual Gifts*, 137–38.

Large churches tend to attract people who like to take comfort in the shadow of larger-than-life pastors. Sunday services of megachurches, whether in America or any part of the world, tend to be professionally produced entertainment featuring fancy bands, singers, and dynamic preachers. As a result, the larger the church, the more unlikely it is for the laity to participate in central ministry.

Even in churches that try to give ministry opportunities to laypeople, such opportunities are reserved for exceptionally gifted individuals, making the ministry an even more exclusive domain. Ordinary people in the pews cannot attempt to imitate them. For example, Vineyard Christian Fellowship distinguished itself from typical churches by vowing to equip the laity for ministry. Nonetheless, those who could pray for people during the "ministry times" were individuals with extraordinary spiritual gifts. They were not just looking for people to sing in choirs or to take care of preschool children. Instead, they were looking for people who could prophesy and cast out demons. Not every church member can do that. They were looking for exceptional gifts from people, which were rare. Not even ordinary pastors can prophesy and heal the sick like that. By trying to equip the laity for the works of ministry, Vineyard Christian Fellowship made it much more exclusive and off-limits to the vast majority of Christians. This is an ironic result. Allowing the Holy Spirit to appoint and use people to do exceptionally spiritual ministry narrows the pool of available people, not widens it. Although Vineyard proposed a novel idea, it could not be replicated everywhere. Given the nature of spiritual gifts, when someone with exceptional gifts appears, those with smaller gifts tend to step back. At least the congregation prefers someone with more noticeable gifts. The congregation tends to put the spotlight on "stars."

Therefore, we should read Ephesians 4:11–13 with a grain of salt. Many excitedly wanted to emphasize that the purpose of apostles, prophets, evangelists, pastors, and teachers was to prepare God's people for works of service. They emphasized preparing or equipping people for works of ministry. They have a point. But that does not mean that the equipped saints will replace the apostles, prophets, evangelists, pastors, and teachers. The charismatic churches that emphasized the equipping of the saints produced the ironic result of reinforcing the offices of apostles and prophets. While claiming that laypeople must be equipped, they wanted to claim that they were apostles and prophets. Toward the end of John Wimber's career at Vineyard, for example, putting star prophets like Paul Cain and the Kansas City prophets on the pedestal was a deviation from the original vision of the Vineyard movement. Placing the emphasis on the spiritual makes for an exciting and dynamic ministry, but it does not necessarily widens the pool of ministers and leaders. Instead, the majority of people step back in awe. The so-called signs and wonders ministry can accentuate the spectator mentality of church services.

One old pastor reflected in his essays that geniuses are rare among believers, and believers are rare among geniuses.[14] Not many Christians are frank enough to make such a statement. Jesus lamented the lack of workers, although the harvest is plentiful. Jesus also lamented his disciples' inability to perform necessary tasks well. What churches desperately need are believers who are also highly gifted. Christians easily give up looking for geniuses on the pretext that God chooses the foolish to shame the wise (1 Cor 1:27–31). Christians almost require Christian workers to be imperfect so that they may give credit to God. There is a difference between being imperfect and incompetent. King David was a flawed man but was nonetheless a genius. The Renaissance artists were devout men; they were at the same time geniuses. Without their ingenuity, the Renaissance would not have been possible. Bach and Handel were all faithful people, but also musical prodigies.

Ministry suffers when churches begin to distance themselves from gifted people on the pretext of humility. The secular world attracts the most talented people in music, art, literature, film, entertainment, academics, science, technology, finance, and all the other conceivable endeavors. But churches consider such selectivity to be secular and proud. How do churches expect to compete with the world for the hearts and minds of people in that way? If churches want to win back the hearts and minds of people in the twenty-first century, churches need the most talented and gifted workers possible. The brightest graduates from top universities should be encouraged to consider careers in the Christian ministry. We need the most talented people to make church music. We also need the best literary minds to write scripts for Christian plays and literature. Every good and perfect gift is from above (Jas 1:17). We need to use all the good and perfect gifts from God to edify the church and preach the gospel. Anything short of it is doing a disservice to God. If recruiting talented people costs money, churches should be willing to foot the bill. Artists and musicians spend much money and time building

---

14. Lee, *Geniuses without Faith*, 28.

their skills and deserve to be fairly compensated for their abilities and churches should not be stingy about it.

What Will Draw People to Church?

The spiritual condition of Europe is more complicated than it seems because the empty pews do not necessarily represent the lack of faith. While the church attendance rate stays at 5 percent, the proportion of the population expressing religious belief is 50 percent, which suggests that a high percentage of people believe but do not attend church.[15] The condition of Christianity does not correspond with the situation of the church. But this fact clarifies the task of the church. Not all those who are unchurched are unbelievers. Reviving Christianity involves drawing unchurched believers to church.

When I was a college freshman, there was a big convocation at the university chapel on the first Sunday of a new school year. People in academic robes filed into the sanctuary in a procession resembling a commencement. The president of the university, the late A. Bartlett Giamatti, was one of them. The chaplain of the university turned to the president during the sermon and expressed his wish to see him more often on Sundays. The president squirmed in his seat while the congregation chuckled. But as far as I remember, the president never showed up again for the rest of the academic year. If the university chapel services were boring for me, they would have been boring for him, too. It might have helped if President Giamatti preached at the university chapel instead of the university chaplain. Mr. Giamatti's theology might not have been as informed as the chaplain, but he would have had no trouble attracting a crowd every Sunday. It was not as if the university community was not interested in religious issues because the chapel was packed when the German theologian Hans Küng came to speak at Yale. More people are interested in Christianity than we realize, although that number does not necessarily translate to church attendance. Churches have much work to do.

Attempting to get people into church buildings has led some churches to hold raffle nights, youth dances, yoga classes, cooking schools, and other imaginable events. In the film *The Man Who Was Not There*, a black comedy depicting a modern man's alienation, the protagonist drily narrates that he and his wife attend church usually on Tuesday nights—for

---

15. Kaufmann, "End of Secularization in Europe?," 85.

bingo games. In the film, attending bingo games at church accentuates the spiritual distance between the modern man and Christianity. It would have been better if the church did not hold such events. The familiarity of the church makes it even more irrelevant to unbelievers.

What will draw people to church for the right reasons? The presence of God in the church will. This is the only obvious answer. Because the church is supposed to be the house of God, it must maintain the minimum amount of holiness. Unwarranted familiarity with the church will only reduce its sacred nature. Jesus drove out money changers and cattle from the temple, saying, "My house shall be called the house of prayer" (Matt 21:13).

Pastor Jack Hayford of The Church on the Way recollects that, one Saturday evening, as he entered the sanctuary to turn the thermostat on, he saw some kind of mist within the sanctuary. He thought to himself, "There cannot be any mist inside of a building." Looking more carefully, he realized that it was not either mist or fog, but the presence of God.[16] The next morning, the church attendance doubled without any explanation. There were several times that God mystically manifested his presence to his church after that event.

What can we say? Christianity must be accompanied by mystical elements that can only be attributed to God. That does not mean that every pastor must witness the mysterious mist in the church building every Saturday evening. But every pastor must be able to say what Peter said to the man at the Gate Beautiful: "Silver and gold I have none. But what I have I give to you" (Acts 3:6). This is the role of a minister. Peter did not say, "what *we* have," but "what *I* have." On a personal level, every minister should have something to give to others. It may not be the same thing that other ministers have. It does not have to. But each minister has his unique gift. The better he is aware of his gift and role, the more effective he will be. If a minister is not sure of what he has to give to others, he has little to offer.

The film *The Exorcist* depicts a priest who is wrestling with his doubt. Though he is a psychiatrist and a well-educated man, he is also a helpless son of a slowly dying mother. The gradual dimming of his mother's consciousness eats away his faith. It is at this point that he is asked to perform an exorcism for the little girl Regan. There is very little he can do for her because he is wrestling with his own demons. The demon inside

---

16. Dart, "His Way."

Regan knows this fact and mocks the priest. The arrival of the more experienced priest, the exorcist, helps the younger priest to combat the evil spirit inside the young girl.[17] Sometimes, the stark spiritual condition of humanity makes us realize the true nature of our work and our need to be spiritually equipped. The demon inside the girl cannot be persuaded to leave. It must be chased out with spiritual authority. Therein lies the essence of Christian ministry. If we miss this essence, we miss everything.

People do not come to church to see the pastor. They come to meet God. They are not interested in the pastor's personal opinions or charming personality. They can find similar things elsewhere. What they expect from the pastor is to help them to experience God's love. Ultimately people are looking for God. A pastor cannot take God out of his pocket and give to people. That is not how it works. But he can help his flock to approach God in faith. When people feel that God is meaningfully present at church, they will fill the pews. God is the most precious asset of the church.

European pastors seem to be reluctant about the so-called marketplace of religion or spiritual consumerism. Secular scholars are better informed about the need for the marketplace than Christian pastors. Secular scholars know that lack of competition, mainly due to the state regulation of religion, deprives churches of spiritual vitality on account of scarcity, unpopularity, and clerical sloth.[18] The government funding of state churches may very well be the reason for the loss of churches' competitive spirit.[19] Christianity that triumphed over the Roman Empire was competitive, but the Christianity that came out of the Roman Empire was heavily dependent on state patronage.[20] Competition is necessary and healthy because it motivates pastors. People cannot be made to come to church; they must want to go to church. If religious marketing seems reprehensible to pastors, they can call it something else: competing for the minds of people. Although pastors are responsible for motivating people to want to come to church, they do it by presenting Jesus Christ to people. Jesus Christ has an irresistible appeal to any person, any time, anywhere. Instead of trying to get people to come to church, we must try to get Jesus into the church.

17. Friedkin, *Exorcist*.
18. Bruce, *God Is Dead: Secularization in the West*, 152.
19. Edwords, "Faith and Faithlessness by Generation."
20. Stark, "Secularization, R.I.P.," 260.

This is always the first spiritual task of each church. If people discover the trace of Jesus at church, they will want to come.

A Church Should Be Able to Disband and Restart

The Church of Jesus Christ on earth stands forever. Local churches, on the other hand, have natural life spans like people.[21] This is one of the most remarkable, surprising, and unpleasant aspects of the church growth theory. Just as a person grows into maturity, spends active years of productive service, retires from work, grows old, and eventually dies, a local church goes through similar stages. The difference is that while people die naturally, local churches refuse to die even though their lives have ended. The ability of churches to disband and restart according to needs is probably the most radical concept of the new church of the twenty-first century. This idea goes against the grain of traditional ecclesiology. The idea that churches should be able to disband at the right time is based on the theory that local churches have natural life spans. Churches without any visions, energy or strength to carry on the Great Commission effectively nonetheless remain out of the sense of duty. Such a sense of responsibility, though noble, is not effective for church growth or strength.

The non-church movement is attractive because it is free from organizational rules. Non-church movement has regular meetings and Bible studies like ordinary churches. It also has lay teachers who are theologically well trained. But it does not have a separate church building, and when a teacher dies, the gathering disbands. This is where the non-church movement differs from ordinary churches. Sometimes it will be better for the kingdom of God if congregations can dissolve—not reluctantly but voluntarily. Dismantling a church simply means that it has completed its job for an appointed time. Someone else can start a church elsewhere to begin a new necessary work more effectively without debts and obligations to the prior church.

Churches in the post-Christian era should not have too much attachment to buildings. New Christians should be able to exchange architectural esthetics with substance. When Jesus was teaching a multitude by the Sea of Galilee, he did not have expensive hardware that we take for

---

21. Saarinen, *Life Cycle of a Congregation*.

granted today. That did not stop him from doing the work of God. Early Christians traveled light. Buildings were afterthoughts to them.

Post-Christian churches can meet in coffee shops, living rooms, classrooms, and office conference rooms. Where two or more people gather in Jesus's name, Jesus is in their midst. Post-Christian churches should be light, mobile, and efficient. It does not cost an enormous amount of money to do the essential church ministry. Money is never a problem for the church. Perhaps too much money has been the problem. The Covid-19 pandemic has already made Christians worldwide experiment with small-group meetings at homes. Although they had to meet at homes out of the health necessity, they may find home churches to be viable alternatives to church-centered worship services in the future.

Making it easier for churches to disband and restart will lift the psychological burden and guilt from pastors and congregants. Disbanding an existing church does not mean that they have failed. It just means that they are relocating and regrouping. During the Battle of Midway, the command ship of the admiral-in-charge was hit by Japanese bombers and began to sink. According to the old naval tradition, the captain of a boat has to go down with the boat. But the admiral-in-command simply relocated to another ship. The battle was still going on, and he had to keep commanding—from another ship. Sinking of the command ship simply meant that the command ship suffered a loss, not that the battle was lost. We need this kind of flexibility about church ministry. We should not lament over empty cathedrals being sold off in European cities. It is not Christianity that is being sold off. The true church can meet elsewhere. Christianity is not tied to real estate. This is the liberty afforded in the post-Christian era.

Always Make the Messages Relevant

Preachers should present the same gospel with new perspectives to make it relevant to the audience. Instead of repeating the same old familiar doctrines, present variations of the theme which answer the contemporary audience's existential questions. If preachers repeat the same old doctrines, congregants will hear them not as "good news" but as "old news."[22] But the word of God is living and active, which means that each person can hear it as a personal word to him. Those who meditate on the Bible

---

22. Van de Poll, *Europe and the Gospel*, 279.

discover that familiar verses often present new, unexpected illuminations every time they read them. The Bible is not a list of dead religious rules but a living book. Preachers can present the living aspect of God's word to the audience so that the audience can feel that God is speaking to them through the preacher. The common characteristic of famous preachers everywhere is that the audience thinks that the message was tailor-made for them. Preachers did not prepare their messages with specific people in mind. Still, the Holy Spirit, who knows the personal situations of the sheep, gave insights to preachers. Preachers speaking under the illumination of the Holy Spirit can feel that their words are specially directed to someone, even though they may not know who.

Church's messages should correlate with the questions in people's hearts. They may not want to hear how their sins can be forgiven so that they can go to heaven. But they may be interested in hearing what Jesus has to say about the temptations they are struggling with. If the church does not believe that Jesus has anything valuable to say to people, the church has nothing to offer them. To be relevant to post-Christian Europe, the church must believe that Christ has something valuable and pertinent to give to the world. Perhaps the seeker-sensitive approach adopted by Willow Creek Church offers a new alternative to the messages of the new European church. Ministers need to believe that the Father has something precious to give to those who ask him. This faith makes all the difference in the world.

Denominations in the Global Era

Until mixed martial art tournaments became popular, traditional martial arts insisted on their unique styles and traditions. There were many traditions—karate, kung fu, taekwondo, jujitsu, judo, Muay Thai, and traditional boxing. All of them kept their mystical allure until fighters from various martial art backgrounds began to test their skills with one another in the octagon. In the octagon, fighters realized that they needed roughly the same skills to overpower their opponents: punching, kicking, and wrestling. It does not matter what martial arts traditions they come from. They all need to make those basic moves well to win. As a result, regardless of their background, they all adopted a similar method of fighting. Some fighters lean more on traditional boxing skills, while other fighters employ more kicks. Eventually, though, they must wrestle on the floor where jujitsu skills seem to rule. Sophisticated kicks that once appealed to people did not seem to be all that useful in actual fighting situations.

Denominations are like those diverse martial arts. Although they come from different theological and liturgical backgrounds, they all need the same skills to be effective in actual ministry. The commonly required skills are preaching, praying, and pastoring skills. Theological seminaries and Bible schools should equip their students to do these basic ministries well.

Theological distinctions seem to grow hazy in this age of denominational pluralism. Preachers do not follow the official theology of their denominations but the spiritual needs of their congregations. When a person listens to famous preachers on YouTube, he cannot tell their denominational background. A hearer cannot tell whether the preachers are Calvinist or Arminian. Sometimes hearers cannot even tell whether they are evangelical or mainline. After listening to a good sermon, one does not say, "That was a good Presbyterian sermon," or "That was a good Lutheran sermon." One simply says, "That was a good sermon." The best compliment will be, "That was truly a word from the Lord."

Worship styles are also becoming similar around the world. This trend does not only reflect theological changes but sociological changes—the need to be closer to the congregation. Seeker-sensitive orientation requires the pulpit to resemble a stage rather than a platform. Also, the traditional clergy vestments seem to lose meaning in an age where church-goers do not dress up in traditional Sunday clothes.

Church music is in transition. This transition reflects the public taste in music. The number of classical music majors is decreasing around the world. The number of organ majors is declining. Fewer churches are using hymn books. That does not mean that church music is becoming less sophisticated. People across cultures appreciate the power of sacred music. The future of church music will continue to need creativity and spirituality.

Church architecture is also changing. The most significant determinant of church architecture is money and space. New churches start in rented theaters or empty halls. When they grow and have more money, they build their buildings. But no church will intentionally go back to the old conventional church architecture, which placed the pulpit on the pedestal looking down on the congregation and the pews facing the pulpit form a long rectangle. The popular democratic sentiment will not allow it. Also, many people express doubt about spending so much money to build sanctuaries that are used only once a week. It seems to be an inefficient use of money and space. As a result, many church buildings double as school auditoriums or public culture centers.

In the past, denominational labels meant something to the public. Those were the times when the public identified with traditions. Those days are gone. Many churches are calling themselves community churches. Saddleback Community Church, for example, is originally Southern Baptist, but Rick Warren decided that the denominational label was irrelevant to the postmodern people. Bill Hybels, who was from the Christian Reformed Church, dropped the denominational name from Willow Creek Community Church. Chuck Smith, originally from the Four Square Church, dropped the denominational affiliation when he started the Calvary Chapel.

That does not mean that denominations are useless now. They are still relevant. Without denominational affiliations, it is impossible to tell if a church is a cult. To show that a church has a credible foundation, every pastor needs a denomination to back him up. Flocks have the right to ask where the minister went to seminary, where he was ordained, and what his theology is. If a pastor cannot answer any of these questions clearly, he is a suspect.

Denominations are here to stay for those reasons. But they will increasingly take the back seat in the postmodern era. Denominational names play minor roles when people are deciding where to go to church. People are looking for Jesus, not a denomination. Ministers' loyalty should be to Jesus first and foremost, not to their denominations. Those who demonstrate unusual dedication to their denominations are anachronistic. It is true ecumenism when ministers can trust one another and work together for a common goal. Institutional unity is not our goal, but the unity of purpose is.

— 11 —

A New Paradigm of World Mission

WHAT QUALIFIES A PERSON as a missionary necessarily involves crossing national, cultural, and linguistic boundaries away from his family and familiar surroundings to preach the gospel. According to this definition, international relief organizations do not qualify as mission agencies because they do not preach the gospel. The role of a missionary does not appear in the Bible. All the apostles and evangelists performed missionary tasks, but they were not called missionaries. Abraham can be construed as the first missionary in the Bible because he left his people and father's household to possess his inheritance in a foreign land. Joseph can also be considered as a missionary because he testified to Yahweh in an alien and gentile culture. The most characteristic missionary in the Old Testament was Jonah, and his counterpart in the New Testament is Paul.

Paul was a quintessential global citizen. He was a Christian intellectual, speaking multiple languages, well versed in Greek philosophy, and able to engage in scholarly discussion with learned people. He was capable of interpreting the gospel in ways that gentiles could understand. He was an Asian sent by the Lord to Europe to evangelize Europeans. His vision of the Macedonian man opened Paul's European missionary adventure.

Paul's paradigm of missionary work did not include additional activities like education, medical assistance, or economic relief. He did not consider his work to bring a more advanced form of culture or knowledge to less-developed nations. Europe in the first century AD was more advanced than Asia in terms of philosophy, culture, and political power. Alexander the Great had conquered the known world and imposed the

Hellenistic culture and language on his empire. Greek, as a result, was the language of the learned. The Roman Empire was the mighty political power ruling over the entire known world, including Judea at the time Jesus was born. When Paul brought the gospel to Macedonia, he was not going from a more advanced culture to a less advanced one. By all measures, Europe at that time was more advanced culturally and politically than Asia. Therefore, Paul did not bring with him any additional tools commonly found in missionary projects today: education, medical support, and economic relief. He did not go to a poor country to set up a school or dig up wells to help local people. He did not bring with him an advanced form of culture to help backward people. Paul had one purpose: preaching the gospel to get people to the faith in Jesus Christ.

The concept of modern missionary work is different. Missionaries go from rich countries to less well-off countries. Their work involves not only religious instruction, but also medical assistance, educational help, and economic aid. In the past, missionaries followed the colonizers to save the souls of "uncivilized" peoples. This concept of missionary work persists to this day. The 10/40 Window, located between ten and forty degrees north of the equator, has been the target of concentrated missionary effort. This region also includes some of the poorest nations in the world.

But the religious landscape of the twenty-first century requires a different paradigm. While the 10/40 Window still contains unreached countries, the most spiritually needy world falls outside the window. Christianity is no longer the religion of the rich and advanced nations. Instead, the meek of the world are inheriting the earth. The kind of help that the new mission fields require does not include extra help. They do not need medical aid or financial help. The focus is back on the gospel. In the past, when a western mission agency built a school in a mission field, many students were expected to embrace Christianity. When western mission agencies built a hospital in a mission field, it would have a tremendous evangelistic effect on the local population. This model does not apply to Europe, which already has excellent schools and hospitals. They do not need help in material terms. What they need is not more bread, but more of the word of God.

This is the first time such a situation has occurred in the history of Christianity. The paradigm of mission applicable to other parts of the world does not apply to western societies.[1] We need a new paradigm. That is also

---

1. Wrogemann, "Mission as Oikumenical Doxology," 60.

why the gospel must go around the world one more time. We need new methods of doing world missions. The new method is perhaps simpler and less cumbersome than the old method. It does not require much financial investment. It is more software-oriented than hardware-oriented. We need people who understand the postmodern western mindset and present the gospel message to those who are not necessarily unfamiliar with Christianity but drifted away from it. We need philosophers, psychologists, sociologists, authors, artists, musicians, journalists, opinion leaders, scholars, and media experts. We need people with spiritual insight and cultural insight—someone like Blaise Pascal, who was a mathematician and a Christian mystic. We need more Daniels—someone who was well versed in secular learning and able to interpret dreams and spiritual visions. Western civilization has reached the zenith of material advancement, but its spirit has become poor. Japheth needs the tents of Shem (Gen 9:27). Apostle Paul said his messages and preaching were not in words of human wisdom but the demonstration of the power of the Holy Spirit. Why do people think that they have to choose between intellect and spirituality?

Even though Europe was at one time the center of the western Christian civilization, Christian tradition and heritage without the substance of faith is an empty shell. There must be many Macedonians today saying, "Come over here and help us," as in Paul's vision. This help means spiritual help, not other kinds. Europe is still the center of the world in terms of culture, tradition, education, science and technology, democratic values, and peaceful politics. Everyone in the world wants to drive European automobiles, wear European-designed clothes, send children to European schools, learn European know-how in music and arts, and spend his retirement years in Europe. The accomplishment of the European civilization is unparalleled in history. Nonetheless, the inner man is void. Man cannot live by bread alone.

This is an exciting time to be alive. We have never traveled this road before (Jos 3:4). It will be exciting just for that reason alone. Old ways of doing things do not apply anymore. People must fasten their safety belts because the ride ahead is going to be fast and bumpy. Only those who put their trust in Jesus need to apply. Blessed are those who are ready for the work that lies ahead of them. If we believe, we will see the glory of God. As Sergeant Horvath excitedly exclaims in *Saving Private Ryan*, "We are back in business."[2]

---

2. Spielberg, *Saving Private Ryan*.

— 12 —

Lessons for America

THE PROPHECY OF JOHN Winthrop, the Puritan lay preacher and founder of the Massachusetts Bay Colony, that America would be the "city on a hill" became America's destiny. Very few nations in the world began with such a prophetic vision inspired by God. Like his prophecy, America has really become like a shining city on a hill. Although America has made many mistakes throughout its history, it also was in America that Martin Luther King Jr. declared, "I have a dream." God inspired both the city-on-a-hill prophecy and the dream speech. It is not a coincidence that many revivals took place throughout America's history to keep its faith on the right course when the rest of western civilization went spiritually off course.

Europe has had no such prophetic vision to guide its destinyin recent years. The lack of spiritual content is strongly felt. America is still the center of Protestantism. America has most of the famous churches, preachers, and theological seminaries. Christians all over the world listen to American preachers more than preachers from any other country. Americans still send out more foreign missionaries than any other nation on earth. English, the language of the King James Version, is honored above any different languages because it is the tool for communicating the word of God. Even German Christians prefer to use English when praising God.[1] More people want to learn English than any other language. As a result, English will continue to be the dominant language for communicating the truths of the gospel.

1. Chitwood. "Why German evangelicals are praising God in English."

America has a spirit of optimism that arises from its Christian faith. It is not a coincidence that the positive thinking movement began in America. Positive thinking goes well with the spirit of America. Even though many Americans complain that the American Dream is dead, other countries cannot even talk about such a dream. America is still a country where any Johnny boy can become a millionaire or President. This optimism arises from the faith in God, which exists at the base of American society.

America is still a country where Presidents, government officials, social leaders, and entertainment figures can publicly claim their faith in Jesus. Whether they are genuine or not is of secondary importance. How many countries exist in the world where public figures proclaim their Christian faith—except perhaps South Korea? In America, people can run into Christians in almost all corners of society. People can find thriving churches to attend in most communities. Christian television broadcasts still thrive in America.

Faith is alive and well in America. This is in stark contrast to Europe. It is as if God took faithful remnants from the Old World and transported them to the New World to preserve the faith. While Latin and South Americas were populated by the conquistadors searching for gold, the United States was first inhabited by the Puritans in search of religious freedom. Europe does not have the equivalent of the Bible Belt of America. This is a tremendous asset for Christianity in America.

The spirit of America is what has made America great. Although people from other parts of the world may not admit it, people worldwide admire America and want to come to America. The famous lyrics from *The West Side Story* apply to all people in the world: "I wanna live in America." Even the Chinese President Xi Jinping confessed, before being sworn in as President, that he preferred American films like *Saving Private Ryan* to the Chinese martial arts films. Until he swore in as President, he was educating his daughter at Harvard. General Yamamoto and Fidel Castrol, who antagonized America, both studied there at one time.

Christianity in America faced the same challenges of secularism as Europe. But Christianity in America did not suffer the corresponding decline as Europe. What has saved Christianity in America is the series of spiritual revivals that have succeeded in keeping the spiritual zeal. Although the US is a western culture like Europe, Christianity in the US did not fall into the trap of dry intellectualism devoid of spirituality like in Europe. There was no countervailing spiritual energy in Europe to resist the dry liberal theology that took all spiritual convictions out of the clergy and theologians. There must be a healthy balance between intellectual rigor and spiritual power. Europeans had intellectual rigor but not spiritual power. America maintained a healthy balance, which is a real blessing from God. As a result, people come from all over the world to learn theology as well as spirituality. Even Bonheoffer came to study at Union Theological Seminary and was mesmerized by the black church music he experienced at Harlem. The Christian character of America attracts Christian people to want to come to America. As a result, conservative Christians tend to congregate in America. Birds of a feather flock together. Benny Hinn, a Lebanese immigrant to Canada, started his healing ministry in Toronto but eventually relocated to America.

America also has a sound capacity for self-criticism. Whenever there are excesses by overzealous Christian ministers, Americans can discern them and correct them. For example, American Christians are aware of the excesses of the prosperity gospel. There is a healthy tension between various styles of faith, which make sure that Christianity does not go into any extremes. There was a large group of conservative evangelicals who not only supported Donald Trump during the 2020 Presidential Election, but also claimed that Trump was God's choice. But there was also an equally large group of Christians who were deeply concerned about the radical politicization of the evangelical community.

The mix of ethnic and racial groups in America is another asset. Christianity in America benefits from the gifts and talents of various ethnic and racial groups. The Azusa Street Revival, which gave birth to the pentecostal movement, was racially mixed. African Americans offer a valuable musical contribution to American Christianity. The Asian-Americans are beginning to contribute leadership to churches and Christian organizations. The Dutch immigrants brought with them a very pure and conservative form of faith untainted by secularism.

Religious liberty is prized above any other form of freedom in America. It is unthinkable in America, for example, to arrest a healing evangelist for practicing medicine without a license as in Europe. Only in America could major television networks broadcast Billy Graham's crusade during prime time. Such things are unimaginable in any other country in the world, including Europe.

Comparing Canada with the US will provide the keys to understanding the difference between Europe and America. Though similar to the US in many ways, Canada is not like the US in spiritual terms.

Canada is closer to Europe in spiritual terms than the US The mainline Protestant denominations in Canada have all gone in the same direction as the European churches. Canadians do not seem to have as many alternatives to the dwindling mainline denominations as Americans do. Canadians do not have conservative Christian voices to resist the liberal political agendas like the US.

Americans have honored God, and God has honored America. America can be likened to Jacob, while Europe can be likened to Esau. The immigrants who left their fatherlands to inhabit America were like Jacob, who left home searching for God's blessings. Jacob's fortune was the result of God's blessings. Esau, however, stayed home and inherited his father's property. Esau and Jacob were twins, sharing the same father and mother. But their orientations were the opposite. As a result, America possesses the rights of the first-born son, which used to belong to Europe. God has blessed the Americans with material blessings as well as spiritual blessings. As God appeared in Jacob's dream at Bethel, where he promised to bless Jacob, God gave his promise to bless Americans, making them like the city on a hill.

Nevertheless, there are some troubling signs about the spiritual state of America. The first sign is that Americans are trying on their own to lift their status in the world instead of allowing God to do it for them. America did not become a city on a hill by boosting its stature in the world. It was the result of God's blessing. The "America First" policy of Donald Trump went against this principle. America cannot keep up its status if she seeks her interest first over and against the common interests of humanity. Making America great again at the cost of its responsibilities goes against the spirit of the city on a hill.

When Americans try to emphasize Christian heritage in political events, it looks like showmanship instead of a genuine expression of faith. Christian ministers invited to pray at Presidential inaugurations seem more interested in advertising Christianity than in genuinely praying for the President and the nation. Foreigners can see through their showmanship.

Americans like big-name brands in everything, including churches and ministries. The phenomenon of megachurches started in America. People seem to implicitly trust churches with big names as they trust Wall-Mart. Their trust is misdirected. Spiritual integrity is not to be found in size or celebrity. Instead, smaller and less well-known churches are doing the important work. Fame and success are always dangerous temptations to God's ministers.

American evangelicalism seems to keep running by its initial momentum without engaging the intellectuals in frank dialogues. As a result, intellectuals in America are left out of the evangelical movement. Students at top American universities do not take evangelicalism seriously. To them, evangelicalism is too dogmatic and exclusive. The evangelicals have not been successful at avoiding this negative image. America needs figures like C. S. Lewis to engage thinking Christians in frank religious dialogues.

Like Europe, the element of suffering is absent in American Christianity. The prosperity gospel mostly rejected the suffering of sickness and poverty as a lack of faith. The only group that has included the element of suffering in its theology is the African American church. The black preachers do not only speak about the sufferings due to racism; they also speak about sufferings from broken marriages, dysfunctional homes, and poverty. It cannot be just African Americans who have those pains. Still, the white churches do not seem to know how to discuss them from the perspective of faith. As a result, American churches do not know how to discuss the real pains of ordinary people, making evangelical Christianity distant from the existential conditions of people.

Eleven o'clock Sunday morning is still the most segregated time of the week in America because the ethnic groups and races are divided in their church attendance. The presence of diverse ethnic groups and races is a tremendous asset for American Christianity, but it does not know how to profit from this asset. Even on-campus churches are divided along the racial line on Sunday mornings.

God has blessed Americans with much spiritual blessing. Instead of using it to serve other nations by evangelism and mission, American Christians are tempted to turn inward and seek their material blessing. The most famous American preachers are prosperity preachers. Even the most prominent African American preachers seem to imitate the prosperity gospel. Though not the exact replica of the prosperity gospel, their messages are based on self-improvement principles, which appeal to the public. Americans do not know what to do with their excess spiritual energy. God gives spiritual gifts to edify the church and preach the gospel; instead, Americans use their spiritual energy for their benefit. Not only are they making this mistake for themselves, but they are spreading this error to the rest of the world. The prosperity gospel is equated with

Americanism. This is a critical error because the spiritual credibility of American Christianity is damaged in the eyes of the Europeans.

Those who use the spiritual gifts from God for their material blessing are falsely equating the free-enterprise values of America with Christianity. Instead of being transformed by the renewing of their minds, they are conforming to the values of American society. The megachurch pastors resemble CEOs of Fortune 500 companies instead of John the Baptist or Elijah. As a result, even though the number of Christians is high in America, they are diluting the effect of their Christian testimony. The American version of Christianity does not have the power and purity that it could have had.

Despite all such problems, America has a God-given destiny. No other nation on earth is like America in spiritual terms. Americans should consider it their blessing as well as mission. If they are faithful to the gifts and calling placed on them by God, God will continue to use America as the spiritual lighthouse of the world. I would not have to write this book if the entire western civilization were like the United States. The spiritual benefit of America is that she is not like her European cousins.

That does not mean that Europe should try to imitate America at this stage. Instead, European Christians should pray to God to give them a vision of their own. Europeans, especially Germans, have been burned once by Hitler, who excited them with his diabolical vision and oratory. As a result of this negative experience, Germans may be wary of any kind of mass excitement. It is an unfortunate event in their past which blocks spiritual revival among them. Europeans must overcome their unhappy past. Europeans must pray for a true revival in Europe. We need more Martin Luther, John Calvin, John Wesley, William Booths, Charles Spurgeon, Dietrich Bonheoffer, and Helmut Thielicke in Europe. Our Catholic brothers should have more St. Augustine, St. Francis, and St. Loyola. It happened once, and it can happen again. Christianity must be reintroduced to Europe. And Europe will be saved once again.

Closing Words

Secularists Have Answered the Question for Us

WE CAN VIEW THE current condition of Christianity in Europe either from the European perspective or from a Christian perspective. From the European perspective, the situation in Europe is pessimistic. From the Christian perspective, the situation in Europe is business as usual. It is nothing new. We have seen worse. When the servants of the Lord try to save the world, this kind of hardship is to be expected. If saving humanity were any easier, God would not have sent his Son. From the Christian perspective, the Christian faith is alive and well on the planet earth. The gospel is progressing with power all over the world. We should not ask why Christianity is doing well in other parts of the world; we need to ask why it is not doing well in Europe. Europe is an exception to what God is doing all over the world. The first shall be last, and the last shall be first, Jesus said. Perhaps Jesus is humbling the European believers who were the first in the world. Humbling is not a bad thing because it promises better things in the future. God gives grace to the humble.

We have to include Jesus in our discussions. We cannot talk about Europe as if Jesus was not there or he did not care. The faith factor is the most valuable part of the discussion. Much of the debate on the spiritual condition of Europe takes place without the faith factor. This fact in itself discloses the reason for the problem. The loss of faith is the reason for the decline of Christianity in Europe. Even discussing the issue lacks faith. How do we expect to find the solution? Without faith, the problem seems insurmountable. As Jesus said, "With man, it is impossible, but not with God. For all things are possible with God" (Mark 10:27). Instead of panicking and worrying, we have to pray and believe. Already there are many signs that European Christians are doing what is necessary. European students are praying for revival in Europe. Their effort is called *Revive Europe*.[1] The Lord works with the church. We must remember that. When the disciples went out to preach, the Lord worked with them, confirming the word with accompanying signs (Mark 16:20). In the Greek manuscript, the term "them" is missing in Mark 16:20. Thus the passage can be read like this: "Then the disciples went out and preached everywhere, and the *Lord worked with and confirmed his word* by the signs that accompanied it." If the church wants to experience the Lord working with it, it must first preach the word of God. The Lord will work with the word of God.

The 20th century was particularly difficult for Christians in the west. Many events occurred which shook their faith. The ground underneath them shook. These troubles were men's troubles and not God's troubles. There was nothing wrong with God, but there were many things wrong with men. These troubles caused the shaking. The shaking was necessary so that what could not be shaken may remain (Heb 12:27). What Europeans took for granted about Christian faith cannot be taken for granted anymore—such as their status as Christians, the role of the church as a social institution, and the religious identity of culture. All of these things must be worked out carefully and deliberately. Unless the Christian faith is protected and treasured, it can be challenged and trampled on. Fierce battles are going on for the souls of men, and men must not lose them.

When Christianity is reintroduced to Europe, things will have to be done differently than before. The church is no longer a state institution. Therefore, the church must rely on the Lord Jesus alone. Secular theorists like Max Weber argued that the church would surely demise when severed from political and economic support. Weber was looking at the old, traditional model of the church. Churches in Europe must run under a different rule. They must be competitive now—not with other churches but with secular, opposing values. Instead of presuming that people are already Christians, the church should bring them to the faith one by one.

The church should once again become the fisher of men. Instead of trying to clean up the fish before catching them, the church should catch them first and allow them to clean themselves. Jesus died for sinners. If the church turns away sinners because they are sinners, the church is not doing a proper job of representing Jesus. In the 20th century, theologians were the first Christians to lose their faith in scripture. The trouble was that their loss of faith in scripture led to the loss of faith in Christianity.

---

1. Breuel. "European students unite in prayer for revival."

Liberal theology was just a school of theological opinions and ideas. Their theological opinions cannot substitute for the word of God. Putting too much stock in liberal theology takes away the confidence to preach the word of God. Instead of helping ministers, liberal theology incapacitated ministers. Liberal seminaries became the first battleground where the devil defeated would-be ministers and preachers. We need more theological seminaries with conservative and evangelical theology.

Jesus is Lord, and he does what he wants us to do. Jesus does not need anyone's approval for his actions. He does not have to prove to anyone why he does what he does. That is how Jesus did it when he was on the earth. He first acted and then explained its meaning. He first forgave the paralytic's sin and then explained that he had the authority to forgive sins on earth. He calmed the wind and the sea first and then explained the need for faith. The religious leaders during Jesus's earthly ministry were always left out of what Jesus was doing. They saw Jesus's miracles but did not personally benefit from them. They saw Jesus saving sinners but did not experience the same grace. Bypassing scholars and intellectuals, Jesus can send the Holy Spirit upon believers and start revivals. If he does that, many of us will be left out of his works. Jesus does not want to leave his friends in the dark about what he wants to do (John 15:15). Jesus will probably want to engage as many clergy and Christians in his discourse so that they can understand and welcome the works of God. Ministers do not want to be like Eli, who could not hear the voice of God that young Samuel heard—especially when the Lord's subject was Eli.

There are signs of significant changes. Secularists used to predict that Christianity would become extinct in modern society. But Christianity did not die as they had predicted. Secularists were not the only people who were wrong about the future of religion. Liberal theologians also predicted the death of Christianity. Instead, it was liberal theology that began to collapse.[2] As a result, scholars had to change their theories. The secularists began to admit that they were wrong.[3] Modernization does not necessarily lead to the decline of religion. People's religiosity does not decrease. The German philosopher Jürgen Habermas, an icon of secular rationalism, pronounced in 2001 that the world had entered a "post-secular age."[4] In the post-secular age, religious and secular world-

---

2. Cox. *Religion in the Secular City.*
3. Berger. *The Desecularization of the World.* p. 2.
4. Gorski. "After Secularization?" pp. 56.

views could coexist and even enter into dialogue with each other.[5] In contrast to the traditional way of studying religion, which analyzed the demand side of religion, the supply side began to analyze the opportunities and restrictions confronting religious leaders.[6] They have found that, where there are powerful religious leaders who supply religious motivations, religion thrives in society. Sociologists Stark and Iannaccone defined the supply side as follows: "To the degree that a religious economy is competitive and pluralistic, overall levels of religious participation will tend to be high. Conversely, to the degree that a religious economy is monopolized by one or two state-supported firms, overall levels of participation will tend to be low."[7] Secularists are doing the job for us. This is the advocacy of this book. To reverse Christianity's decline in Europe, Europe needs Christian leaders who will supply the necessary momentum and motivation. The reason for the decline of Christianity in Europe was its problems on the supply side. Instead of waiting for the demand for religion to increase, strengthening the supply side of Christianity will be able to revive Christianity. It is not just the shepherd who looks for the sheep; often, it is the other way around. Where there are able shepherds, sheep will gather under them. This is how revivals occurred in the Bible. God raised apostles, prophets, evangelists, pastors, and teachers to edify Christians. He has done so in the past, and he will do so today.

The coronavirus epidemic shook European society existentially. Europe is not as strong or invincible as it once thought it was. The scientific and cultural accomplishments of Europe were not built on a firm foundation. The identity crisis of Europe stems from the loss of its spiritual identity. Europeans should not turn elsewhere to resolve this crisis. Jesus is the vine and we are the branches. Separated from him, we lose what we are.

Many great men of faith had to repeat their tasks. David repented of his sins and then took Bathsheba again under the Lord's instruction. Peter accepted his failure and took his calling as an apostle for the second time. Job came out of his trials and received double blessings from God. John Mark overcame his error and returned to his vocation as a servant of the Lord. Jonas repented of his disobedience and succeeded at his task the second time around.

---

5. Gorski. "After Secularization?" pp. 56
6. Finke. "Supply-side explanations for religious change." p. 27.
7. Finke. "Supply-side explanations for religious change." 27.

Jesus said that if we have faith as small as a mustard seed, we can command a mountain to move from here to there. The European continent is indeed a giant mountain. But at the command of believers, it will begin to move. For those who believe, the coming years and decades will be the most exciting times in their lives. Douglas Murray suggests, though he is only a cultural Christian, that now is a great time to start a religion because no one has done it in Europe for quite a long time.[8] Odon Vallet, a professor of religion at the Sorbonne, said that, if he were investing in stocks and bonds, he would buy Christianity. "The price now is very low, so I think it has to go up."[9] The best is saved for the last.

---

8. Rebel Wisdom. "Cultural crisis and the Intellectual Dark Web" *YouTube*.
9. Allen. "Christianity under siege."

About the Author

TED KIM IS A preacher, theologian, and Christian thinker with a vision to reintroduce the gospel to Europe. Born in Seoul, Korea, Ted immigrated to Toronto, Canada, where he finished high school. Afterward, Ted studied philosophy at Yale University and law at Columbia Law School. Nevertheless, all along, he felt a calling to the ministry. Instead of pursuing a career as a Wall Street lawyer, Ted enrolled at Fuller Theological Seminary in Pasadena, California. Ordained in 1991, Ted Kim went back to South Korea, where he worked as an associate pastor at a large Presbyterian church. In 2000, he planted a church at a bowling alley in Seoul with a handful of people, which rapidly grew to more than nine thousand registered members. During twenty years of pastoring Good News Presbyterian Church, he baptized more than one thousand people. He sent out missionaries to China, Japan, Africa, and France. He broadcasts weekly sermons on Christian TV and radio in Korea. Perfectly bilingual in English and Korean, Ted has also taught himself French and German. With more than ten years left until retirement, Pastor Kim felt the leading of the Lord to resign his post to start new missionary work in Europe. Ted will be based in Germany but hopes to work all over Europe wherever his service is welcomed and needed. He wants to coach and train young ministers, consult church planting, and provide prophetic guidance to local churches. Though ordained as a Presbyterian minister, Ted learned from diverse denominations and campus ministries, including the United Church of Canada, Lutherans, Baptists, Holiness, independent charismatics, Methodists, Assemblies of God, Vineyard, Intervarsity Christian Fellowship, Campus Crusade for Christ, and Youth With A Mission.

Bibliography

Allen, John L. "Christianity under Siege." *National Catholic Reporter* 44.21 (Jun 13, 2008) 5–6.
Applebaum, Anne. "The West Has Lost Confidence in Its Values. Syria Is Paying the Price." *The Washington Post*, September 6th, 2019. https://www.washingtonpost.com/opinions/global-opinions/the-west-has-lost-confidence-in-its-values-syria-is-paying-the-price/2019/09/06/b8b73dee-d0ac-11e9-b29b-a528dc82154a_story.html.
Ayer, David, dir. *Fury*. Culver City, CA: Columbia Pictures, 2014.
Bauman, Clarence. *The Sermon on the Mount: The Modern Quest for Its Meaning*. Macon, GA: Mercer University Press, 1985.
Becker, Wolfgang, dir. *Good Bye Lenin!* Adlershof, Berlin, Germany: X-Filme Creative Pool, 2004.
Beeby, H. Dan. "A White Man's Burden, 1994." *International Bulletin of Missionary Research* 18.1 (January 1994) 6–8.
Berger, Peter, ed. *The Desecularization of the World: Resurgent Religion and World Politics*. Grand Rapids: Eerdmans, 1999.
Berger, Peter, et al. *Religious America, Secular Europe? A Theme and Variations*. London: Routledge, 2016.
Boff, Leonardo. *Ecclesiogenesis: The Base Communities Re-invent the Church*. Maryknoll, NY: Orbis, 2012.
Breuel, Sarah. "European Students Unite in Prayer for Revival." *Christianity Today*, October 25, 2019. https://www.christianitytoday.com/edstetzer/2019/october/european-students-unite-in-prayer-for-revival.html.
Brian Holdsworth. "The Reason Christianity Is Dying in the West." *YouTube*, September 1st, 2017. https://www.youtube.com/watch?v=KVSLUJt5yWI.
Brown, Callum. *The Death of Christian Britain*. London: Routledge, 2001.
Bruce, Steve. *God Is Dead: Secularization in the West*. Malden: Wiley-Blackwell, 2002.
Bruce, Steve, and Tony Glendinning. "When Was Secularization? Dating the Decline of the British Churches and Locating Its Cause." *The British Journal of Sociology* 61.1 (2010) 107–26.
Cameron, James, dir. *Titanic*. Los Angeles: Twentieth Century Fox, 1997.
Chadwick, Owen. *The Christian Church in the Cold War*. London: Penguin, 1993.
Chitwood, Ken. "Why German Evangelicals Are Praising God in English." *Christianity Today*, February 17, 2020. https://www.christianitytoday.com/ct/2020/march/why-german-evangelicals-are-praising-god-in-english.html.

Clements, Keith. "Christian Faith in Europe: Residual or Potential?" *International Journal for the Study of the Christian Church* 13.1 (2013) 3–15. DOI:10.1080/1474225X.2013.723897.

Coppola, Francis Ford. *The Godfather: Part III*. Hollywood: Paramount Pictures, 1990.

Cox, Harvey. *Religion in the Secular City: Toward a Postmodern Theology*. New York: Simon & Schuster, 1984.

Cox, Jeffrey. "Master Narratives of Long-term Religious Change." In *The Decline of Christendom in Western Europe, 1750–2000*, edited by Hugh McLeod, 201–17. Cambridge: Cambridge University Press, 2003.

Curtis, Adam, dir. *The Power of Nightmares: The Rise of the Politics of Fear*. Season 1, episode 1, "Baby It's Cold Outside." Aired October 20, 2004 on BBC Two. https://www.bbc.co.uk/programmes/p088s5rv.

Davechappelletv. "Dave Chappelle – Chivalry Is Dead." *YouTube*, July 16th, 2009. https://www.youtube.com/watch?v=ymNdfdQvdVc.

Dart, John. "His Way: Pastor Sparks Rebirth of Pentecostal Church." *Los Angeles Times*, December 15, 1991. https://www.latimes.com/archives/la-xpm-1991-12-15-me-1044-story.html.

"David Cameron Says the UK Is a Christian Country." *BBC*, December 16th, 2011. https://www.bbc.com/news/uk-politics-16224394.

Davie, Grace. "Europe: The Exception that Proves the Rule." In *The Desecularization of the World: Resurgent Religion and World Politics*, edited by Peter Berger, 65–84. Grand Rapids: Eerdmans, 1999.

Di Sabatino, David, dir. *Frisbee: The Life and Death of a Hippie Preacher*. Jester Media, 2005.

Eberstadt, Mary N. S. *How the West Really Lost God: A New Theory of Secularization*

Edwords, Fred. "Faith and Faithlessness by Generation: The Decline and Rise and Real." *The Humanist*, September/October 2018. https://thehumanist.com/magazine/september-october-2018/features/faith-and-faithlessness-by-generation-the-decline-and-rise-are-real.

Faucon, Philippe, dir. *Fatima*. Istiqlal Films, Arte France Cinema, 2016.

Finke, Roger, and Laurence R. Iannaccone. "Supply-side Explanations for Religious Change." *The Annals of the American Academy of Political and Social Science* 527 (May, 1993) 27–39.

Friedkin, William, dir. *The Exorcist*. Burbank, CA: Warner Bros. Pictures, 1973.

Froese, P. "Hungary for Religion: A Supply-side Interpretation of the Hungarian Religious Revival." *Journal for the Scientific Study of Religion* 40.2 (June 2001) 251–68.

Fukuyama, Francis. *The End of History and the Last Man*. New York: Free Press, 2006.

Gill, Robin. *The Myth of the Empty Church*. London: SPCK, 1993.

Gorski, Phillip, and Ates Altinordu. "After Secularization?" *Annual Review of Sociology* 34 (2008) 55–85.

Hallström, Lasse, dir. *Chocolat*. Los Angeles: Miramax, 2000.

Hardy, Rod, dir. *Between Love and Hate*. Burbank, CA: Cosgrove/Meurer Productions, 1993.

Hendrix, E. R. "The Religion of Today." *Herald of Gospel Liberty* 99.44 (Nov 1, 1906).

The Heritage Foundation. "Roger Scruton – The Future of European Civilization: Lessons for America." *YouTube*, October 14th, 2015. https://www.youtube.com/watch?v=WMz3clGp_MY.

Honig, Emily. "Socialist Sex: The Cultural Revolution Revisited." *Modern China* 29.2 (April 2003) 143–75.
Huston, John, dir. *The Man Who Would Be King.* Culver City, CA: Columbia Pictures, 1975.
Jackson, Chris. *Loving God When You Don't Love the Church: Opening the Door to Healing.* Grand Rapids: Chosen, 2007.
Jenkins, Philip. *The Next Christendom: The Coming of Global Christianity.* Oxford University Press, 2007
Kaufmann, Eric, et al. "The End of Secularization in Europe? A Socio-demographic Perspective." *Sociology of Religion* 73.1 (Spring 2012) 69–91.
King, Karen L. "Women in Ancient Christianity: The New Discoveries." *Frontline*, April 1998. https://www.pbs.org/wgbh/pages/frontline/shows/religion/first/women.html.
Kumar, Krishan. "The Question of European Identity: Europe in the American Mirror." *European Journal of Social Theory* 11.1 (2008) 87–105.
Kunovish, Robert M. "An Exploration of the Salience of Christianity for National Identity in Europe." *Sociological Perspectives* 49.4 (2006) 435–60.
Lee, Sang Boum. *Geniuses without Faith; Believers without Genius.* Seoul, South Korea: Korean Christian Publishing, 2003.
Libby, Alger. "Christianity Provided a Foundation for the West's Secular Humanism." *Edmonton Journal*, January 2nd, 2016.
Life Production. "Cindy Jacobs Brings New Prophecy to Europe." *YouTube*, December 14th, 2018. https://www.youtube.com/watch?v=Kg5tvoljvhY.
Linford, John. "Christianity and Outdated Doctrine." *The Times*, November 9th, 2002. https://www.thetimes.co.uk/article/christianity-and-outdated-doctrine-8m7g526ot8l.
Lipka, Michael. "In Some European Countries, Church Membership Means Paying More Taxes." https://www.pewresearch.org/fact-tank/2014/09/22/in-some-european-countries-church-membership-means-paying-more-taxes/.
McLeod, Hugh. *Religion and the People of Western Europe 1789–1989.* Oxford: Oxford University Press, 1981.
———. *The Religious Crisis of the 1960s.* Oxford: Oxford University Press, 2010.
Meddeb, Abdewahab. *Islam and the Challenge of Civilization.* New York: Fordham University Press, 2013.
Mendes, Sam, dir. *Skyfall.* Beverly Hills: MGM, Columbia Pictures, 2012.
Monbiot, George. "Covid-19 Is Nature's Wake-up Call to Complacent Civilisation." *The Guardian*, Mar 25th, 2020. https://www.theguardian.com/commentisfree/2020/mar/25/covid-19-is-natures-wake-up-call-to-complacent-civilisation.
"More Than 220,000 People Left the Protestant Church of Germany in 2018." https://evangelicalfocus.com/europe/6752/germany.
Mulcahy, Robert, dir. *Prayers for Bobby.* Beverly Hills: Daniel Sladek Entertainment, 2009.
Murray, Douglas. *The Strange Death of Europe: Immigration, Identity, Islam.* London: Bloomsbury Continuum, 2019.
Nachtigall, Patrick. "Why Evangelical Churches Struggle in Europe." *Three Worlds*, May 25, 2018.
Nietzsche, Friedrich. *The Gay Science.* Translated by Walter Kaufmann. New York: Vintage, 1974.

O'Neill, Siobhan. "I'm a Committed Atheist, but My Child Has Become Religious and I'm Proud of Her for Challenging My Indoctrination." *The Independent*, March 13th, 2017. https://www.independent.co.uk/voices/christianity-children-confirmation-schooling-atheist-parenting-a7627086.html.

Opfinger, Matthias. "Two Sides of the Medal: The Changing Relationship between Religious Diversity and Religiosity." *Review of Social Economy* 72.4 (2014) 523–48.

Paas, Stefan. "Mission from Anywhere to Europe: Americans, Africans, and Australians Coming to Amsterdam." *Mission Studies* 32 (2015) 1–28.

———. "The Crisis of Mission in Europe—Is There a Way Out?" *Scandinavian Evangelical e-Journal* 3 (2012) 16–51.

Parsons, Gerald. *The Growth of Religious Diversity*. Vol 2, *Britain from 1945*. London: Routledge, 2017.

PastorStudy. "The Tragedy of Mainline Protestantism." *YouTube*, April 19th, 2013. https://www.youtube.com/watch?v=vNE-yo_Ovkk.

Pera, Marcello. *Why We Should Call Ourselves Christians: The Religious Roots of Free Societies*. New York: Encounter, 2009.

Pollock, John. *Moody without Sankey: A New Biographical Portrait*. Hodder & Stoughton, 1963.

Puzo, Mario. *The Godfather*. Reissue edition. New York: Berkley, 2005.

Rebel Wisdom. "Cultural Crisis and the Intellectual Dark Web, with Douglas Murray." *YouTube*, October 5th, 2018. https://www.youtube.com/watch?v=MXS8qkHlhrs.

Reese, Thomas. "The Hidden Exodus: Catholics Becoming Protestants." *National Catholic Reporter*, April 18, 2011. https://www.ncronline.org/news/parish/hidden-exodus-catholics-becoming-protestants.

Scott, Ridley, dir. *Kingdom of Heaven*. Los Angeles: Twentieth Century Fox, 2005.

Stark, Rodney. "A Supply-side Reinterpretation of the 'Secularization' of Europe." *Journal for the Scientific Study of Religion* 33.3 (September 1994) 230–52.

———. *The Triumph of Faith: Why the World Is More Religious than Ever*. Wilmington: ISI Books, 2015.

Stark, Rodney, and Laurence Iannaccone. "Secularization, R.I.P." *Sociology of Religion* 60.3 (Autumn 1999) 249–73.

Stetzer, Ed. "If It Doesn't Stem Its Decline, Mainline Protestantism Has Just 23 Easters Left." *The Washington Post*, April 28, 2017. https://www.washingtonpost.com/news/acts-of-faith/wp/2017/04/28/if-it-doesnt-stem-its-decline-mainline-protestantism-has-just-23-easters-left/.

Stone, Oliver, dir. *Born on the Fourth of July*. Los Angeles: Ixtlan, 1989.

Thome, Stephan. "Was Deutschland von Taiwan lernen kann." *Der Spiegel*, March 28th, 2020. https://www.tagesschau.de/ausland/corona-taiwan-101.html.

Tucker, Garland. "Quo Vadis? The Philosophical, Spiritual Floundering of Europe in 2017." *National Review*, October 21st, 2017. https://www.nationalreview.com/2017/10/europe-christianity-non-believers-cultural-identity-crisis-immigration-assimilation/.

Saarinen, Martin F. *The Life Cycle of a Congregation*. Washington, DC: The Alban Institute, 1986.

Sandford, John, and Paula Sandford. *The Transformation of the Inner Man*. Tulsa: Victory, 1982.

Sarah, Cardinal Robert, with Nicolas Diat. *The Day Is Now Far Spent*. San Francisco: Ignatius, 2019.

Segal, Eric. *Oliver's Story*. New York: Avon, 2012.

Shenk, Wilbert. "New Wineskins for New Wine: Toward a Post-Christendom Ecclesiology." *International Bulletin of Missionary Research* 29.2 (April 2005) 73–79. http://www.internationalbulletin.org/issues/2005-02/2005-02-073-shenk.pdf.

Smith, Mark D. "Ancient Bisexuality and the Interpretation of Romans 1:26–27." *Journal of the American Academy of Religion* 64.2 (Summer 1996) 223–56.

Spielberg, Steven. *Saving Private Ryan*. Glendale, CA: Dreamworks Pictures, 1998.

Van de Poll, Evert. *Europe and the Gospel: Past Influences, Current Developments, Mission Challenges*. Warsaw: Versita, 2013.

Vigne, Daniel, dir. *Le Retour de Martin Guerre*. N.p.: Production Marcel Dassault, 1982.

Wagner, C. Peter. *Your Spiritual Gifts Can Help Your Church Grow*. Glendale: Regal, 1979.

Wandusim, Michael Fuseini. "Christianity in Africa: A Beacon of Hope for Christianity in Europe." *Journal of Advocacy, Research and Education* 2.1 (2015) 92–96.

Winkler, Irwin, dir. *De-Lovely*. Beverly Hills: MGM, Potboiler Productions, 2004.

"The World's Muslims: Religion, Politics, and Society." https://assets.pewresearch.org/wp-content/uploads/sites/11/2013/04/worlds-muslims-religion-politics-society-full-report.pdf.

Wrogemann, Henning. "Mission as Oikumenical Doxology—Secularized Europe and the Quest for a New Paradigm of Mission. Empirical Data and Missiological Reflections." *Missionalia: Southern African Journal of Mission Studies* 42.1–2 (Apr/Aug 2014) 55–71.

Wynne-Jones, Jonathan. "Europe Has Neglected Its Christian Roots, Says Church of England." *The Telegraph*, April 17th, 2010.

Yedroudj, Latifa. "Prince Charles' Views on Religion Could Force Him to GIVE UP Throne—'ABDICATION.'" *Express*, August 25th, 2018. https://www.express.co.uk/news/royal/1008027/Prince-Charles-news-abdication-king-charles-religion-later.

Index

A

abortion, 57, 144
Abraham, 84–85, 97, 102, 140, 169
accomplishments of western civilization, 105–6, 171
Acts, 26, 44, 158
Adam and Eve, 97, 99, 122, 131
adultery, 93, 121, 126
adulthood, rights and duties of, 106
Africa, 8
African Americans, 63–64, 174, 176
  churches, 176
African pentecostals, 61–62
Age of Faith, 142
agnostic religions, 101
AIDS epidemic, 37, 129–30
Alexander the Great, 169–70
Al-Qaeda, 136
"America First" policy, 175
American bishops, 50
American Christianity, 172–77
  decline of mainline denomination in, 61, 72, 74–75
  and diverse ethnic and racial groups, 174, 176
  and evangelicalism, 4–5, 17, 60, 72, 143–44, 174, 176
  and Protestant denominations, 61
American Dream, 173
American Forces Network, 40
Americanism, 9, 177
Ananias and Sapphira, 107, 157

Angley, Ernest, 9
Anglican leaders, 47
Animal Farm (Orwell), 92
Annacondia, Carlos, 43
anonymous Christians, 49, 147
antichrist, 3, 17
Antioch, 94, 109, 145–46
Apartheid, 66
Apollos, 82
apostasy, 28–29, 92, 151
apostles
  and equipping people for works of ministry, 159
  and gentiles, 109
  and loss of faith, 58
  and post-Christian Christianity, 139–41
  preaching the gospel, 41, 154
  spiritual authority of, 157
  See also specific apostles
architecture. *See* buildings
Arminianism, 104
Asian Americans, 174
Asian Christians, 8, 48–49. *See also Korean Christianity*
Assemblies of God church, 40
assimilation, 57
assurance of salvation, 11, 72–74
atomic bombs, 66
Augustine, Saint, 141
authentication process, 25
authoritarian *vs.* authoritative leadership, 157

authority, 11, 74, 91, 156–57, 163
Azusa Street Revival, 60, 174

B

Bannon, Steve, 11–12
baptism, 11, 44, 88
Barnabas (apostle), 33, 67, 145
Barth, Karl, 110
Bartimaeus, 104
Bathsheba, 181
Battle of Midway, 165
Beckett, Samuel, 101
belief
    and conviction, 73, 111–14
    dual system of, 116
    eschatological, 17–18
    fighting against instinct, 36–37
    generational, 23–28
    and intellect, 116–17
    opportunity for, 21–22
    and reason to believe, 45
    and science, 114–15
    and spiritual conditions of Europe, 161
    and unbelievers, 23, 76, 121, 161–62
    See also faith
belonging, 146
Berkhof, Hendrikus, 155
Between Love and Hate (film), 126
Bible
    criticism of, 76
    disagreeing with, 86
    doing things for a second time, 6
    and doubts, 117
    in education, 144
    eschatology, 16–20
    and extrabiblical revelations, 86–87
    and freedom, 97, 100
    French, 31
    and homosexuality, 131, 133
    instances of disobeying God, 22
    missionaries in, 169
    and money, 120
    and natural phenomena, 114–15
    in postmodern era, 149–50
    relevance of, 165–66
    revivals in, 181
    and suffering, 78
    and time, 19–20
    and waiting for God's promises, 101
    and welfare, 118
Bible Belt, 173
Boff, Leonard, 156
Bonheoffer, Dietrich, 174
Bonnke, Reinhard, 9, 61
Book of Job, 19
boredom, 53
born-again experience, 11, 44, 59–60, 143
born of the Spirit, 10, 60
Brexit, 17, 25, 67
Britain, 23, 25, 53, 57, 67, 70
Buddhism, 137
buildings, 5, 29–30, 40–42, 52, 164–65, 167–68. *See also* non-church movement
bursting of the bubble, 38–42
Bush, George W., 9

C

Caesarea, 149
Cain, Paul, 159–60
Cain and Abel, 83–84, 97
callousness, 26, 43
Calvary Chapel, 130, 168
Calvinism, 73, 104
Cameron, David, 57
Canaan, 103
Canada, 57, 174–75
capitalism, 106, 118
Carter, Jimmy and Rosalyn, 124
Catholic Church
    and European Christianity, 49–51
    in Germany, 145
    in Japan, 113
    in Korea, 57
    and the monastic movement, 150
    and Protestant churches, 49–51
    and the Protestant Reformation, 142
    and religious pluralism, 137
    and salvation, 73
    and Vatican II, 34

Index

Catholic Diocese of Orange County. *See* Christ Cathedral
celibacy, 36, 121, 125, 132
certainty, 17, 111
Chappelle, David, 1
charismatic leadership, 73, 156, 158
charismatic movement, 51, 73, 88, 148, 159–60
Charlie Hebdo (magazine), 63
chastity, 36, 113, 121
childhood affection deprivation, 127
children, 23–25
Chocolat (film), 24, 92
Christ Cathedral, 40
Christianity
    as antiquated, 52–54
    and the Bible, 86
    Catholics and Protestants, 50–51
    and charismatic movements, 88
    and church attendance, 47
    and church buildings, 29–30
    and churches, 47, 144–49
    cultural heritage of, 58
    by default, 43–45
    and disappointment of Europeans, 55–56
    and ecclesiology, 153–54
    and eschatology, 17–19
    and European civilization, 33
    and evangelization, 15–16
    exclusive claims of, 111–14
    external expressions of, 38–42
    and familiarity, 8, 59–60
    fatigue and guilt, 62–65
    and freedom, 34–38
    future of, 13
    and generational belief, 23–25
    and God, 83–84
    and humanism, 109
    identity of, 9–10
    and identity of Europe, 67
    and Islam, 134–37
    and LGBT+ people, 128–33
    and maturing of humanity, 103, 105–8
    and money, 117–20
    passivity of, 13
    and personal choice, 104–5
    post-Christian, 139–44
    in the postmodern era, 149–51
    and Protestant Reformation, 142
    and religious hype, 10
    and religious privacy, 48–49
    reviving, 161–63
    and salvation, 84–85
    and science, 114–15
    and secularism, 5
    and secularists, 178–81
    and secularization, 7–8
    and sex, 121–28
    and spiritual temptation, 117
    survival of, 1–6
    and theology, 72–76
    and truth of the gospel, 89–90, 93–95
    usefulness of, 151–53
    and world missions, 170–71
    See also American Christianity; European Christianity; Korean Christianity
churches
    African American, 176
    in America, 175–76
    as antiquated, 52–54
    attendance, 29, 34, 41, 45, 47–49, 51, 52, 60, 79–80, 144–49, 161–62, 176
    buildings, 5, 29–30, 40–42, 52, 164–65, 167–68
    and church growth, 2, 4–5, 39–41, 46, 154, 158, 164
    and cultural changes in Europe, 29
    and denominations, 61
    disbanding and restarting, 164–65
    drawing people to, 161–64
    and European Christianity, 13, 29–30, 76–77
    and evangelicalism, 73
    and hierarchies, 92
    and homosexuality, 133
    horizontal movement between, 80–82, 153–54
    and lay participation, 158–61
    and legalism, 89–92
    and liturgy, 44
    and megachurches, 40, 53, 81–82, 147, 159, 175–77

churches (*cont.*)
    and mobile method of ministry, 41–42
    and money, 118–20
    music, 148, 167
    non-church movement, 145, 151, 164
    and persuasion, 143
    and Protestant Reformation, 44, 142–43
    and race, 174, 176
    reinvention of, 5–6
    and relevant messages, 166
    and return to original priority of preaching the gospel, 154–55
    and secularism in Europe, 179
    seeker-sensitive, 73, 166, 167
    and sermons, 45–47
    and state relations, 42, 52, 55, 56–57, 82, 118–19, 143–44
    and structure of ministry, 156–57
    and truth of the gospel, 94–95
    See also Catholic Church; Protestant churches
Church of England, 52, 67
city-on-a-hill prophecy, 172
civil conversations, 112–13
cleansing of ten lepers, 99–101
clergy
    abuse of authority, 91–92
    and antiquated tradition, 53
    and lay participation, 158–61
    and loss in membership, 50
    and sermons, 45–47
    sex abuse scandals, 63, 67
    vestments, 167
coercion, 92–93, 143
cohabitation, 124
Cold War, 17–18
collectivism, 47–49, 55
colonialism, 64, 78–79
colonization, 63, 66, 170
Columbus, Christopher, 15, 26
comfort, 76, 81
commandments, 39, 98
communism, 4, 18, 36, 65, 118
community of faith, 48–49, 77, 91
compensation, 101–2
competitiveness, 42, 52, 82, 143, 163, 179, 181
compulsion, 100–102
condemnation, 93, 99
confidence, 62–64, 73–76, 140, 154, 180
congregations, 45–46, 89, 90–92, 155, 157, 159, 167
consensus, 97, 138
consent, 104, 125
conservative Christians, 118, 124, 129, 135, 149, 174
conservative evangelicals, 174
conservative theology, 180
Constantine (Emperor), 141–42, 155
Constitution of the Islamic Republic of Iran, 28
Constitution of the United States, 42, 57, 143
consumer mentality, 82, 163
conversion, 26, 43–44, 55, 60, 89–90
conviction, 73–74, 111–13
Coppola, Francis, 58
Corinthian church, 53
Cornelius, 26, 48, 94, 109, 154
coronavirus pandemic. *See* COVID-19 pandemic
counterculture movement, 150–51
courtesy, 91
covenants, 85, 97, 99, 102, 135
COVID-19 pandemic, 3, 7, 48, 70, 165, 181
creation *versus* evolution, 114–15, 143
credibility, 17, 111, 121, 177
Crusade, 63, 142, 152
Crusoe, Robinson, 142
Crystal Cathedral, 40, 52–53
cults, 92, 95, 151
cultural changes, 29, 34
cultural Christians, 58, 59, 87
cultural consensus, 138
cultural expressions, 35
cultural identity, 2–3, 81
Cultural Revolution in Communist China, 36
cynicism, 10

Index

D

dabbling with the spiritual world, 89
Daniel, 171
Darwin, Charles, 115
Darwinism, 76, 115
David (King), 6, 29, 62, 72, 85, 97, 160, 181
deconsecration, 30
dedication, 49, 168
De-Lovely (film), 21
demagogue, 56
denominations
    allegiance to, 6
    decline of, 61, 74–75, 175
    and evangelicalism, 72
    freedom to switch, 82
    in the Global era, 166–68
    and LGBT+ issues, 133
    Protestant, 61, 175
desires, 36–37, 123, 125, 127
desire to go to church, 80
destructive and anarchic behavior, 107
Deuteronomy 28, 102
developed countries, 82
disciples
    accompanied by the Lord, 69, 179
    arrival of kingdom of God, 19
    and community of faith, 48
    at Ephesus, 10, 26
    inability to perform necessary tasks well, 160
    and post-Christian Christianity, 139
    and priesthood of all believers, 158
    relationship with Jesus, 99
    and sexual preferences, 133
    waiting for the coming of the Holy Spirit, 101
discrimination, 108–9
dismantling a church, 164–65
disobedience to God's will, 32–33
Dispensationalism, 17–18, 21–22, 105
divorce, 1, 37, 124, 125–26, 147
dogmatism, 77, 112
dominant culture, 2, 60
doubts, 116–17
dual system of belief, 116

E

early church, 90, 109, 154, 156
earnestness, 78–79
earthly ministry of Jesus, 30–31, 59, 78, 99, 140, 180
earthly power, 141
Eastern Europe, 4, 60, 65
ecclesiology, 153–54, 156, 164
economic prosperity, 79. *See also* money
Edict of Milan, 141–42
Egypt, 102
Eli, 28, 180
Elijah, 3, 5, 32, 64, 84, 156, 158
Elisha, 156, 158
Elymas, 157
"Emily in Paris" (television series), 12
empathy, 121–22
The End of History (Fukuyama), 16–17
English language, 172
Ephesians 4:11–13, 159
Ephesus, 10, 26, 42
Episcopal church, 61
equality before God, 92, 108–10
equipping the saints, 73, 157, 159
Esau, 175
eschatology, 15–19, 21, 105, 120
ethics, 35, 110, 121–24
Ethiopian eunuch, 26, 121, 141
ethnic and racial groups in America, 174, 176
Europe
    and America, 60–62
    and Catholic Church, 49–51
    Christian renewal in, 79, 80, 88, 90
    and church attendance, 47–48, 51, 144–45
    decline of Christianity in, 7–8, 55–56, 178–79, 181
    defending the faith, 65–68
    expressions of Christianity in, 38
    future of Christianity in, 68–71
    guilt and fatigue in, 62–64
    identity crisis of, 181
    immigrant pentecostal churches in, 157
    as major mission field, 1–6

Europe (*cont.*)
  missionaries in, 43
  and Muslim immigrants, 134–37
  reintroducing Christianity to, 33
  and relevance of Christianity, 52–53
  religious freedom in, 42
  and second chance to believe, 21, 27–30
  spiritual condition of, 7–14, 29, 56–59, 161, 178–79
  and western civilization, 171
European Christianity
  and American Christianity, 76–77, 172–77
  as an antiquated institution, 51–54
  and the Catholic Church, 49–51
  and cultural Christianity, 58
  and disappointments, 55–56
  and familiarity, 9, 55–56, 59–60, 162
  fatigue and guilt, 62–65
  generational interest, 23–30
  and importance of worship services, 45–47
  and individualism over collectivism, 47–49, 55
  and receiving the gospel a second time, 31–32
  and spiritual callousness, 43
  and spiritual power, 73
  and spiritual renewal, 79–80
  and theology, 72–76
European Union, 17, 25, 65–67, 70, 136
evangelicalism
  American, 4–5, 17, 60, 72, 143–44, 174, 176
  and eschatology, 16–17
  in Europe, 60–62
  and intellectuals, 176
  in Latin America, 43–44
  and motivation and momentum, 11–12
  and non-evangelical churches, 154–55
  and post-Christian Christianity, 143–44
  and radical politicization, 174
  and reinventing Christianity, 150–51
  and seminaries, 40, 75
  and sex, 121–22, 124
  and theology, 72–76, 180
  and world evangelism, 15–16, 73, 169–70
Evangelical Lutheran Church, 61
Evangelische Kirche in Deutschland, 145
evils in modern history, 66
evolution, 24, 114–15, 143
The Exorcist (film), 162–63
experiencing God, 45, 87–89, 116–17, 163
exploitation, 63, 66
extrabiblical revelations, 86–87
Ezekiel 16:49, 132–33

F

faith
  Age of, 142
  in America, 9, 173
  and biblical scholarship, 76
  and church attendance, 47–48, 145
  and church leadership, 45–47
  community of, 48–49, 77, 91
  and cynicism, 10
  by default, 43–44, 56–58
  defense of, 65–68
  and evangelicalism, 73
  external expressions of, 38
  and generational belief, 23–26
  and God's promises, 97
  and the Holy Spirit, 88
  and intellect, 116–17
  and legalism, 92
  and liberal theology, 74
  and local churches, 149
  loss of in Europe, 7–8, 64, 178–79
  and money, 120
  motivation for, 80, 96
  and participation, 155
  and personal choice, 103–5
  and prophecy, 69
  and prosperity gospel, 90–91, 176
  and the Protestant Reformation, 142
  public demonstration of, 49
  righteousness by, 103, 108
  and spiritual passivity, 11–13

Index

and suffering, 78–79
See also belief
faith and works, debate between, 26
false gospel, 90, 94
false prophets, 84, 95, 151, 157
family, 35, 124, 147
fanaticism, 76, 144
fatigue, 62–65, 68
Fatima (film), 135
favoritism, 69, 92
fear, 18, 99
feminism, 75
financial crisis of 2008, 106
First Commandment, 39, 98
First Jerusalem Council, 94
flesh, 94–95
flexibility, 165
folklore, 29
foolishness, 93
Fourth Commandment, 98
fragmentation, 138
Francis, Saint, 150
freedom
   and adulthood, 106
   explosion of, 34–37
   and love, 152–53
   meaning of, 96–103
   of movement between religions, 82, 153
   of religion, 5, 38, 52, 56, 95–96, 143, 173–74
   restriction of, 106–7
   understanding, 104–5
free market, 106–7
free societies, 106–7
free will, 104
Freud, Sigmund, 36, 84
Frisbee, Lonnie, 129–30
Fukuyama, Francis, 16–17
fundamentalist Christians, 17, 57
Fury (film), 11

G

Galatia, 90, 94
Galatians 4:1–7, 105
Galileo, 115
Gandhi, Mahatma, 66
gay Christians. *See* homosexuality
gay marriage, 57, 144
gender identity, 130
Genesis, 19, 65, 83, 84–85, 103, 114–15
Genesis 3:15, 84
Genesis 24, 103
geniuses, 160
gentiles, 94, 108–9, 141, 169
Germany
   and church attendance, 145
   and church music concerts, 148
   and English language, 172
   and European arrogance, 48
   and evangelists, 9
   and expression of Christianity, 67
   and Muslim immigrants, 134
   and spiritual leadership, 61
   and spiritual revival, 177
   and state-sponsored religion, 52
Giamatti, A. Bartlett, 161
gifts and calling. *See* spiritual gifts
globalization, 13
Global South, 4, 14, 61, 63, 66, 69–70
glorification, 75
God
   and American Christianity, 172–77
   and anonymous Christians, 49
   belief in, 112
   calling a second time, 32–33
   callings of, 155–57, 160
   and charismatic churches, 148
   and church attendance, 162–63
   and clergy authority, 91–92
   and eschatology, 16–20
   and Europe, 69–71
   and European Christianity, 1–6
   and evangelicalism, 144
   experienced through the Holy Spirit, 87–89
   experience of, 116–17
   and fatigue, 32, 64–65
   and freedom, 96–103, 107
   and generational belief, 27–29
   and homosexuality, 128–29
   and human desires, 37–38
   and humility, 127–28, 178
   and Islam, 135

God (cont.)
   and Jesus Christ, 84–86
   living aspect of, 53–54, 166
   and local churches, 41
   and man's weakness, 141–42
   and maturing of humanity, 105–6, 107
   and money, 117–20
   and opportunity for faith, 21–23
   patriarchal aspect of, 67
   and prosperity gospel, 90–91
   and radical equality, 108–10
   revelation of, 83–84, 86–87
   and revivals, 181
   and salvation, 73–74
   and science, 114–15
   and sermons, 45–47
   and sex, 122
   and suffering, 78–79
   will of, 103–4
   word of, 44–45, 75–76, 153, 154–55, 179–80
Godfather (films), 24, 58–59, 127–28
golden lampstands, 153
Goliath, 62, 72
good news, 27, 100
gospel
   and Apostle Paul, 10, 71, 140
   and Christianity by default, 43–44
   and English language, 172
   and guilt, 68
   and the law, 89–95
   and liberal theology, 74
   and local churches, 148–49
   and loss of Jerusalem church, 141
   in modern missionary work, 169–71
   presenting to new generation, 24–27
   prosperity, 90–91, 120, 174, 176–77
   and Protestant Reformation, 90, 150
   relevance of, 165
   and sermons, 46–47
   truth of, 46, 89–90, 93–95, 150
   understanding of, 35, 37–38
   See also preaching the gospel
governments, 96–97, 106–7, 118–19
The Graduate (film), 150
Graham, Billy, 12, 43–44, 59, 72, 125–26, 143, 174
Graham, Ruth, 125–26
Great Commission, 2, 15, 32, 65, 69, 164
Guccione, Bob, 122
guilt, 37, 46, 62–65, 66, 68

H

Habermas, Jürgen, 105–6, 180–81
Hagar, 102
hardening of the population, 55
Hardy, Miki, 61
harvest is plentiful, 57, 158, 160
Hayford, Jack, 162
healing movement, 60
"healing" of homosexuals, 130
health and wealth, 72–73
Hebrews, 91
Hebrew servants, 95, 102
Hefner, Hugh, 122
Hegel, Georg Wilhelm Friedrich, 87, 96
hesitation to repeat the work, 30–32
hierarchies, 55, 91–92, 156
Hillsong, 61–62
Hindu believers, 115
Hinn, Benny, 174
hippie counterculture movement, 60
Hispanic people, 63–64
Holocaust, 63, 64, 66
Holy Laughter revival, 73
Holy Spirit
   and Apostle Paul, 10, 171
   and charismatic churches, 148
   and Cornelius, 26
   and Day of Pentecost, 101
   and ecclesiology, 153
   and experiencing God, 87–89
   gifts of, 48–49, 148
   and Jesus, 180
   lying to, 107
   movement of, 22–23
   in post-Christian Christianity, 139–40
   preachers speaking under illumination of, 166
   and priesthood of all believers, 156
   and the pulpit, 155
   Reformed movement, 45

and spiritual ministry, 159
and spiritual renewal in Europe, 10, 80
and theology, 72-76
in worship services, 53
home churches, 165
homogeneity in society, 138
homogeneous unit principle, 81
homophobia, 129
homosexuality, 128-33
horizontal movement of church members, 81, 146-47
Hour of Power broadcast, 40
human instinct, 36-38, 122-23, 125
humanism, 109-10
humanity, maturing of, 103, 105-8
humanity, sin of, 131-32
human rights, 109-10, 123
humility, 4-5, 70-71, 79, 127-28, 160, 178
Hybels, Bill, 41, 168
hypocrisy, 28, 109, 121

I

Iannaconne, Laurence, 181
identity
  crisis of in Europe, 2, 56, 63, 67, 181
  cultural, 2-3, 81
  gender, 130
  and immigration, 2, 70, 134
  national, 95
  religious, 56-57, 67, 95, 134, 138, 181
ideological evolution, 16-17
idolatry, 3
illness, 34, 152
immigrants, 2, 4, 57, 63, 69-70
immoderation, 127
inclusivity, 85-87, 112-13
individual consciousness, 55
individual conversions, 44
individualism over collectivism, 47-49, 55
Innocent III (pope), 150
Inshallah, 104
institutional changes, 108
intellect and faith, 116-17

intellectualism, 173-74
international relief organizations, 169
intolerance, 113
intuition, 116
Iran, 28, 136
Is Europe Christian? (Roy), 62
Islam, 28, 56, 103-4, 134-37
Israel, 28-29, 39, 59, 87, 97-99, 102, 135

J

Jacob, 54, 120, 175
James (apostle), 92
Japan, 78-79, 113, 136, 145, 151
Japheth, 171
Jefferson, Thomas, 149-50
Jehovah's Witnesses, 61
Jerusalem church, 41, 92, 140-41, 154
Jesus Christ
  and anonymous Christians, 49
  chooses his servants, 156
  and churches, 47, 145, 148-49
  and community of faith, 48
  and denominations, 168
  and divorce, 126
  earthly ministry, 180
  and European Christianity, 5, 68-69, 77-78, 178-79
  and evangelicalism, 72, 74
  and freedom, 98-101
  and gifted believers, 160
  and God, 84-86
  and homosexuality, 133
  knowledge of, 26-27
  leaving out of discussion, 13
  and legalism, 89-95
  and liberal theology, 74-76
  living water, 80
  and loss of faith, 58
  love for, 96
  and marriage, 124
  and maturing of humanity, 105
  and mobile method of ministry, 29-30, 41-42
  and money, 117-20
  as motivation for church attendance, 163-64

Jesus Christ (*cont.*)
    and opportunity for belief, 21–22
    and personal choice, 104
    and Peter, 23, 32–33
    and politics, 56–57
    and popularity, 24–25
    and post-Christian Christianity, 139–40, 164–65
    and preaching the gospel as original priority, 154–55
    and radical equality, 108–10
    redeeming humanity from curse of law, 102–3, 105
    and relevant messages, 53–54, 166
    repeating his work, 23, 30–32
    representation of to current generation, 153
    return of, 15–20
    and revelation of God, 83, 86–87
    and salvation, 11
    and sexual ethics, 121–22
    and spiritual condition of Israel, 59–60
    and suffering, 78
    and temptations, 116
    and true disciples, 158
    and true faith, 44
    and the true gospel, 89–95
    and usefulness of Christianity, 152
Jesus People movement, 60, 68, 130, 150–51
Jews/Judaism, 67, 108–9, 135, 140
Jezebel, 64
Jim Crow, 66
Job, 19, 79, 120, 181
John 4:24, 88–89
John 9:21, 106
John (apostle), 3, 50, 85, 140
John Mark, 33, 181
Johnson, Magic, 127
Jonah, 6, 169
Jonas, 181
Joseph, 169
Judas Iscariot, 39, 117
Jude 1:7, 131–33
Judeo-Christianity, 3, 114

K

Kansas City prophets, 159–60
Khomeini, Ayatollah, 136
Kierkegaard, Søren, 26
King, Martin Luther Jr., 66, 172
Kingdom of Heaven (film), 142, 152
Kinsey Reports, 35
knowledge, 26–27, 43, 46, 114–17
Korean Christianity
    and church growth movement, 39–40
    history of, 63
    and the Holy Spirit, 22
    and religious identity, 57
    and religious pluralism, 137–38
    and suffering, 78–79
    "voting with feet" concept, 80–81
Korean War, 79
Kuhlman, Katherine, 60
Küng, Hans, 161

L

Laban, 103
L'Abri movement, 68
laity, 155–56, 158–59
Laodicean Church, 79
Larkin, Philip, 36
Last Adam, 86
Latin America, 8, 43, 50
law/legalism, 37, 89–95, 97–99, 101–3, 105–6, 108, 123
lay Christians, 73
leadership
    authoritarian *vs.* authoritative, 157
    charismatic, 73, 156, 158
    and men, 66–67
    religious leaders, 109, 180–81
    spiritual, 61, 66–67, 156–57
legalism. *See* law/legalism
Le retour de Martin Guerre (Vigne), 125
lesbianism, 133
Leviticus 20:13, 131
Lewis, C. S., 176
LGBT+ people, 49, 75, 128–33
liberal seminaries, 75–76, 180

Index

liberal theology, 45–46, 74–76, 87, 174, 180
library of Tyrannus, 42
limiting civil liberties, 106–7
liturgy, 44
"live-and-let-live" mindset, 73
living water, 80
local churches, 41, 148–49, 154, 164
Lord's Supper, 44
love
    and adulthood, 106
    and freedom, 95–96, 99–103, 152–53
    and Jesus's commands, 93
    overcoming guilt and fatigue, 68
    and pastors, 90
    and preaching, 155
    and sex, 126
Love Story (Segal), 24
Luther, Martin, 44, 46, 91
Lydia, 154

M

MacArthur, Douglas, 145
Macedonian man in Paul's vision, 62, 169–71
magicians of the Pharaoh, 84
mainline denominations in America, 61, 72, 74–75
Malcolm X, 66
male-dominated society, 66
Mandela, Nelson, 66
The Man Who Was Not There (film), 161–62
The Man Who Would Be King (film), 36
Mark 8:22–26, 30–31
Mark 16:20, 179
market economy, 119
marketplace, 163
marriage, 123–26, 147
martial arts, 166–67
Mary Magdalene, 109
mass migration, 134–35
mass piety, 29
mass trends, 24
material blessings, 90, 175–77
maternal aspect of God, 67

maturing of humanity, 103, 105–8
means of the flesh, 94
megachurches, 40, 53, 81–82, 147, 159, 175–77
men and spiritual leadership, 66–67
Merkel, Angela, 67, 134
Methodist church, 40, 61
#MeToo era, 67, 125
migrants, 136
military hierarchy, 69
ministry
    and charismatic churches, 148
    and competition, 82
    and denominations, 167–68
    effectiveness of, 51
    equipping lay people for, 73, 158–60
    and fatigue, 62
    flexibility in, 165
    gifts and calling, 155–57, 162
    innovations in, 27–30
    and liberal theology, 180
    and liturgy, 44
    and men, 66
    mobile methods of, 41–42
    monopoly of by church hierarchy, 55
    perseverance in, 31–32
    and preaching the gospel as original priority, 154–55
    and sermons, 45
    and showmanship, 175–76
    and unchurched people, 147
mission
    and American Christianity, 172
    and Constantinian church, 155
    and eschatology, 15–16, 21
    in Europe, 43
    and evangelicalism, 74
    and lost sheep, 33
    new paradigm of world mission, 169–71
    and 10/40 Window, 15, 21, 170
mobile method of ministry, 41–42
moderation, 127
modernization, 8, 42, 180–81
modern missionary work, 170
modesty, 9, 13
momentum, 11–12
monasteries and convents, 36

monastic movement, 150
money, 117–20, 160–61, 165, 167–68
monopoly of the ministry by the church hierarchy, 55
monotheism, 112
Moody, D. L., 8
morality, 35–37, 121–23
moral leaders, 66
Moral Majority, 143
Mormonism, 60, 86, 151
Moses, 5, 29, 32, 84, 95, 97–99, 156
Mother Theresa of Calcutta, 66
motivation, 11–12, 80, 90, 95–96, 99, 181
mourning, 79
Murray, Douglas, 64, 76, 182
music, 148, 167
Muslims, 2, 43, 57, 115, 134–37
mustard seed, 104, 182
mutual exclusivity, 115
mystical elements, 162

N

Nadab and Abihu, 87, 89
The Name of the Rose (film), 142
national identity, 95
native Europeans, 69–70, 80
native Indians in North America, 66
natural phenomena, 114
newcomers, 147
New England colonies, 144
New Testament
    and authority, 91, 156–57
    and beginning of Christianity, 44
    church services, 53
    and discipleship, 158
    and giving up privileges, 120
    God's covenant, 85, 99
    and the gospel, 23
    and mission work, 169
    prophecies of, 16
    and revelation, 86
    and sexuality, 121
    and sinful woman who washed Jesus's feet, 93
    and weakness, 141
New World, 9, 15, 77, 173

Nicodemus, 60
Niebuhr, Reinhold, 76
Nietzsche, Friedrich, 1–2, 116
9/11, 135–36
nine lepers, 101, 152
Noah's flood, 18, 20, 84
Nobel Peace Prize, 8
nobility, 29
nomads, 41
non-Christians, 16, 63, 105, 109–10
non-church movement, 145, 151, 164
nondenominational churches, 61
non-evangelical churches, 154–55
non-practicing people in the west, 43
non-white people, 66
Normandy invasion, 27

O

Obama, Barack, 8–9
obedience, 23, 49, 92, 97, 102
Old Covenant of the law, 102
Old Testament, 29, 101, 120, 121, 135, 169
Old World, 9, 77, 143, 173
Oliver's Story (Segal), 24
on-campus churches, 176
"once again" phrase, 31
optimism, 17, 173
Orban, Viktor, 67
organizational rules, 164
Orwell, George, 92
otherness of God, 84, 110
outdated doctrines, 54, 118
outside help, 12

P

Parable of the Vineyard, 22
paradigm of missionary work, 13, 169–71
Pareto Principle, 156
Paris, France, 52–53
parish, 146
partial knowledge, 117
Pascal, Blaise, 171
passivity, 11, 13, 74

Index

pastoral ministry, 27, 29
pastors
    authoritative leadership of, 157
    charismatic role of, 158–59
    and church growth movement, 39–41, 156
    and denominations, 168
    and drawing people to the church, 147–48, 162–63
    European, 26
    and hierarchy, 91–92
    and the Holy Spirit, 88–89
    and liberal theology, 74
    and motivation, 90
    and preaching, 155
    and religious monopoly, 82
    and social agendas, 75–76
    and spiritual power, 94–95
    and theological seminaries, 174
    and unchurched people, 147–48
patriarchal aspect of God, 67
patriotism, 144
Paul (apostle)
    and approaching people as novices, 10
    and Caesarea passage, 149
    and church attendance, 145–46
    and disciples at Ephesus, 10, 26
    and false gospels, 3, 90, 94
    and God's grace, 107
    and grace, 105
    and homosexuality, 131–32
    and Jews, 67
    and John Mark, 33
    and legalism, 91, 94, 102, 108
    and love, 68
    and Macedonian man in vision, 62, 169–71
    method of preaching, 43–44, 71, 155, 171
    and mobile method of ministry, 30, 41–42
    paradigm of missionary work, 169–70
    as a post-Christian Christian, 140
    and preaching the gospel a second time, 6
    and priesthood of all believers, 158
    and religious liberty, 82
    second letter to Corinthians, 53
    and spiritual leadership, 156–57
    and starting a church, 154
Paulson, Henry, 106
Pearl Harbor, 136
peasant class, 29
pedagogical element in conversion, 89
pederasty, 132
Pentecost, day of, 48, 101, 141, 154
pentecostal churches, 50, 157
pentecostalism and spiritual energy, 72–73
pentecostalism from the Global South, 61–62
pentecostal movement, 8, 60, 88, 174
permissible human sexuality, 123, 128
persecution, 113, 140–42
perseverance, 32
personal conversion, 26, 55
personal knowledge, 26–27
personal morality, 35
personal salvation, 73, 150
persuasion, 143
Peter (apostle)
    called for a second time, 23, 32–33, 181
    and clergy, 91
    and Cornelius, 26, 109, 154
    and gentiles, 94, 109
    judgment of Ananias and Sapphira, 107
    loss of faith, 58
    and love, 93, 96
    and preaching the gospel, 154
    and role of the pastor, 162
    sermon of, 139–40
    spiritual authority of, 156
    and temptation, 116–17
Pharisees, 98–99, 108
Philip, 26, 141, 158
Philippi, 154
piety, 26, 29, 37, 115
piousness, 37
Pitt, Brad, 11
plurality of churches, 81
political correctness, 67, 87, 95, 112

politics
    and American evangelicalism,
        143–44, 174
    and certainty of belief, 111–12
    and Christian heritage, 175
    and Christian seminaries, 75
    and conservative political
        movements in Europe, 67
    as idol, 65
    and outside help, 11–12
    and religious freedom, 95
    and religious identity, 56–57
    and religious pluralism, 138
polygamy, 125
polyphony, 44
polytheism, 112
Pompidou Center, 52
pornography, 37
Porter, Cole, 21
positive thinking movement, 173
post-Christian Christianity
    and American evangelicalism,
        143–44
    and church attendance, 148
    and deconstructing Christianity,
        6, 118
    and ecclesiology, 153–54
    and the gospel, 89
    and liturgy, 44
    and non-church movement, 164–65
    and Protestant Reformation, 142
    understanding, 139–44
    and what belongs to Christianity, 38
postmodern era, 6, 25, 51, 117, 149–51,
    168, 171
post-secular age, 180–81
poverty, 78–79, 119–20
pragmatism, 77
Prayers for Bobby (film), 130
preachers
    African American, 176
    American, 60–61, 172, 176
    and belief, 111
    conservative, 122
    and denominational pluralism, 167
    and evangelists, 60–61, 68
    gifted, 156
    and legalism, 90–91
    making gospel relevant, 165–66

prosperity, 176
    and religious hype, 10
    and sermons, 45–47
    social agenda, 76
preaching the gospel
    and baptism, 44
    and church attendance, 47
    to the end of the world, 2, 15–16,
        19–20
    in Europe, 10
    and gifts, 160
    and liberal theology, 74
    and local churches, 148–49
    and mission, 169–70
    priority of, 154–55
    for a second time, 23, 30–32
Preamble to the Ten Commandments, 98
prejudice, 105, 113
premarital sex, 124
pre-Reformation society, 90
Presbyterian church, 40
presumption, 38–39, 44, 60
priest-episcopal-papal structure, 156
priesthood of all believers, 155–58
priestly class, 99
Prince Charles, 67
Prince William, 77
priority of preaching the gospel, 154–55
privacy, 11, 49
privileged status of the church, 55
progressive theology, 75
promiscuous gay culture, 129
prophecy, 16–18, 69, 76, 172
prophets, 159–60. *See also false prophets*
prosperity, 79, 142
prosperity gospel, 90–91, 120, 174,
    176–77
Protestant churches, 49–51, 61, 81, 91,
    137, 153, 155, 158
Protestant denominations in Canada, 175
Protestantism, 63, 81, 137, 158, 172
Protestant Reformation, 44, 90, 142,
    150, 155
Proverbs, 120
proximity, 22, 59
psychology, 18, 36, 84, 99, 146
public school education, 144
punishment, 99, 106–8
Puritans, 39, 173

Index

Puzo, Mario, 58, 127

Q

Qing Dynasty, 64
Queen Elizabeth II, 67
questions, 117, 166
Qutb, Sayyid, 136

R

racism, 176
radical equality of men before God, 108–10
Rebekah, 103–4
reconciliation, 83
Reformed movement, 44–45
refugee problem in Europe, 63
relevance of church's messages, 165–66
religion
    and covenant, 99
    and diversity, 51, 57, 81–82
    and equality, 108–10
    and exclusive claims, 111–14
    and freedom, 5, 38, 52, 56, 95–96, 143, 173–74
    and hype, 10
    and identity, 56–57, 67, 95, 134, 138, 181
    and inclusivity, 87
    and participation, 81–82, 155, 181
    by presumption, 39
    and religious differences, 137–38
    and religious economy, 52, 181
    religious leaders, 109, 180–81
    religious liberty, 56, 82, 174
    religious monopoly, 52, 82
    and religious pluralism, 57, 81, 113, 137–38, 167
    religious privacy, 49
    religious zeal, 90, 108
    and science, 114–15
    and values, 136, 147
religious belief. *See* belief; faith
repentance, 19–20, 22, 59, 79, 109, 181
repetition, 30–32
representation of Christ, 153
repression, 36

Republican political agenda, 72, 144
resurrection, 23, 32, 48, 78, 93, 96, 109
revelation, 53–54, 83–87
Revelation 2:5, 153
Revelation 2:21, 19–20
revival movements. *See spiritual revivals*
Revive Europe, 179
rewards, 82, 90, 94, 97, 101–2
righteousness, 48, 94, 99, 102–3, 108–10, 144
right to leave, 152
Roberts, Oral, 60–61
Roman centurion, 108
Roman Empire, 22, 141–42, 163, 170
Romans 1:27, 131–32
Rousseau, Jean-Jacques, 96
Roy, Oliver, 62
rules, 35, 83–84, 91, 97–98, 123, 164

S

Sabbath, 98–99
sacraments, 44
sacrifice, 152–53
Saddleback Community Church, 168
salvation, 11, 72–74, 85–86, 104, 143, 150, 154
Samaria, 141, 158
Samaritan, 108
Samson, 130
Samuel, 28, 180
Sandford, John and Paula, 130
Sarah, 102
satire, 63, 121
Saul, 62, 72
Saul of Tarsus, 23
Schaeffer, Francis, 68
Schweitzer, Albert, 77
science and religion, 114–15
second coming of Christ, 15–18, 101
Second Commandment, 39, 98
secularism
    challenges of, 173–74
    and Christian culture, 38–39
    and Christianity, 5
    and freedom, 38, 96
    and gifted workers, 160
    and religious identity, 56–57
    and revival, 60, 62

secularism (cont.)
    and scientists, 115
    and separation of church and state, 42, 143
    and westernized Muslims, 136
secularization, 7–8, 60, 81–82, 142
Secularization Hypothesis, 81–82
secular scholars and theorists, 163, 178–82
seeker-sensitive churches, 73, 166, 167
Segal, Eric, 24
selectivity, 160
self-actualization of Spirit, 96
self-control, 127–28
self-criticism, 174
self-expression of Spirit, 87
self-restraint, 121
self-revelation, 84
Seoul, Korea, 40, 80–81
separation of the church and state, 42, 57, 143–44
sermons, 45–47, 139–40
service, 95, 155, 159
servitude, 95–96
seven deacons, 154
Seventh-Day Adventists, 61
sexuality, 35–37, 121–28, 128–33
The Shoes of the Fisherman (film), 77–78
showmanship, 175
sin of humanity, 131–32
slavery, 63, 66, 98, 102
small-group meetings, 165
Smith, Chuck, 130, 168
social agendas, 75–76
social contract theory, 97
Sodom and Gomorrah, 13, 18, 20, 132–33
South Africa, 66
South America, 50, 156
Southern California, 52–53
sovereignty of God, 73, 104–5
Spanish Inquisition, 92–93
spectator mentality of church services, 160
spiritual authority, 156–57, 158, 163
spiritual condition of Israel, 28–29, 59
spiritual energy, 72–73, 173–74, 176
spiritual gifts, 32–33, 48, 148, 155–57, 159–61, 162, 174, 176–77

spiritual leadership, 61, 66–67, 156–57
spiritual needs, 50–51, 75, 81–82, 89, 150, 167
spiritual power, 47, 73, 91, 94–95, 142, 148, 174
spiritual purity, 51, 141
spiritual revivals, 4, 8–11, 29, 43–44, 60–62, 80, 172–73, 177, 179–81
"sprinkle" Christians, 44
Spurgeon, Charles, 68
Stark, Rodney, 113, 181
state and church relations, 42, 52, 55, 56–57, 82, 118–19, 143–44, 155
Stephen, 92
The Strange Death of Europe (Murray), 64
A Streetcar Named Desire (film), 37
suffering, 78–79, 176
superstition, 142
Swaggert, Jimmy, 121–22
syncretism, 87

T

Taiwan, 48
Taizé Communauté, 68, 77
Tarsus, 145
tax collectors and prostitutes, 108–9
temptations, 7–8, 88, 116–17, 166
Ten Commandments, 39, 98
tents of Shem, 171
10/40 Window, 15, 21, 170
terrorism, 63, 135–36
theological discussions and propositions, 61–62, 88
theological seminaries, 51, 74–75, 167
theology, 72–76
theoretical knowledge, 26–27
Thielicke, Helmut, 61, 68
Thomas (apostle), 48, 78
time, 19–20, 22, 70, 105
Titanic (film), 11, 54
tithing, 118
Tokugawa, 113
tolerance, 73, 113
Tower of Babel, 65–66
transnational projects, 62
trauma, 117
trends in religious matters, 24–25
true believers, 48, 145

Index

true church, 165
true gospel, 37, 90
Trump, Donald, 9, 17, 174–75
truth, 111–12, 117
truth of the gospel, 46, 89–90, 93–95, 150

U

unchurched people, 146–48, 161
unhappy experiences at church, 147
United Church of Christ, 61
United Kingdom, 67
United Methodist Church, 61
United States
    Constitution of, 42, 57, 143
    lessons for, 172–77
    and Muslims, 136
    and religious identity, 56–57
    and secularization, 8
    and separation of church and state, 42, 57, 143–44
    and split between liberal theological and evangelical seminaries, 75
    See also American Christianity
universal church, 10
universal human rights, 62
Universalism/Unitarianism, 150
unjust war, 112
US Government, 106

V

vaccination, 55–56
Vallet, Odon, 182
Vatican II, 34
Versailles Treaty, 63
Vineyard Christian Fellowship, 73, 130, 159–60
VIP treatments, 91–92
virtuous Christians, 123
"voting with feet" concept, 80–82, 112, 153–54
vulnerability, 116–17

W

Waiting for Godot (Beckett), 101
Wall Street banks, 106
Warren, Rick, 168
wars for the souls of men, 3
ways to God, 83–84
weakness, 93, 141
wealth, 72–73, 119–20. *See also* money
Weber, Max, 179
welfare, 118
Wesley, John, 28, 43
western civilization, 95, 105–8, 110, 115, 151–52, 172
western democracy, 16–17, 107
westernization, 8, 40
western society, 36, 122, 134, 138
western values, 62
western world, 28–30, 34–54, 60, 70, 95–96, 136–37
white men, 66
wholeness, 100
Wigglesworth, Smith, 70, 88
willfulness, 85
Willow Creek Community Church, 40–41, 166, 168
Wimber, John, 73, 159–60
Winthrop, John, 172
women, 66–67, 108–10, 126, 131–32
word of Christ, 26
working class, 98
world evangelism, 15–16, 73, 169–70
world mission paradigm, 13, 16, 33, 169–71
World War II, 60, 69
world wars, 63, 65–66
worship services, 45–47, 53, 89, 148, 165
worship styles, 167

X

Xi Jinping, 173

Y

young people, 5, 35, 68, 123–24, 146–47, 150